DAN TOOMBS

THE CURRY GUY BIBLE

Recreate over 200 Indian Restaurant and Takeaway Classics at Home

Photography by Kris Kirkham

Hardie Grant

QUADRILLE

For Caroline, Katy,
Joe and Jennifer

CONTENTS

PREFACE

I didn't eat my way around curry houses in the UK and street-food places in the Indian subcontinent to find shortcuts to making Indian food. I wanted the whole shebang, and since starting my blog in 2010, I've acquired a massive catalogue of authentic and British-style recipes. Many made it into my first three cookbooks, whereas others had to be held back until the time was right. That time is now! I have also come across some good shortcuts, which are explained here as well.

I'm happy to now give you *The Curry Guy Bible*: a collection of more than 160 of the most popular recipes from my first 3 books and 50 new mouthwatering recipes that will get you the results you're looking for – and perhaps a few tasty surprises. I'll warn you that some of my new recipes could be considered to be way out there and even unhealthy by some! Being a big believer that everything is fine in moderation, I couldn't bring myself to give you watered-down versions of spectacular recipes. I have given you the most authentic versions, but you can easily adjust the recipes to your personal preferences – just read the following few pages for how to do this.

Think of this as a greatest hits cookbook. If you already have one or both of my first two books (*The Curry Guy* and *The Curry Guy Easy*), you will now have all of the most popular curries, starters and sides in one place along with new, previously unpublished recipes to top up your recipe library. If you also have a copy of my third book, *The Curry Guy Veggie*, you will not only see a few of the recipes from there but also some exciting new veggie options.

Choosing which recipes to feature in a cookbook called 'The Bible' wasn't a job to be taken lightly. I revisited recipes from my blog as well as my larger collection of recipes and started cooking. What made this task easier was all the fantastic feedback I received from the readers of my blog and subscribers to my YouTube channel. I enjoyed putting new recipes out there to see how they were received. I was sent new recipes, advice and tips from home cooks and chefs all around the Indian subcontinent, the UK and the rest of the world, which is a great advantage of living in the times we do. Connecting with, and learning from, people like this just wasn't possible even a couple of decades ago, and I feel so lucky to be able to learn and progress as a cook in this way and pass that knowledge on to you.

In the four years that I've written five books, I have been asked a lot of questions and also learned so much about the food I love. I cook these recipes so often that I have been able to stand back and think about what I like about them and how I can introduce new ideas that will keep my recipes fresh, unique and interesting. Many of the questions I received about recipes in my previous books have been answered in this book. I've also reread my books and made changes where necessary to ensure that the instructions are super-clear.

I love doing what I do and hope you enjoy this new collection of recipes. The idea behind this book was to give you one large collection of all the most-loved curries, starters and sides, and I think I've done it here. Cooking should be fun, so get in there and start cooking! People love a good curry feast and you really can make meals that are just as good as, if not far better than, going out or picking up a takeaway. You might even find you save a lot of money if you're a curry-head like me.

Of course, I still love going out to a great Indian restaurant – what curry fan doesn't? But there's something really satisfying about knowing that you can stay in and make your own takeaway for friends and family. I enjoy shopping for new ingredients and really getting to know how to use them, and it is my hope that you will find that almost as enjoyable as cooking the actual recipes.

If you have any questions about any of the recipes in this book or my previous cookbooks, please get in touch. Getting to know the people who read my books is one of the things I enjoy the most. I manage all my social accounts, so when you ask a question it will be me who answers. I'm @TheCurryGuy on Twitter, Facebook and Instagram, and would love to hear from you. I can also be contacted by email at dan@thecurryguy.com. Don't forget to look me up on YouTube too, as I am in the process of filming each of the recipes from my books, so that not only can you read them but you can also cook along with me.

Happy Cooking!

Dan

HOW TO USE THIS COOKBOOK

To help you more easily find the recipes you want to try, each recipe has been labelled with one or more badges:

 Gluten-free: I am always asked which of my recipes are gluten-free. Most are. Just look for this badge.

 Vegetarian: Look for this badge for vegetarian recipes. Most other recipes can easily be made vegetarian. Substitute veggies, legumes, lentils and/or the veggie kebabs as you see fit.

 Vegan: Most of the recipes can be made vegan, but look for this sign for those that are already vegan.

 BIR: Along with the British Indian Restaurant (BIR) section, you will also find recipes throughout this book that are favourites at UK curry houses, and they have all been labelled with this badge.

 30 minutes or less: Look for this when you want to whip up something quickly.

 Fermenting, marinating or soaking time: Just follow the preparation instructions and let nature take its course. I have included this badge so that you know you will need to do a little forward preparation.

 Low and slow: Longer cooking times are required for these recipes.

 Consume at your own risk: There are two reasons you will see this badge. Usually it's because a lot of oil or other fat is used to make it authentic. If you prefer, you can simply reduce the amount of fat you use in these recipes and you will still get an amazing flavour, although the end result will be different. The other reason you may see this badge is when the curry is really spicy. Again, that is in your hands. You can reduce the amount of chillies or chilli powder to your liking. There's no point making a curry that's too spicy to eat – even if it is the authentic way of making it.

ABOUT THESE RECIPES

Whether you're a fan of British Indian Restaurant (BIR) food, authentic Indian cuisine or both, the fun is about to begin. In this book I have featured all of the most popular recipes from my previous books and also added more of my favourite authentic Indian and BIR recipes. As I love being in contact with so many readers of my books and blog, I have been in an excellent position to really think about which recipes to feature. I have taken requests and also answered the questions asked of me to write a book that I hope you will turn to again and again for recipes for the dishes you love.

As authentic as the following recipes may be, please don't feel like you have to follow them to the letter. They are a good starting point, but everyone's tastes are different. How much time you have to spend on cooking is also a big factor in how much you will enjoy cooking the recipes. For this reason, I have given alternatives to making all the preparation ingredients, such as curry house-style base sauce and pre-cooked meats. Spending a little time making these is time well spent if you want to make BIR food like you get at your local curry house, but I have offered alternative cooking methods should you just want to whip up a chicken tikka masala without the need to make a base sauce. Although the forward preparation does take some time, you will actually be able to recreate your curry-house favourites in minutes once you've made them.

If you are new to my books, I should explain how these recipes came to be and how you should use them. I developed the majority of these recipes after watching them being made many times at restaurants, taking notes and photographs and, of course, through a good deal of experimentation. I found the experimentation the most enjoyable. Like me, you will learn not only the famous recipes but how to tailor them to your own tastes and dietary requirements.

With this in mind, please feel free to adjust the recipes to your own personal tastes. If you want more coconut or sugar in your chicken korma, add it. If my lamb madras isn't spicy enough for you, add some more chilli powder or fresh chillies. If lamb vindaloo doesn't appeal but king prawn (jumbo shrimp) and mushroom vindaloo does, why not? This is the beauty of BIR sauce recipes. Think about it... when you go out for a curry, you see all the famous sauces like tikka masala and madras, along with a list of main ingredients like chicken, lamb, prawns (shrimp) or vegetables that you can have in them. Although I have given popular combinations, there is no reason why the chicken tikka masala on page 186 can't be changed to a paneer tikka masala, and I give instructions on how to do this on page 183.

I'm going to state the obvious when it comes to curries and marinades – we're not baking cakes here! An extra teaspoon of curry powder or a little less garlic and ginger paste than called for won't ruin your curry. Just be careful with the chillies and chilli powder. If you're not sure about the spiciness, always use less than called for. You can always add more to taste, but it is difficult to cool down a curry once added.

WEIGHTS AND MEASURES
I'd like to emphasize that during my many visits to restaurant kitchens, I was rarely given exact ingredient measures for different recipes. Carefully measuring a tablespoon of this or a teaspoon of that just isn't done in busy curry houses. I have yet to see a curry-house chef using kitchen scales, measuring spoons or jugs. Everything is eyed up on the spot and added until the dish looks, tastes and smells just right. The only measuring tool they use is their handy chef's spoon. This is a long-handled spoon that holds 30ml (2 tablespoons). They dip this spoon into large sauce, spice and paste containers and take out what they need. It's like watching a conductor, with the containers of spices and other ingredients all part of the symphony orchestra.

When writing these recipes, I used heaped generous tablespoon and teaspoon measures. After watching these chefs simply dipping their big spoons into this or that ingredient and transferring it to the curry, it just didn't feel right to take a tablespoon of a spice and then carefully level it off. This isn't that kind of cooking; it's much freer. So please use my recipes as a guideline. They are the way I make them at home; though admittedly I worked out the exact measures for this book. After you make a few recipes, you'll soon learn how much of this or that ingredient to add to make the perfect curry feast for you and your family and friends.

A NOTE ABOUT INGREDIENTS
Copying the recipes as I learned them was not always an option. I had to decide whether to show you the recipes as I most often saw them prepared, with commercial pastes and sauces, or go for homemade alternatives used by many chefs hoping to make their mark. I chose the latter. When you consider how busy curry houses get at weekends, it's no wonder many chefs choose to use commercially available pastes, spice masalas and other products. It would be a full-time job to produce homemade spice blends and pickles, which just wouldn't be economically viable for a low-cost curry house. Personally, I enjoy experimenting with my own spice masalas and pastes and have included some of my recipes. To simply tell you to use a brand name spice paste didn't seem right for a cookbook.

What I have on offer for you here are my own homemade alternatives, just as many of the chefs I've met only use their own masalas and pastes. That said, if you're in a rush or simply don't like spending a lot of time in the kitchen, the ready-made products are there for you, and from time to time I choose to use them too.

WHICH OILS?
I usually use rapeseed (canola) oil for frying. This is a personal choice, as research has shown that it is one of the healthiest oils you can use. It can be used to cook at the required high temperatures and has a neutral flavour.

Rapeseed oil is not actually the same as canola, but it is made from rapeseed and is supposedly even better for you, so it can be substituted. In the UK, rapeseed oil is often sold as vegetable oil (check ingredients on the packaging); this is the oil you are looking for. The more expensive virgin rapeseed oil is not recommended for these recipes as it has a stronger flavour.

Ghee and mustard oil are also recommended in some recipes. Recipes just seem to taste better with ghee, but I do consider it a treat and not the norm. There was a time when ghee was used a lot more in restaurant curries, but these days people are more concerned about their health, so it is used less often. I love the sharp and pungent flavour of mustard oil. It has been used in Indian cookery for centuries; however, it has not been approved for human consumption here in the UK yet, though it is available from Indian shops in the hair section, and is purchased both for hair and cooking. If you've ever dined out at a curry house or high-end Indian restaurant, you've probably been served dishes that were prepared with this oil. You can of course substitute rapeseed (canola) oil, but the flavour will not be the same. If using, it is best to bring mustard oil to a boil and let it cool before heating it up again to use in your cooking. In the recipes where lots of oil or rendered animal fat is called for, you can use less and/or use the oil you prefer.

SEASONED OIL
Seasoned oil is made and used at most good Indian restaurants. It is the byproduct of several recipes in this book. The fried onion recipe (see page 173), onion bhaji recipe (see page 24) and the skimmed oil from the base curry sauce (see page 164 or 166) can be used to add flavour to curries in place of plain vegetable or rapeseed (canola) oil.

HOW AND WHEN INGREDIENTS ARE ADDED
I add ingredients as I was taught, using authentic subcontinent cooking techniques to achieve optimum flavour. I want to point this out because, as you begin to create your own recipes, the order in which you add ingredients is important.

Oil is added first, followed by whole spices, if using. To that, chopped vegetables like onions, peppers and chillies can be added and fried before other aromatics like garlic and ginger paste go in. Some ingredients burn faster than others, which is why they need to be added in a specific order to the hot oil. Inexpensive spices such as turmeric, chilli, cumin and ground coriander can withstand heat and cook happily from the beginning of cooking. More expensive and delicate spices such as ground cardamom seeds, nutmeg, saffron, mace, dried fenugreek leaves (kasoori methi) and homemade garam masala are best added at the end of cooking just before serving, as prolonged cooking results in them losing a lot of their flavour.

When and how you add the base sauce in the classic British curry recipes is also important. Just a little is added at first, which quickly begins to boil down and caramelize in the pan. There is so much flavour in this caramelized sauce and it needs to be stirred in before the rest of the base sauce and stock are added. With more liquid in the pan, this second batch can simmer away untouched unless it looks like it is burning. Some of this batch will caramelize too, which again can be scraped into the sauce for even more mouthwatering flavour.

Don't worry, all is explained in each recipe, so there's no need to grab your highlighter.

COOKING HEAT
In the following recipes, I suggest cooking over a medium–high heat. In most restaurants, the chef cooks over intensely high heat, much hotter than most domestic hobs can achieve. Once you get to know the recipes, you might like to try turning the heat up, but while you're practising, medium–high will be just fine. I have adjusted my recipes so that you should be able to get great results whether you are cooking on a gas or electric hob.

SERVING SIZES
When curries are prepared in curry houses, they are usually cooked in small one- to two-person portions. With the exception of a few recipes, I have chosen to write my recipes to serve four. All the recipes can easily be scaled up or down, but if scaling up, don't just scale the chilli powder up as you do the other ingredients. Add it to taste.

EQUIPMENT AND PRESENTATION

No special 'Indian' cooking equipment is needed to prepare these recipes. You will probably already have everything you require to cook. This is a list of useful utensils, pots and pans that will come in handy, both for cooking and presentation:

- 3-litre (3 US quarts) heavy-based saucepan with tight-fitting lid
- Food processor
- Spice grinder or pestle and mortar
- Blender (jug or hand-held)
- Large frying pan
- Large wok
- Large roasting tray with a wire rack
- Large mixing bowls
- Wire mesh spoon
- Good-quality chef's knife – please don't go for one of those inexpensive knife sets! If you're on a budget, get one good-quality chef's knife and you'll have everything you need
- Measuring jug
- Barbecue with flat metal skewers – the skewers are optional as you can always cook on the grill, but skewers add a lot to the presentation.
- Spice dabba – this is a large, air-tight container that holds several smaller containers for storing spices. They are designed for the home cook and wouldn't be used at most restaurants. Any air-tight containers will do for storing spices.
- Balti pans, karahis and/or handis – these are totally optional but do add a lot to the presentation of your meal. They can be picked up quite inexpensively at Asian shops and online. There is more information on them on page 237.

YOUR INGREDIENT MISSION CONTROL PANEL

Every Indian restaurant chef has their most important spices, pastes and sauces within easy reach so that they can dip their chef's spoon into them and take out what they need as they cook. To watch a professional chef do this is quite impressive. Often they are cooking many different curries at once. With some practice, you will be able to do this too. You will use a lot of different ingredients in the following recipes; I have included a list in the ingredients section on pages 340–2.

Some ingredients, however, are used more often than others. Here's a list of ingredients that most chefs have in close proximity:

- Mixed powder (see page 169)
- Garam masala (see page 167)
- Tandoori masala (see page 168)
- Garlic and ginger paste (see page 172)
- Chilli powder
- Ground cumin
- Ground coriander
- Ground turmeric
- Dried fenugreek leaves (kasoori methi)
- Coconut flour
- Ground almonds
- Spice pastes (depending on chef)
- Sugar
- Salt*

*A good dose of salt helps bring out the flavours of the spices. Many people are reducing their salt intake these days, but a generous sprinkling of the stuff is needed to brighten up any curry. The amount you use is a personal thing, so I haven't included exact measurements in most recipes. Even when used liberally, your homemade curries will probably have one heck of a lot less salt and taste much better than those ready meals found at the supermarket.

5 ESSENTIAL COOKING RULES

In my first cookbook, I listed five rules to follow and I thought it would be good to mention them again here.

RULE #1

Only use the freshest ingredients you can get your hands on. Even the best chefs in the world can't do much with stale spices and poor-quality meat and vegetables. We are so lucky to have excellent farmers' markets, butchers, fishmongers and spice suppliers here in the UK. Use them.

RULE #2

Take an afternoon to make the base ingredients if you really want to get your curry-house curries right. Out of all these recipes, only the base sauces (pages 164 and 166) need to be made from scratch to get that awesome texture, aroma and flavour that is the BIR curry. I have given new instructions on how to make the curries without the base sauce (see page 163), but taking time to make it will get you more authentic results and will actually save you time if cooking often. Other base ingredients like garlic and ginger paste and the spice blends can be purchased commercially. Remember, though: fresh is best and you will notice a difference in the end result.

RULE #3

Add the ingredients in the order I've specified.

RULE #4

Have fun! Choose a time to cook when you really feel like cooking. You'll enjoy it much more.

RULE #5

Other than rules one to four, there are no rules. Along with the recipes, I included many alternative ideas for making them your own. Just go for it! If it sounds good, it probably is.

STARTERS

Who doesn't like a good starter or two when dining out at an Indian restaurant? In this section you will find recipes for the most popular starters out there. From crispy onion bhajis to delicious prawn puri, you are almost certain to find your favourite.

All of these popular starters are easy to make, and many can be prepared in advance. Some of these starters go fantastically well with a good pickle, chutney and/or raita, and I have recipes for those too on pages 328–39.

PAPADAMS
MAKES 8 PAPADAMS; SERVES 4–8

Almost everyone loves a papadam or two while eagerly awaiting their curry dinner. Most good Indian restaurants fry their own as they are much better than pre-packed papadams. The great news is that they aren't difficult to prepare. Many supermarkets and Asian food shops sell papads, which are flat lentil discs that when fried turn into lovely papadams. You could purchase papad flour and make your own – I have a few times and it's a lot of work. Ready-made papads are the way to go. Papads are available plain or with whole spices – I love cumin papads, black pepper papads and chilli papads. Make sure you use a pan that is at least 4cm (1½in) wider in diameter than the papads you are using as they expand.

PREP TIME: 5 MINS
COOKING TIME: 10 MINS

Rapeseed (canola) oil, for deep-frying
Papads (1–2 per person)

Heat 10cm (4in) of oil in a large pan or wok until hot. When a piece of papad puffs up quite quickly when dropped into the oil, you know the oil is hot enough. Papads are usually cooked in pairs, which speeds up the process and also helps keep them uniformly flat. Drop the papads in the oil. They will very quickly expand into full-size papadams. Be careful not to overcook or burn the papadams; they will quickly begin to turn brown so remove them from the oil before this happens. It only takes seconds to overcook papadams, so be ready to get them out of that oil. Remove from the oil with tongs or a wire-mesh spoon and place on paper towel to absorb the excess oil.

You can leave them to cool flat, or fold them into your own preferred shapes while they are still hot. Serve or store in an air-tight container.

TIP

When planning a curry night in with friends, I cook papadams earlier in the day so I can check them off my to-do list. This is what they do at busy restaurants too, often making enough for three or more days in one go.

Clockwise from top left:
Papadda vada (page 14); green coconut chutney (page 331); mango pickle (page 330); masala papads (above) with tomato, onion and mint salad (page 326); tajah badam (page 52) and posh Bombay mix (page 52)

MASALA PAPADS
SERVES 2 OR MORE AS PART OF A
MULTI-COURSE MEAL

I think you'll like these roasted papads topped with this simple but tasty masala. I like to stack them up and serve them like a salad, but simply topping a papad with the masala is equally as good. They are pictured opposite. You can prepare them a couple of days ahead: just store the roasted papads in an air-tight container and the masala in the fridge.

PREP TIME: 10 MINS
COOKING TIME: 10 MINS

1 large tomato, diced
½ red onion, finely chopped
2–3 green chillies, finely chopped
Juice of 1 lime
3 tbsp finely chopped coriander (cilantro)
Salt and freshly ground black pepper, to taste
½ tsp chaat masala (see page 168) (optional)
3–4 tbsp rapeseed (canola) oil
2–3 papads per person

Mix the tomato, onion, green chillies, lime juice and coriander (cilantro) in a large bowl. Season with salt and black pepper and add a little chaat masala if you like. Remember that most papads and chaat masala already have salt in them, so it is a good idea to try one first so that you don't over-season the masala. Cover and place in the fridge while you roast the papads.

Heat a dry frying pan over a medium heat. Using a brush or your hand, spread a little oil over both sides of a papad. Place it in the centre of the pan and press it down with a spatula. You will be able to see the papad cooking through. When this begins to happen, flip it over and press it down again with the spatula. Continue flipping until the papad is nicely roasted on both sides and cooked through – about 30–45 seconds. Transfer to a wire rack and continue cooking the remaining papads in the same way.

To serve, top each papad with about 2 tablespoons of the masala.

PAPADDA VADA

MAKES 20 – FEEDS A CROWD

Papadams are delicious, but this Keralan recipe takes them to the next level. The papads are dipped into a spicy batter before deep-frying. Unlike plain papads, these battered papads stay about the same size when fried. They are delicious served with a selection of pickles, sauces and chutneys. Papadda vada are pictured on page 12 in the top left corner.

PREP TIME: 10 MINS, PLUS SOAKING TIME
COOKING TIME: 20 MINS

Rapeseed (canola) oil, for deep-frying
20 papads

FOR THE BATTER
275g (scant 1½ cups) basmati rice, rinsed and soaked in
    water for 5 hours, then drained
½ tsp ground turmeric
1 tsp chilli powder
1 heaped tbsp black sesame seeds
1 tsp cumin seeds
1 tbsp dried chilli (hot pepper) flakes (optional)
½ tsp salt

To make the batter, place the soaked rice in a food processor and add just enough water to blend it into a thick batter. Whisk in the rest of the ingredients. The batter should be thick enough to adhere to the papads when dipped into it. If it is too thick to easily dip, add a drop more water – it should be the consistency of double (heavy) cream.

Heat the oil in a large saucepan or wok until hot enough to deep-fry. The oil is ready when a piece of papad dropped into the oil sizzles and floats to the top immediately.

Dip the first papad into the batter, ensuring that it is very well coated, and gently place it into the oil. Fry for about 40 seconds until the batter coating turns light brown. Transfer with a slotted spoon to a wire rack over a tray or to a piece of paper towel. Allow the excess oil to drip into the pan or drain into the paper while you finish cooking the remaining papads.

SPICY STUFFED GREEN CHILLIES

SERVES 4 OR MORE AS PART OF A
MULTI-COURSE MEAL

Green chillies stuffed with spiced gram flour? You're just going to have to trust me here if you don't already know how good these are! These stuffed chillies make the perfect appetizer.

PREP TIME: 10 MINS
COOKING TIME: 10–15 MINS

125ml (½ cup) rapeseed (canola) oil
100g (heaped ¾ cup) gram (chickpea) flour
½ tsp ground turmeric
½ tsp chilli powder
½ tsp ground cumin
½ tsp ground coriander
1 tsp amchoor (dried mango powder)
Salt (I use just under 1 tsp)
350g (12½ oz) long green chillies
Raita or coconut chutney, to serve (optional)

Heat 1 teaspoon of the oil in a large frying pan over a medium–high heat. Tip in the flour and work it with a whisk or fork in the pan so that it toasts evenly. The flour is ready after about 2 minutes when fragrant and lightly browned. Don't worry if you see small balls of untoasted gram flour. Break them up as best you can, but any remaining are fine.

Add the turmeric, chilli powder, cumin, coriander, amchoor and salt and transfer to a mixing bowl. Pour in 70ml (¼ cup) of water and work with your hands into a thick paste.

Slit the green chillies down the middle and remove most of the seeds with your thumb. Stuff the chillies with the gram flour paste.

Heat the remaining oil in a frying pan over a low heat. Fry the chillies for 2–3 minutes until browned all over. You should see a few blackened spots and blisters on the chillies. Serve immediately on their own or with a good raita or coconut chutney.

Spicy stuffed green chillies

POTATO AND ARTICHOKE SAMOSA PINWHEELS

SERVES 4 OR MORE AS PART OF A MULTI-COURSE MEAL

I'm a big fan of samosa pinwheels. Not only do they look great, they're also a lot easier to prepare than regular samosas. This potato and artichoke combo is a good one, but feel free to experiment with other fillings. The black bean samosa filling on page 18 works really well cooked this way. Unlike other samosas, these pinwheels do not freeze well, so it is best to make and fry them on the same day.

PREP TIME: 30 MINS,
   PLUS RESTING TIME
   FOR THE DOUGH
COOKING TIME: 15 MINS

2 tbsp rapeseed (canola) oil or ghee
1 onion, finely chopped
2 tbsp garlic and ginger paste (see page 172)
2 green chillies, finely chopped
1 tsp ground cumin
1 tsp ground coriander
1 tsp garam masala (see page 167)
½ tsp ground turmeric
400g (14oz) mashed potato (about 1 large potato)
200g (7oz) cooked artichoke hearts, diced
2 tbsp lemon juice
3 tbsp finely chopped coriander (cilantro)
Rapeseed (canola) oil, for frying
4 heaped tbsp plain (all-purpose) flour, plus extra for dusting

FOR THE PASTRY
150g (heaped 1 cup) plain (all-purpose) flour
1 tbsp rapeseed (canola) oil
1 tsp cumin seeds
½ tsp salt

TO SERVE
Mint and coriander sauce (see page 335)
Tamarind sauce (see page 336)
Yoghurt sauce (see page 338)

To make the filling, heat the oil in a large frying pan over a medium–high heat. When hot, add the onion and fry for about 5 minutes until soft and translucent. Stir in the garlic and ginger paste, green chillies, cumin, coriander, garam masala and turmeric. Now add the mashed potato and artichoke and stir until well combined. It should have a nice yellow glow because of the turmeric. Stir in the lemon juice and chopped coriander (cilantro) and set aside to cool.

Now make the pastry. Mix the flour, oil, cumin seeds and salt in a bowl and slowly add about 80ml (5½ tablespoons) of water while working with your hands until you have a soft but dry dough. Let it sit for about 30 minutes, covered with a wet tea (dish) towel.

To make the pinwheels, roll the dough out on a lightly floured surface into a 20cm (8in) diameter circle that is slightly thicker than a chapatti. Spread the potato and artichoke mixture evenly all over the surface – it should look like a big potato pizza. Starting at one end, roll it into a tight cylinder, then slice into 2.5cm (1in) rounds.

When ready to cook, heat about 10cm (4in) of oil in a large wok or saucepan. The oil is ready when a piece of pastry sizzles and rises to the top immediately when placed in it. If you have an oil thermometer, aim for 170°C (340°F).

Mix the 4 tablespoons of flour with 100ml (scant ½ cup) of water in a bowl to make a thick paste.

Dip one of the pinwheels in the flour paste so it is nicely coated and carefully lower it into the oil. Repeat with the rest of the pinwheels and fry for about 3 minutes per side until nicely browned all over. You may need to work in batches to avoid overcrowding the pan. I usually turn the pinwheels over in the oil a few times for more uniform cooking. Transfer to paper towel to soak up the excess oil, then serve with the sauces.

NOTE

For a lighter option, preheat the oven to 200°C (400°F/Gas 6), omit the flour paste and just brush each samosa pastry with a little oil, then bake for about 20 minutes, or until heated through and browned to your liking.

Top plate: Samosa pinwheels (above); smoked toor dhal samosas (page 19); and tomato, onion and mint salad (page 326)
Bottom chopping board: Black bean and Cheddar samosas (page 18) with tomato, onion and mint salad
Left: Mint and coriander sauce (page 335) and a smoked toor dhal samosa

BLACK BEAN AND CHEDDAR SAMOSAS

MAKES ABOUT 20

These samosas, pictured on page 17, are great with tomato salsa or coriander sauce (as per the recipe on page 335 but leaving out the mint and adding more coriander/cilantro). In this recipe I have used ready-made samosa wrappers – available at most Asian shops in the freezer section. If you want to make your own wrappers, I explain how to do this in the lamb or vegetable samosas recipe on page 21. I've also made a smoked toor dhal samosas video on my YouTube channel, Dan Toombs, where you can watch me folding the samosas. The wrapped (but unfried) samosas can easily be frozen: simply spread out on a baking tray, transfer to a freezer bag once frozen and thaw fully before frying.

PREP TIME: 25 MINS
COOKING TIME: 20 MINS

2 tbsp rapeseed (canola) oil, plus extra for deep-frying
½ onion, finely chopped
2 garlic cloves, minced
2 x 400g (14oz) tins (cans) black beans, drained and rinsed
½ tsp chilli powder
½ tsp ground cumin
Handful of grated Cheddar cheese
Salt, to taste
20 shop-bought rectangular samosa sheets
3 tbsp plain (all-purpose) flour

Heat the oil in a saucepan over a medium–high heat. When hot, add the onion and fry for about 5 minutes until soft and translucent. Stir in the garlic and fry for a further 30 seconds, then add the beans, chilli powder and ground cumin. Reduce the heat to medium and start mashing it all up with a potato masher until you have a mixture the consistency of mashed potatoes. Whisk in the cheese and season with salt. Allow to cool. The bean mixture will become thicker as it cools.

To make the samosas, take a samosa sheet and place it on a clean surface with one of the short ends closest to you. Mix the flour with enough water to make a thick paste, ready for sealing the samosas. Take the top left corner of the samosa sheet and bring it about halfway down to meet the right-hand side, creating a kite-like shape at the top. Now fold the top right corner down to meet the left-hand side, creating a triangular pocket with a small flap. Fill the pocket with a generous tablespoon of the filling and fold the small triangular flap and pastry over to close. Now rub the flour paste all over the surface of the remaining pastry, and fold it into a neat triangle to seal. If there are any holes in the corners, use the paste to seal them too. Repeat with the rest of the samosa wrappers and filling.

Heat about 10cm (4in) of rapeseed (canola) oil in a large saucepan or wok to 170°C (340°F) – or until a piece of samosa sizzles immediately when dropped in the oil. You don't want to overcrowd the pan so you might need to work in batches. Fry for about 2 minutes, turning the samosas a few times as you do, until they are crisp and light brown. Keep warm while you fry any remaining batches.

NOTE

For a lighter option, brush them with a little oil and bake at 200°C (400°F/Gas 6) for 20 minutes, or until heated through and browned.

MAKE IT VEGAN

These are excellent without cheese, or you could use a vegan cheese.

SMOKED TOOR DHAL SAMOSAS
MAKES ABOUT 25

I tried smoked toor dhal samosas at a little street-food stall in Mumbai. They were so good I had to try making them at home. Samosa pastry is available at most Asian shops in the freezer section, but if you want to try making your own, look at my lamb or vegetable samosas recipe on page 21. If you would like to see how I fold them, watch my samosa video on my YouTube channel, Dan Toombs. To try these samosas smoked you will need to light charcoal, as described below, or use a home smoker for an easier and smokier process. They are pictured on page 17.

PREP TIME: 1 HOUR, PLUS
  SOAKING AND RESTING TIME
COOKING TIME: 35 MINS

150g (1 cup) toor dhal
½ tsp salt
½ tsp ground turmeric
2 tbsp finely chopped ginger
1 tsp amchoor (dried mango powder)
1 tsp garam masala (see page 167)
3 tbsp finely chopped coriander (cilantro)
½ tsp rapeseed (canola) oil, plus extra for deep-frying
25 shop-bought rectangular samosa sheets
Your favourite chutneys and lime wedges, to serve

FOR THE TEMPERING
2 tbsp rapeseed (canola) oil
1 tsp mustard seeds
1 tsp cumin seeds
2 green chillies, finely chopped
10 curry leaves, roughly chopped

Rinse the dhal several times, cover with water and soak for 30 minutes.

Meanwhile, light a few pieces of lumpwood charcoal outside to become white-hot (optional).

Tip the dhal into a pan with the salt, turmeric and ginger and cover with 1 litre (4½ cups) of water. Bring to a boil over a high heat, then reduce the heat and simmer for 30 minutes, or until the dhal is really soft. Stir in the amchoor and garam masala. You want the dhal to be really thick as it is a stuffing, so reduce the water down until good and thick. Stir regularly so it doesn't burn to the bottom of the pan. Set aside to cool; it will thicken more as it does.

Now heat the tempering oil over a high heat in a separate pan until visibly hot. Add the mustard seeds. When they begin to pop (after about 30 seconds), reduce the heat to medium and stir in the cumin seeds, chillies and curry leaves. Temper for about 40 seconds, then pour it over the cooked dhal and whisk it in, along with the coriander (cilantro).

By this time, the charcoal should be ready. Using tongs, place the hot charcoal on a piece of foil and carefully transfer to the pan with the dhal. Drizzle the ½ teaspoon of rapeseed (canola) oil over the charcoal – it will begin to smoke heavily. Cover the pan and let the dhal smoke until all the smoke is gone. I usually smoke mine in my Traeger or smoker, which I find more convenient. Feel free to use a smoker if you have one.

Take a samosa sheet and wrap the filling up as explained on page 18. Repeat with the remaining samosa wrappers and filling.

When all the samosas are wrapped, you can freeze them if you wish. Spread them out on a baking tray and transfer to a freezer bag once frozen. Be sure to thaw them first before frying.

If frying immediately, heat about 10cm (4in) of oil in a large saucepan or wok to 170°C (340°F) and fry in batches for about 3 minutes until crispy and lightly browned. Keep warm while you fry the remaining samosas.

Serve with your favourite chutneys and lime wedges for squeezing.

NOTE

For a lighter option, preheat the oven to 200°C (400°F/Gas 6), brush each samosa with a little oil and bake for about 20 minutes, or until heated through and browned to your liking.

EASY CHICKEN TORTILLA SAMOSAS

MAKES 12, SERVES 4 OR MORE AS PART OF A MULTI-COURSE MEAL

Many people don't attempt making samosas because they don't want the mess of making their own pastry, and/or samosa wrappers are hard to come by without a special trip to an Asian grocer. Long before I ever tried Indian food, I was a big fan of Mexican food, and this recipe came to me because of my fondness for deep-fried chimichangas. You could use this method with other filled samosa recipes in this book too.

PREP TIME: 15 MINS
COOKING TIME: 15 MINS

6 x 25cm (10in) flour tortillas or chapattis
2 tbsp rapeseed (canola) oil, plus extra for deep-frying
1 tsp black mustard seeds
1 tsp cumin seeds
10 fresh or frozen curry leaves, roughly chopped (optional)
2 onions, finely chopped
2 green chillies, finely chopped
1½ tbsp garlic and ginger paste (see page 172)
1 tomato, diced
1 tbsp tandoori masala (see page 168) or garam masala (see page 167)
1 tsp Kashmiri chilli powder (optional and to taste)
4 tbsp finely chopped coriander (cilantro)
500g (1lb 2oz) skinless chicken breasts or thighs, roughly chopped
Juice of 1 lime
Salt, to taste
200g (7oz) green cabbage, thinly sliced and chopped
1 carrot, grated
1½ tbsp plain (all-purpose) flour
Raita, hot sauce and/or chutneys, to serve

Cut the tortillas in half so that you have 12 half circles. Set aside. Heat the oil over a medium–high heat and when visibly hot, stir in the mustard seeds. When the mustard seeds begin to crackle (after about 30 seconds), reduce the heat to medium and add the cumin seeds and curry leaves (if using). Sizzle for about 30 seconds, but be careful not to burn the cumin seeds. To cool the pan down, add the onions and fry over a medium heat for about 5 minutes until soft and translucent. Now add the chillies and garlic and ginger paste, and stir it all up to combine. Cook for a further 30 seconds to cook the rawness out of the garlic and ginger.

Add the tomato and stir well. Then stir in the tandoori or garam masala and the chilli powder (if using). Stir in 2 tablespoons of the coriander (cilantro) and the chicken. Cook until the chicken is cooked through, about 7 minutes, and then squeeze in the lime juice and season with salt. Tip everything into a bowl to cool.

Place the pan back on the heat and add the cabbage and carrot. Fry in whatever oil remains in the pan until just cooked through but still crunchy – 2–3 minutes should do the job. Pour into the bowl with the chicken and stir well to combine.

In a small bowl, whisk 4 tablespoons of water and the flour with a fork to make a paste. This paste will be used to seal the samosas. Take one tortilla half and place it on a clean surface with the flat cut at the top. Bring the two corners together. Apply a generous amount of the paste to the exterior of one of the straight edges and press the two sides together to form a cone shape. You will need to press firmly so the cone sticks together. Fill the cone almost to the top with the chicken mixture and seal the top using more paste. Repeat with the remaining tortillas.

Heat the oil to 170°C (340°F), or until a piece of tortilla begins to sizzle immediately when added to the oil and floats to the top. Cooking in batches, add the samosas to the hot oil and cook for about 4 minutes, or until they are crispy brown and heated through. Transfer to paper towel to soak up the excess oil and serve hot with a good raita, hot sauce and/or chutney.

LAMB OR VEGETABLE SAMOSAS
MAKES 18–20

Shop-bought filo pastry or samosa wrappers are most often used at Indian restaurants. They do the job, but there's nothing like homemade pastry, so I have included my pastry recipe here. If you want to make these samosas ahead of time, you can freeze them once shaped but not fried, on a plate, wrapped tightly in cling film (plastic wrap). Once frozen, transfer to a freezer bag and store until ready to fry, defrosting them first. You can see the lamb version pictured on page 23.

PREP TIME: 30 MINS
COOKING TIME: ABOUT
30 MINS

Rapeseed (canola) oil, for deep-frying

FOR THE PASTRY
400g (2¾ cups) plain (all-purpose)
   flour
Pinch of salt
1 tbsp rapeseed (canola) oil
1 tbsp melted ghee

FOR VEGETABLE FILLING
2 tbsp rapeseed (canola) oil
1 tsp cumin seeds
1 onion, finely chopped
2 green bird's eye chillies, finely
   chopped
1 tbsp garlic and ginger paste (see
   page 172)
2 floury potatoes, peeled and cut into
   1cm (½in) cubes
2 tsp mixed powder (see page 169)
About 250ml (1 cup) water or spice
   stock (see page 167) – enough
   to cover
1 carrot, finely chopped
3 tbsp finely chopped coriander
   (cilantro)
125g (1 cup) frozen peas
Salt, to taste

FOR THE MEAT FILLING
1 quantity pre-cooked keema (see
   page 178)*

*You will probably have some keema
left over. Go ahead and use it in a curry
or refrigerate/freeze for later use.

Mix 350g (2½ cups) of the flour in a large bowl with the salt, oil and ghee. Slowly drizzle enough water into the mixture to make a firm but sticky dough. Sprinkle the remaining flour on a clean surface, tip out the dough and knead for about 5 minutes until it no longer sticks to your hands. Cover the dough and let rest for 30 minutes.

To make the vegetable filling, heat the oil in a large frying pan over a medium–high heat until bubbles appear. Add the cumin seeds. When they become fragrant in the oil, toss in the onion and chillies, and fry for 5–7 minutes until the onion is translucent and lightly browned. Add the garlic and ginger paste and fry for a further minute.

Add the potatoes and mixed powder, and just enough water or spice stock to cover. Simmer until the potatoes are soft, topping up the stock if needed. Add the carrot and continue cooking until cooked through but still al dente. Reduce the stock until you have a dry potato mixture. Stir in the coriander (cilantro) and peas and season with salt. Set aside to cool.

To make the lamb or vegetable samosas, tear off a piece of dough the size of a golf ball and place on a floured surface (keep the remaining dough in the bowl covered so that it doesn't dry out). Roll the dough into a very thin rectangle, the thinner the better, about 5 x 12cm (2 x 4½in).

Place about 1 tablespoon of lamb or vegetable filling at the top of the pastry rectangle. Fold the top left corner over the filling to make a small triangular pocket. There will still be about 6cm (2½in) of pastry under this triangular pocket. Fold the top of the triangle over onto the remaining pastry and then again to create a little triangular samosa. Press the seams together tightly and repeat until all of the samosas are made.

When ready to cook, pour 10cm (4in) of rapeseed (canola) oil into a deep saucepan and heat to 170°C (340°F). Fry the samosas in batches until nicely browned. Remove with a slotted spoon and transfer to a wire rack. Keep warm while you fry the remaining samosas.

BORA AND PODINA

MAKES ENOUGH FOR 4 AS A SNACK

You won't find bora and podina on many curry-house menus, but I think they're missing a trick. This Bangladeshi snack food is an excellent alternative to papadams. It does take a little longer to make but it's worth every extra minute.

This recipe was emailed to me by Eshan 'Mo' Miah. Mo and I have never met face to face but I feel like we're great friends. Back in the early days of my blog, Mo started sending me his family recipes as well as recipes from his family's restaurant, Table Talk, which is local to me. At the time, Mo was living and working near London, but he arranged for me to visit the Table Talk kitchen to learn from his father, Manik Miah. I picked up so many tips and recipes that day.

Mo has been a great source for recipes, a few of which you'll find in this book. He has also opened a new restaurant in Newquay called Zaman's. If it is anywhere near as good as Table Talk, he's on to a winner!

PREP TIME: 1 HOUR
COOKING TIME: 20 MINS

100g (½ cup) masoor dhal (red lentils)
½ onion, finely chopped
1 tsp salt
½ tsp ground turmeric
380g (scant 3 cups) rice flour
Rapeseed (canola) oil, for deep-frying
Podina coriander and mint chutney (see page 334), refrigerated until really cold

To make the bora, wash the lentils and soak them in cold water for 30 minutes. Drain and transfer to a saucepan. Add 550ml (scant 2½ cups) of fresh water, the onion, salt and turmeric. Cook over a medium heat until the lentils are soft and the water is almost all gone.

Tip the lentils into a bowl and stir in the rice flour. Mix thoroughly with your hands until you have a smooth dough. (Mixing everything while still warm makes it easier.)

On a flat surface, roll out the dough to a 2–3 mm thickness (separate the dough into smaller balls to make this easier if you like). Cut out bite-size pieces of the dough, either in long triangles or use cookie cutters to make different shapes.

Heat at least 10cm (4in) of rapeseed (canola) oil in a heavy-based saucepan to about 170°C (340°F). When a piece of dough sizzles immediately when dropped into the oil, you're ready to cook. Fry in batches, transfer to a plate lined with paper towel and keep warm while you deep-fry the rest. Season with a little more salt if you like. Serve piping hot with the fridge-cold podina.

MAKE IT VEGAN
The bora are already vegan. Leave the yoghurt out of the podina or use a vegan substitute, to taste.

On plate, clockwise from top:
Bora (above); lamb samosas with homemade wrappers (page 21); and onion bhajis (page 24)
Below plate: Podina coriander and mint chutney (see page 334)

ONION BHAJIS
SERVES 4–8

Onion bhajis and vegetable pakoras are best cooked in two stages. The first cooking is in oil that is hot enough to sizzle and cook them through. They are then removed to rest, the oil temperature is increased and they are fried again in the hotter oil to give them a darker and crispier exterior. The bhajis are pictured on page 23.

Mixing the onions with salt at the beginning of the recipe is key to making the perfect bhajis. If you were to bend a fresh onion slice, it would snap. The salt releases moisture from the onion slices so they become limp and no longer snap when bent, making it easier to form your bhajis.

PREP TIME: 15 MINS, PLUS
SITTING TIME
COOKING TIME: 15 MINS

3 onions (slightly larger than tennis balls), sliced
1 tsp fine sea salt
4 tbsp rice flour
140g (1 cup) gram (chickpea) flour
1 tbsp garlic paste*
2.5cm (1in) piece of ginger, peeled and cut into matchsticks
2 fresh green chillies, roughly chopped
1 tbsp panch poran (see page 171)
2 tbsp rapeseed (canola) oil, plus extra for deep-frying
3 tbsp finely chopped coriander (cilantro) leaves

*To make this blend 1–2 cloves of garlic with just enough water to make a smooth paste.

Place the onions in a bowl, sprinkle over the salt and mix it all up with your hands to ensure the onions are evenly coated with the salt. Let them sit for 30 minutes–2 hours; the salt will release the moisture from the onions, which will become part of your batter.

When ready to form the bhajis, sift the flours over the onions and add the garlic paste, ginger, chillies, panch poran, 2 tablespoons of oil and the coriander (cilantro). Begin to work these ingredients into the onions with your hands until they are nicely coated. There should be enough moisture from the onions and oil, but if you are finding it a bit too sticky, add just a little water. When you can easily form a bhaji with your hands, you're ready to go.

Heat about 10cm (4in) of rapeseed (canola) oil to 160°C (320°F) in a large frying pan. Form the onion mixture into bhajis about the size of golf balls, or larger if you prefer. Fry in small batches until lightly browned and cooked through, then remove them with a slotted spoon to a wire rack to rest while you fry the remaining bhajis.

When all the bhajis are cooked, raise the heat of the oil to 180°C (355°F) and fry them again in small batches until you are happy with the colour of the exterior. Serve immediately or, if working ahead, place the bhajis on a wire rack placed over a foil-lined dish in a low oven for up to 30 minutes.

OTHER IDEAS

You can make vegetable pakoras in the same way, adding whichever vegetables you like to the mix. Broccoli and cauliflower cut into small pieces both work well. Diced potatoes, chopped green chillies, courgettes (zucchini) and aubergines (eggplants) are also good.

SEASONED OIL

Don't throw all of the delicious cooking oil away. Save some and use it as seasoned oil for your curries. This adds another delicious layer of flavour.

VEGETABLE PAKORAS

SERVES 4 OR MORE AS PART OF A MULTI-COURSE MEAL

Vegetable pakoras can be made in lots of ways with many different variations. In fact, if you have tried the onion bhaji recipe opposite, it can be made into vegetable pakoras too. Simply follow that recipe and add a few chopped vegetables of choice and voilà... you've got vegetable pakoras! Below is a recipe that is completely different to that one but just as delicious. If you want to make this recipe gluten-free, just leave out the panko breadcrumbs.

PREP TIME: 15 MINS
COOKING TIME: 15 MINS

1 green (bell) pepper, thinly sliced and cut into 2.5cm (1in) pieces
A generous handful of cabbage, shredded (about 90g/1 cup)
1 medium carrot, peeled and julienned
450g (2 cups) shredded baby spinach leaves, large stems removed
3 tbsp finely chopped coriander (cilantro)
170g (1 cup) gram (chickpea) flour, plus extra if needed
80g (⅓ cup) rice flour
1 tsp ground turmeric
½ tsp salt, plus extra to taste
1 tsp Kashmiri chilli powder
1 tbsp lemon juice (optional)
90g (1 cup) panko breadcrumbs (optional)
Rapeseed (canola) oil, for deep-frying
Pakora sauce (see page 338), to serve

Place the vegetables in a large mixing bowl and add the coriander (cilantro).

Sift the gram flour, rice flour, turmeric, salt and Kashmiri chilli powder into a separate bowl and add the lemon juice (if using). Begin slowly pouring about 125ml (½ cup) of water into the flour mixture while whisking until it is about the same consistency as whisked natural yoghurt.

Tip the vegetables into the batter and mix well. Sprinkle the panko breadcrumbs (if using) onto a plate.

Using your hands, form the battered vegetables into balls slightly larger than golf balls and dip them in the panko breadcrumbs. If you are finding the mixture too wet to work with, sift in a little more gram flour. If too dry, add a drop more water.

Heat about 10cm (4in) of oil in a large saucepan or wok to 180°C (355°F). If you don't have an oil thermometer, the oil is ready when a small piece of the battered vegetables sizzles immediately and rises to the top. You might need to cook the pakoras in batches. Fry until they are crispy, brown and cooked through. This will take about 4 minutes. Serve hot with pakora sauce.

NOTE

In this recipe I give measurements in both grams and US cups but there's no need to go rifling through your cupboards for your kitchen scales or cup measures! This isn't that kind of cooking. Just use any tea cup and adjust, adding more or less of the vegetables should you wish to do so.

PRAWN BUTTERFLIES
MAKES 8–10

You can't beat a good prawn (shrimp) butterfly. They may not be good for you but they are quite moreish and worth every calorie. I recommend using the largest prawns (shrimp) you can find – they are easier to prepare and there is a lot more to them.

If you are serving these to friends as part of a multi-dish curry feast, heat the oven to about 150°C (300°F/Gas 2) and fry them a good 30 minutes before everyone arrives, placing them on a wire rack placed over a foil-lined dish in the oven. Then simply transfer them from the oven to a warm plate to serve.

PREP TIME: 15 MINS
COOKING TIME: 10 MINS

8–10 unpeeled raw large prawns (shrimp)
4 tbsp gram (chickpea) flour
2 tbsp rice flour
1 tbsp baking powder
½ tsp roasted cumin seeds (see page 163)
1 tbsp mixed powder (see page 169)
1 tsp chilli powder, or to taste
Salt, to taste
Rapeseed (canola) oil, for deep-frying

Using a sharp knife, slice down the centre of the back of each prawn (shrimp) and remove the black or clear vein. Peel off the head and the rest of the shell down to the tail. Leave the tail intact as it makes a good and attractive handle. Continue to make a shallow incision into the back to butterfly each prawn. Place cling film (plastic wrap) over the butterflied prawns and lightly pound them flat with a mallet.

For the batter, mix the flours, baking powder, cumin, mixed powder and chilli powder together in a bowl. Slowly whisk in about 125fl oz (½ cup) of water until you have a batter the consistency of double (heavy) cream and thick enough to coat the back of a spoon but slowly drip off. If it is too thick, add a little more water, or a pinch more gram flour if too thin. Season the batter with salt.

Heat about 15cm (6in) of oil in a deep, heavy-based saucepan or wok until hot enough for a drop of batter to sizzle immediately when dropped in the oil. Dip and coat the prawns with the batter, slowly lower each battered prawn into the hot oil and fry for about 3 minutes until nicely browned on the exterior and cooked through. You might need to do this in batches.

If cooking ahead (see introduction) remove to a cooling rack placed over a foil-lined dish for any excess oil to drain off, and place in a warm oven (they will stay nice and crisp for 30 minutes). Transfer to a warm plate to serve.

TIP
These are great served with my pakora sauce (see page 338).

PRAWN PURI

SERVES 4 OR MORE AS PART OF A MULTI-COURSE MEAL

After I wrote my first two books, so many people asked 'but where's the prawn puri recipe?' Well, here it is! You can judge how good a curry-house meal is going to be by their prawn puri. Some chefs simply deep-fry chapattis and call them puris. They taste good but simply can't stand up to the real thing. So if you want to cheat, fry up some chapattis and follow the prawn sauce recipe below. If you want to try this recipe the way I love it and make it at home, take some time and make homemade puffy and crispy puris, following my recipe on page 311.

PREP TIME: 10 MINS
COOKING TIME: 15 MINS

2 tbsp rapeseed (canola) oil or ghee
1 star anise
5cm (2in) piece of cinnamon stick
1 onion, finely chopped
2 tbsp garlic and ginger paste (see page 172)
1 green bird's eye chilli, finely chopped
½ tsp Kashmiri chilli powder
1 tsp ground cumin
125ml (½ cup) tomato purée (see page 172)
700ml (3 cups) base curry sauce (see page 164 or 166), heated
450g (1lb) small peeled raw prawns (shrimp)
2 tomatoes, quartered
1 tsp dried fenugreek leaves (kasoori methi)
2 lemons (1 quartered)
Salt, to taste
4 homemade puris (see page 311) or fried chapattis
3 tbsp finely chopped coriander (cilantro)

Heat the oil in a large frying pan or wok over a medium–high heat. Add the star anise and cinnamon and let the flavour of the spices infuse into the oil for about 30 seconds. Add the onion and fry for about 5 minutes until soft and translucent. Stir in the garlic and ginger paste along with the chilli and cook for another minute. Add the Kashmiri chilli powder and the cumin, followed by the tomato purée and about 250ml (1 cup) of the base sauce. Bring this all to a rolling simmer, only stirring if it looks like the sauce is catching on the pan.

Now add the prawns (shrimp) and another 250ml (1 cup) of the base sauce and simmer until the prawns are pink and almost cooked through. The sauce will reduce. You can add a little more base sauce if you like a thinner sauce, but you may not want to use it all. Stir in the tomatoes.

When the sauce consistency is to your liking, add the dried fenugreek leaves (kasoori methi) by rubbing the leaves between your fingers into the sauce. Squeeze the juice of one of the lemons into the sauce and season with salt. To serve, place one puri or fried chapatti on each of four plates. Divide the prawn curry between the plates and garnish with the coriander (cilantro) and a lemon wedge.

Bottom: Prawn puri (above)
Top right: Black pepper and lime rava mussels (page 30)

BLACK PEPPER AND LIME RAVA MUSSELS

SERVES 4 OR MORE AS PART OF A MULTI-COURSE MEAL

These mussels make the perfect starter course. They're crispy and, as very little spice is used, fuss-free too. You can work ahead as all the preparation up to actually frying the mussels can be done 1–2 hours beforehand. Then just 4 minutes of shallow-frying and your starter is on the table. They are pictured on page 29.

PREP TIME: 10 MINS
COOKING TIME: 15 MINS

25 fresh mussels
1 tsp freshly cracked black pepper
¼ tsp Kashmiri chilli powder
½ tsp fine sea salt
1½ tbsp lime juice
1 egg
5 generous tbsp fine semolina flour
4 tbsp rapeseed (canola) oil
Flaky sea salt, to taste
Lime wedges, to serve

Run cold water over the mussels, clean and debeard them. The mussels should close tightly when washed; if they don't, discard them. Bring about 250ml (1 cup) water to a boil in a saucepan with a tight-fitting lid. Place the mussels in the boiling water and cover. In about 5 minutes, they should all open. Discard any that don't.

Break open the mussel shells and carefully remove the meat. Place the meat in a bowl and allow to cool slightly. Sprinkle with the cracked black pepper, Kashmiri chilli powder and salt. Mix well and stir in the lime juice.

Now whisk the egg in a bowl and sprinkle the semolina on a plate. Take one mussel and dip it in the beaten egg, then roll it in the semolina to coat. Repeat with the remaining mussels.

Heat the oil over a medium–high heat in a preferably non-stick frying pan. Fry the mussels on one side for about 2 minutes, then turn them over to fry the other side, until the mussels are golden brown. This shouldn't take more than about 4 minutes.

For a nice presentation, serve the fried mussels in half shells. Season with flaky sea salt and serve hot with lime wedges.

TANDOORI CHICKEN LEGS

SERVES 4 OR MORE AS PART OF A MULTI-COURSE MEAL

One of the things about making Indian food daily and then blogging about it is that inevitably you come across recipes you want to make all the time. Tandoori chicken legs are a family favourite and my basic recipe has changed very little over the years. Red food colouring is often added to the chicken to give it that familiar appearance, but it is being used a lot less these days – it adds no flavour and is solely there for appearance.

PREP TIME: 15 MINS, PLUS
  MARINATING TIME
COOKING TIME: 15 MINS

8 skinless chicken legs, including
  thighs
Juice of 2 limes
1 tsp salt
1 tsp red food colouring powder
  (optional, see introduction)

FOR THE MARINADE
100g (scant ½ cup) Greek yoghurt
1 tbsp ground cumin
3 tbsp garlic and ginger paste (see
  page 172)
1 tsp ground coriander
1 tsp garam masala (see page 167)
1 tsp tandoori masala (see page 168)
1 tsp chilli powder
1 tbsp green chilli paste (see page 172)
½ tsp amchoor (dried mango
  powder)

Cut 3–5 shallow slits in each chicken leg and place in a large bowl. Squeeze the lime juice over the chicken and rub it into the meat along with the salt and red food colouring (if using). Set aside while you make the marinade.

Place all the marinade ingredients in a bowl and work them together with your hands until smooth. Coat the chicken with the marinade and allow to marinate for 2–48 hours – the longer the better.

When ready to cook, skewer the chicken legs onto flat skewers and heat the barbecue. Grill using the direct grilling method (see page 255) until the chicken is nicely charred and then turn. This is important when using skewers, as the meat needs to cook so that it expands and doesn't move around on the skewers.

If you can't be bothered to fire up the barbecue? No worries! Preheat the oven to 200°C (400°F/Gas 6) and cook the chicken on a wire rack placed over a foil-lined oven tray for about 20 minutes, or until cooked through. To get a nice black char, you can finish the cooked chicken directly under the grill (broiler) heated to maximum temperature for a minute or so.

CHICKEN PAKORAS
SERVES 2 OR MORE AS PART OF A MULTI-COURSE MEAL

Chicken pakoras are served in so many different ways at restaurants across the UK. The chicken breast meat can be cut into long strips or simple bite-size cubes that are perfect served as finger food. Often, the meat is dyed bright red to make it look spicy hot, although usually it's not very spicy at all. After trying many different possibilities, I decided to revisit my friend Bob Arora's recipe from Sachins in Newcastle. It's simple but the spices all work together so well. Bob recommends only ½ teaspoon of chilli powder, but I added a whole teaspoon because I like my pakoras on the spicy side. I'll leave that one up to you.

I like to serve this Indian fried chicken with coriander, garlic and chilli raita (page 339). You might like it with that sweet-and-sour red sauce that pakoras are often served with, and I have included a nice one on page 338. It's so good! The chicken pakoras in the accompanying photo were made by cutting the chicken into very small cubes and then squeezing them together in the batter. These really went down a treat once the photo was taken.

PREP TIME: 20 MINS
COOKING TIME: 30 MINS

250g (1½ cups) skinless and boneless chicken breast, cubed or sliced
½ tsp ground turmeric
½ tsp ajwain (carom) seeds
¾ tsp garam masala (see page 167)
½–1 tsp chilli powder, to taste
Salt, to taste
¾ tsp garlic and ginger paste (see page 172)
2 tbsp finely chopped coriander (cilantro)
White of 1 small egg
65g (½ cup) gram (chickpea) flour
Sparkling water
Rapeseed (canola) oil, for deep-frying
Lemon wedges, onion rings and lettuce, to serve

Place the chicken in a large bowl and mix with the turmeric, ajwain (carom) seeds, garam masala, chilli powder and a little salt so that the meat is evenly coated. Let this sit for about 20 minutes.

Stir in the garlic and ginger paste, coriander (cilantro) and egg white. Now start adding the gram flour a little at a time, coating the meat, adding a splash of sparkling water from time to time. Continue until all the flour is used up and it has the consistency of ketchup.

Heat enough oil for deep-frying in a deep, heavy-based saucepan or deep-fat fryer, to between 170–180°C (340–355°F). Using a wire mesh spoon, slowly lower the pakoras into the hot oil. You may need to fry in batches and cooking times will depend on the size of the chicken chunks, but they should only take a few minutes to cook through.

Serve with lemon wedges, onion rings and lettuce.

CHICKEN 65

SERVES 6 OR MORE AS PART OF A MULTI-COURSE MEAL

I'm asked often why this dish is called 'Chicken 65'. There is no one definite answer, but there are two explanations I've heard that I think are better than most. One is that the original recipe had 65 ingredients in it. The more likely explanation is that in India, where the menus can be very long and people order by number, this dish began showing up as the sixty-fifth option on numerous menus, making it easy to go out and order the very popular number 65 without even looking at the menu.

The deep-frying in this recipe can be done ahead of time, so if you are serving this curry-house classic to dinner guests, you won't need to be standing over hot oil when everyone arrives.

PREP TIME: 20 MINS, PLUS
MARINATING TIME
COOKING TIME: 10 MINS

1kg (2lb 3oz) chicken breasts
Rapeseed (canola) oil, for deep-frying
1 tsp black mustard seeds
1 tsp cumin seeds
20 curry leaves
3 green chillies, sliced
12 garlic cloves, finely chopped
10cm (4in) piece of ginger, peeled and
    julienned
3 spring onions (scallions), roughly
    chopped
2 tbsp lemon juice
2–3 tbsp chilli sauce (optional)

FOR THE SPICED BATTER
2 eggs, beaten
2 tbsp garlic and ginger paste (see
    page 172)
3 tbsp cornflour (cornstarch)
3 tbsp rice flour
1 tsp ground turmeric
1 tbsp ground cumin
1 tsp ground coriander
2 tsp chilli powder
1½ tbsp tandoori masala (see page
    168)
1 tsp salt
1 tbsp freshly ground black pepper

Slice the chicken breasts into small bite-size pieces (tikka). Mix all the batter ingredients into a paste, then rub it evenly into the chicken pieces. If time permits, let this marinate for about 30 minutes or overnight, but this isn't crucial.

When ready to deep-fry, heat about 10cm (4in) of oil in a large wok. The oil is ready when a small piece of chicken sizzles immediately upon putting it in the oil. If using an oil thermometer, aim for 190°C (375°F).

Fry the chicken in batches until the exterior is nice and crispy and the meat is almost cooked through. This should take 2–3 minutes per batch. Place the finished chicken pieces on a wire rack to rest while you fry the remaining batches. The frying can be done ahead of time. Store the fried chicken covered in the fridge until ready to use.

Once cooled a bit, remove all but about 3 tablespoons of the oil from the wok. Place over a high heat and toss in the mustard seeds. When they begin to pop (after about 30 seconds), reduce the heat to medium–high, add the cumin seeds, curry leaves and green chillies and fry for a further 30 seconds. Stir in the garlic and ginger and fry until fragrant and soft – about 1 minute should do the job.

Tip in the chicken and spring onions (scallions) and stir well to coat. Fry over a high heat until the chicken is completely cooked through. Squeeze the lemon juice over the top and add the chilli sauce (if using). Give it all one last good stir, check for seasoning, adding a little more salt if needed, and serve.

FRIED CHICKEN LOLLIPOPS

Chicken legs are the juiciest part of the chicken, but there is one thing that stops them being the most popular cut: those six stringy tendons. Luckily they aren't difficult to remove, and I think you will love serving these crispy chicken lollipops. The lollipops are also nice marinated in a chicken marinade, such the tandoori chicken tikka marinade on page 259, and then cooked over direct heat on the barbecue. These are delicious served simply with lime wedges or a good raita, or a hot sauce of your choice.

PREP TIME: 45 MINS, PLUS
    MARINATING TIME
COOKING TIME: 10 MINS

12 chicken legs
Rapeseed (canola) oil, for deep-frying

FOR THE MARINADE
1 egg
1 tbsp tandoori masala (see page 168)
    or garam masala (see page 167)
1 tsp chilli powder
1 tbsp coarse black pepper
2 tbsp garlic and ginger paste (see
    page 172)
1 tbsp soy sauce (use gluten-free if
    liked)
3 tbsp plain (all-purpose) flour
1 tbsp cornflour (cornstarch)
Salt, to taste

Hold a paring knife perpendicular to the end of a chicken leg, just before the ankle, and slice around the skin. Grab the skin and tear it off the ankle. A pair of good pliers will help with this, but I do it by hand. Begin sliding the skin and meat up the leg to form the lollipop end. As you do this, you will see the six stringy white tendons: grasp each tightly with your hand or pliers and pull them off the bone. You could also use a knife to cut any bits you missed. Continue moving the meat and skin up the bone until you have a nice ball at one end. Repeat with the remaining legs.

Whisk all the marinade ingredients together in a large bowl. Coat the chicken lollipops with the marinade and marinate for 30 minutes–24 hours – the longer the better.

When ready to fry, heat about 10cm (4in) of oil in a saucepan until a bit of the batter/marinade sizzles immediately when dropped in. Fry the chicken lollipops in batches until cooked through – about 5 minutes should do the job, but be sure to check. The internal temperature should be 75°C (165°F). If you don't have a meat thermometer, stick a sharp knife in – the chicken is ready when the juices run clear.

CHICKEN CHAAT
SERVES 4 OR MORE AS PART OF A MULTI-COURSE MEAL

This British curry-house classic is hugely popular and also quick and easy to make. I like to add tandoori chicken tikka (see page 259) or any of the grilled chicken recipes in this book as the smoky flavour really adds to the dish. You could really add any leftover cooked chicken. It's a great way of giving new life to your leftover Sunday dinner chicken roast! You can also cook the chicken from raw. Just cut the raw chicken into bite-size pieces and be sure to cook it through in the sauce.

PREP TIME: 10 MINS
COOKING TIME: 20 MINS

3 tbsp rapeseed (canola) oil
1 onion, finely chopped
2 tbsp garlic and ginger paste (see page 172)
2 tbsp mixed powder (see page 169)
1 tsp chilli powder
2 tbsp chaat masala (see page 168)
150ml (generous ½ cup) tomato purée (see page 172)
400ml (scant 1¾ cups) base curry sauce (see page 164 or 166), heated
700g (1lb 9oz) pre-cooked chicken (see introduction above)
½ cucumber, peeled, deseeded and cut into 2.5cm (1in) pieces
½ red (bell) pepper, roughly chopped
100g (3½oz) tinned (canned) chickpeas (garbanzo beans), drained and rinsed
1 large tomato, cut into 8 wedges
Salt, to taste
1 tsp garam masala (see page 167)

Heat the oil in a frying pan over a medium–high heat. When it's visibly hot, add the onion and fry for about 5 minutes until soft and translucent. Add the garlic and ginger paste and give it all another good stir.

Spoon in the mixed powder, chilli powder and chaat masala, followed by the tomato purée. This should sizzle when it hits the pan. When it does, add half the base sauce. Allow this to bubble for a minute or so, only stirring if the sauce begins to stick to the pan. Add the chicken pieces and the rest of the base sauce and simmer until the chicken is cooked through – about 10 minutes should do the job.

To finish, stir in the cucumber, red (bell) pepper, chickpeas and tomato wedges. Season with salt and sprinkle with the garam masala.

INDO-CHINESE SWEET-AND-SOUR CHICKEN

SERVES 4 OR MORE AS PART OF A MULTI-COURSE MEAL

Put simply, Indo-Chinese fusion food just plain gets it and I love this Chinese–Indian combo. The cooking time for this one is a bit long, but there is really very little work to do. When we cooked these during the photo shoot for this book, they went down a treat! We were running short on time but they were so good we decided to make another batch. I'm telling you... this sweet-and-sour chicken is addictive!

PREP TIME: 20 MINS
COOKING TIME: 1 HOUR

1kg (2lb 3oz) boneless and skinless chicken thighs, cut into thirds
Garlic salt, to taste
½ tsp amchoor (dried mango powder)
Rapeseed (canola) oil, for browning the chicken
Cornflour (cornstarch) or rice flour, for dusting
100g (½ cup) caster sugar
125ml (½ cup) rice wine vinegar or white wine vinegar
2 tbsp red chilli hot sauce
4 tbsp tomato ketchup
1 tbsp dark soy sauce or coconut amino*
65ml (¼ cup) orange juice
Salt and freshly ground black pepper, to taste

Preheat the oven to 175°C (350°F/Gas 4) and line a baking pan with foil or baking parchment to make clearing up easier.

Sprinkle the chicken pieces with garlic salt and the amchoor and set aside for about 10 minutes. Meanwhile, heat about 2.5cm (1in) of oil in a saucepan set over a medium–high heat. Roll the chicken pieces in cornflour (cornstarch) to coat well, then fry them in the oil for about 3 minutes, or until lightly browned. Set aside.

Mix together the sugar, vinegar, chilli sauce, ketchup, soy sauce or coconut amino and orange juice with a dash of salt and black pepper in a saucepan. Over a medium–high heat, stir the sauce until the sugar has dissolved.

Place a single layer of the chicken on the prepared baking tray and pour the sauce over. Bake for 1 hour until browned and crispy. For best results you will need to turn the chicken pieces a few times during cooking, but I often forget and have never been disappointed.

Transfer the cooked chicken to a serving plate and serve, or just serve in the tray! It will save you washing up and I really don't think anyone will complain.

NOTE
*Most soy sauces are not gluten-free. If this is important to you, use coconut amino instead.

SWEET AND SPICY CHICKEN WINGS
SERVES 4 OR MORE AS PART OF A MULTI-COURSE MEAL

Chicken wings are becoming a popular starter at lots of Indian restaurants. You might have seen many delicious options, from spicy garlic salt to Portuguese piri piri. They may not all be flavoured with the ingredients you would expect at a curry house, but I've never heard anyone complain! This is a recipe I developed after picking up some chicken wings at a food festival. The chef was happy to tell me what went into his marinade, and I think I got it just right.

Usually chicken is served skinless at Indian restaurants. Skinless chicken wings are available from most halal butchers. I tried skinning them myself once and won't again. It was way too much work. Of course, unskinned chicken wings are a lot fattier, but the crispy chicken skin is worth every calorie.

PREP TIME: 15 MINS, PLUS
    MARINATING TIME
COOKING TIME: 40 MINS

1kg (2lb 3oz) chicken wings,
    preferably skinless
3 tbsp chilli sauce
Raita of your choice, to serve

FOR THE MARINADE
2 tbsp garlic and ginger paste (see
    page 172)
1 tbsp green chilli paste (see page
    172), or 2–3 green chillies, finely
    chopped
1 tsp tamarind concentrate
2 tbsp cider vinegar
3 tbsp Worcestershire sauce
4 tbsp honey
1 tsp chilli powder, or to taste
1 tbsp ground cumin
Juice of 3 limes
Salt and freshly ground black pepper

Mix all the marinade ingredients together in a large bowl. Add the chicken wings and coat well with the marinade. Leave to marinate for 2–48 hours.

When ready to cook, preheat the oven to 200°C (400°F/Gas 6). Arrange the chicken wings on a lightly greased baking tray and place on the middle rack. Cook for about 30 minutes and then give the chicken a good shake and cook for another 10 minutes, or until cooked through and slightly blackened on the outside. Stir in the chilli sauce and serve with a good raita like the coriander, garlic and chilli raita on page 339.

KASHMIRI LAMB CUTLETS

SERVES 4 OR MORE AS PART OF A MULTI-COURSE MEAL

Kashmiri lamb cutlets are irresistible; cooking the meat in the spiced milk makes them melt-in-the-mouth tender. The succulent pieces of lamb can be eaten by hand like chicken nuggets... I bet you can't eat just one. I used boned lamb chops for this recipe, but any good meaty lamb cut will do. You could even cut the chops in half if you are serving a selection of starters to a group.

PREP TIME: 15 MINS
COOKING TIME: 50 MINS

12 lamb chops
500ml (2 cups) full-fat (whole) milk
2.5cm (1in) piece of cinnamon stick or cassia bark
6 green cardamom pods, lightly bruised
1 tsp cloves
2.5cm (1in) piece of ginger, peeled and grated
1 large onion, finely chopped
1 tsp ground cumin
1 tsp freshly ground black pepper
1 tbsp mixed powder (see page 169)
Rapeseed (canola) oil, for deep-frying
Flaky sea salt and 3 limes, quartered, to serve

FOR THE BATTER

4 tbsp gram (chickpea) flour
1 tbsp baking powder
1 tbsp rice flour
1 tbsp chilli powder
150g (generous ½ cup) plain yoghurt
1 tsp garam masala (see page 167)
Pinch of salt

Remove the bone from the chops and pound the meat with a meat mallet into small, flat steaks. Refrigerate until ready to use.

Pour the milk into a saucepan and add the cinnamon, seeds from the cardamom pods, cloves, ginger, onion, cumin, black pepper and mixed powder. Bring to a boil, then add the meat to the milk mixture and simmer for 30 minutes. Remove the meat from the milk and pat dry with paper towel.

Now whisk the batter ingredients together. It should be quite thick, like double (heavy) cream, so that it clings to the cutlets, so add a little more gram flour if it is too thin or more yoghurt if too thick.

Heat about 15cm (6in) of oil in a deep, heavy-based saucepan or wok to about 170°C (340°F) until a little batter dropped in sizzles immediately. Coat one of the lamb cutlets with the batter and slowly ease it into the oil. Repeat with the rest of the meat, but don't overload the pan – you may need to cook the lamb in batches.

Deep-fry until nicely browned, then remove with a wire-mesh spoon to a plate lined with paper towel to soak up any excess oil. Sprinkle with a little flaky sea salt and serve with the lime wedges. They are also great dipped into your favourite raita or chutney.

TIP

If cooking ahead of time, you can place the finished cutlets on a wire rack placed over a foil-lined baking tray in a low oven, for up to 30 minutes.

LAMB SHAMI KEBABS

SERVES 4 OR MORE AS PART OF A
MULTI-COURSE MEAL

When you bite into these shami kebabs, they simply melt in your mouth. Crisp on the outside and fall-apart tender inside; I can't get enough of them. There are few things as toothsome as a hot shami drizzled with coriander, garlic and chilli raita (see page 339) or spicy tomato chutney. Although I use lamb for this recipe, mutton is a popular alternative. If you've got the bone from the shoulder, simmer it with the meat for even more fantastic flavour.

PREP TIME: 15 MINS
COOKING TIME: 1 HOUR 20 MINS

1kg (2lb 3oz) lamb shoulder, roughly chopped and trimmed of excess fat
150g (1 cup) chana dhal, rinsed and soaked for 30 minutes
3 tbsp garlic and ginger paste (see page 172)
3 Kashmiri dried red chillies
1 onion, roughly chopped
2 tsp mixed powder (see page 169)
2 tsp garam masala (see page 167)
Small bunch of coriander (cilantro)
2 tbsp chopped mint leaves
2 green bird's eye chillies, or to taste
Salt, to taste
Rapeseed (canola) oil, for shallow-frying
2 large eggs, beaten

Place the lamb in a large saucepan, add water to cover and bring to the boil, skimming off the foam that rises to the top. Add the chana dhal, garlic and ginger paste, dried chillies, onion and mixed powder.

Cover and simmer for about 1 hour until the water evaporates and the meat is fork-tender, stirring in the garam masala after 45 minutes. Watch the pan carefully so that the dhal doesn't scorch on the bottom, adding more water if required.

Allow to cool, then transfer the mixture to a food processor with the coriander (cilantro), mint and chillies. Blend until fine, with the consistency of thick clay. Season with salt and form into patties. This can all be done well ahead of serving.

When ready to fry, heat about 2.5cm (1in) oil in a large frying pan. Brush both sides of each patty with the beaten egg, place in the hot oil and cook for about 1 minute per side until browned. Remove from the oil to a plate lined with paper towel.

BEEF CHAPLI KEBABS

SERVES 4 OR MORE AS PART OF A
MULTI-COURSE MEAL

Chapli kebabs are, in my opinion, the king of all kebabs. They are traditionally cooked in beef dripping, but you could opt for a healthier oil such as rapeseed (canola) oil, if you wish. You can serve these on their own with a salad and some mint and coriander sauce (see page 335), or wrap them up in homemade naans topped with salad, vegetables and chutney or raita.

PREP TIME: 15 MINS
COOKING TIME: 3 MINS

800g (1lb 12oz) minced (ground) beef (preferably 20% fat)
2 medium red onions, very finely chopped
3 tomatoes, peeled, deseeded and finely chopped
2 tbsp garlic and ginger paste (see page 172)
3 green bird's eye chillies, very finely chopped
1 tsp Kashmiri chilli powder
1 tbsp ground cumin
1 tbsp ground coriander
½ tsp salt, plus extra to taste
2 tbsp gram (chickpea) flour
200g (7oz) beef marrow (available from most butchers and many supermarkets)
Beef dripping, for shallow-frying
Salt, to taste
2 limes, quartered

Place the minced beef in a large baking tray and add all the ingredients down to and including the gram flour. Knead the meat with all the ingredient with your hands for about 10 minutes, pushing it all down into the tray as you do. The idea here is not only to combine the ingredients but to super-mince the meat.

Finely chop the beef bone marrow into 5mm (¼in) pieces or smaller. Work this into the meat as well so that it is all well combined, but you still want to see the chunks of marrow. Divide the meat mixture into four large equal-size patties, or smaller patties if you wish.

When ready to cook, heat about 7.5cm (3in) of beef dripping over a medium–high heat. When visibly hot, carefully submerge the beef patties into the boiling oil. Fry for 2–3 minutes until crispy on the exterior and cooked through. Season with salt and drizzle each with a squeeze of lime juice.

Lamb shami kebabs

RED LENTIL AND VEGETABLE KEBABS

SERVES 4 OR MORE AS PART OF A MULTI-COURSE MEAL

I find myself eating a lot less meat these days and I'm not all that crazy about meat substitutes. That's why I love veggie kebabs like these. They are both filling and delicious. Serve as a snack with a good raita or chutney. Here I have served them with homemade mango pickle (see page 330) and garnished them with flaky salt and coriander (cilantro). If you form the kebabs into small bite-size balls, they are also good stirred into any of the sauces in the curry-house section of this book (see pages 182–235).

PREP TIME: 15 MINS, PLUS
    SOAKING TIME
COOKING TIME: 20 MINS

1 tbsp rapeseed (canola) oil
1 medium red onion, grated
1 medium potato, peeled and grated
80g broccoli (1 cup), grated
1 medium carrot, grated
80g (3oz) cauliflower (1 cup) grated
½ tsp salt
225g (1 cup) masoor (red) lentils, washed and soaked in water for 30 minutes
2 tbsp garlic and ginger paste (see page 172)
5 tbsp finely chopped coriander (cilantro)
50g (½ cup) ground almonds
1 tsp tandoori masala (see page 168) or garam masala (see page 167)
1 tsp chaat masala (see page 168) (optional)
3 green chillies, finely chopped
½ tsp Kashmiri chilli powder (more or less to taste)
1 tsp ground coriander
1 tsp ground cumin
2 tbsp lemon juice
Salt and freshly ground black pepper, to taste
Rapeseed (canola) oil, for shallow-frying

Heat the oil in a large frying pan over a medium–high heat. Add the grated vegetables and the salt and fry, stirring regularly, for 5–7 minutes. You not only want to soften the vegetables but also cook out most of the moisture. They should be quite dry.

Drain the lentils and dry them on paper towel. Place in a food processor with the remaining ingredients up to and including the lemon juice and blend until you have a chunky paste – it should be smooth, but not pâté smooth and there should still be some small chunky bits.

Place this lentil mixture in a mixing bowl and add the fried vegetables. Mix well with your hands to combine and season with salt and black pepper. Form the mixture into the shape of your choice – they could be small and round like meatballs, or made into sausage shapes.

Heat the oil in a large frying pan. I usually use about 5cm (2in) of oil, but you could use a lot less if using a non-stick pan. Fry the kebabs for about 3 minutes until browned on one side, then flip them over and brown the other side for 2–3 minutes.

ALOO TIKKI CHAAT

SERVES 4–8

I absolutely love this chaat! The tamarind sauce and the mint, coriander and mango chutney can be purchased from most good Asian grocers or online. If you fancy a go at making your own, I have included recipes on pages 336 and 335. Phoa (rice flakes) are also available at Asian shops. You could leave them out, but they really do help give the aloo tikki an amazing crispy texture.

PREP TIME: 10 MINS
COOKING TIME: 20 MINS,
   PLUS THE TIME IT TAKES
   TO PAR-COOK POTATOES

250g (1 cup) Greek yoghurt
1 tsp chaat masala (see page 168)
½ tsp red chilli powder
Juice of 1 lime
Salt, to taste
4 medium potatoes, unpeeled
4 heaped tbsp rice flour
4 heaped tbsp phoa (rice flakes),
   soaked in 2 tbsp water for
   30 minutes (optional)
Rapeseed (canola) or vegetable oil,
   for frying
Pinch of asafoetida*
½ tsp cumin seeds
3 green chillies, finely chopped
2.5cm (1in) piece of ginger, peeled
   and finely chopped
1 tsp ground coriander
½ tsp ground turmeric
½ tsp chilli powder
Small bunch of coriander (cilantro),
   finely chopped
Tamarind sauce (see page 336), to
   serve
Mint, coriander and mango chutney
   (see page 335), to serve

Whisk the yoghurt for about 2 minutes until airy and light. Stir in the chaat masala, chilli powder and lime juice and season with salt. Set aside.

Boil the potatoes in their skins until almost tender, but still with a little resistance when a knife is inserted. Allow to cool a little, then peel and grate the potatoes into a mixing bowl. Stir in the rice flour. Squeeze any excess liquid from the soaked rice flakes (if using) and add them too.

In a small frying pan, heat about 2 tablespoons of oil over a medium–high heat until hot. Add the asafoetida and cumin seeds to the hot oil and fry for about 30 seconds, then add the chillies and ginger. Fry for a further minute or so, then stir in the ground coriander, turmeric and chilli powder.

Sauté until the chillies and ginger are cooked through – about 2 minutes should be enough – then remove from the heat to cool slightly. Pour this mixture and the coriander (cilantro) into the bowl with the grated potatoes and mix well by hand. Season with salt.

Mash the mixture lightly with a potato masher or by hand. The mixture shouldn't be completely mashed and you should still be able to see that the potatoes have been grated. Form the mixture into golf ball-size balls, then press down on them gently to form them into patties (tikki).

Shallow-fry the tikki in about 2.5cm (1in) of hot oil for 2 minutes on one side, then flip over to fry the other side for 2 minutes. If needed, fry for a little more time to brown to your preferred colour. Season with salt and top generously with the yoghurt mixture, along with some tamarind sauce and mint, coriander and mango chutney.

NOTE
*If you are gluten-free, please check the asafoetida packaging as some brands contain wheat flour.

MULLIGATAWNY SOUP
SERVES 4

There is no one recipe for Mulligatawny soup and it can vary greatly in flavour and colour. This recipe is up there with the best. It is delicious served with broken idlis. You can purchase instant idli mix at most Asian shops or follow my recipe on page 311.

PREP TIME: 10 MINS
COOKING TIME: 30 MINS

25g (2 tbsp) butter
3 bay leaves
5cm (2in) piece of cinnamon stick
6 cloves
1 large red onion, finely diced
1 stick celery, diced
1 carrot, diced
50g (1¾oz) tinned (canned) plum tomatoes, roughly chopped
½ leek, diced
1 tbsp plain (all-purpose) flour
1 litre (4½ cups) salt-free chicken or vegetable stock
400ml (14fl oz) tin (can) thick coconut milk
Salt, to taste
4 broken idlis (see page 311) (optional)
4 lemon wedges, to serve

FOR THE SPICE PASTE
1 tbsp ground cumin
1 tbsp ground coriander
1 tbsp freshly ground black pepper
1 tsp ground turmeric
6 garlic cloves, peeled
4cm (1½in) piece of ginger, peeled and roughly chopped
Handful each of coriander (cilantro) and mint leaves

Put all the spice paste ingredients into a food processor or blender. Add a splash of water and blitz to a paste. Leave to one side.

Melt the butter in a large heavy-bottomed saucepan. Add the bay leaves, cinnamon and cloves and fry for a minute or so to flavour the butter. Add the onion and cook for 5 minutes until soft and translucent.

Add the vegetables and cook for a further 5 minutes. Stir in the spice paste and fry for a few minutes until fragrant. Stir in the flour followed by the stock. Cover and simmer for 15 minutes until thickened. Pour in the coconut milk and mix. If you like a creamier texture, as I do, blend the soup and run it through a sieve. Adjust the seasoning and add more stock if it is too thick.

Season with salt and serve with idli pieces, if desired, and lemon wedges.

MANGO LASSI
SERVES 2
PREP TIME: 5 MINS

Way back when I first started my blog, it was the mango lassis that got my kids excited about going out for a curry. I was happy with the pints of cold lager, but for them it was those thick mango milkshakes that they craved more than the curries and rice. So this is one of the first recipes I taught them. Lassis are the perfect accompaniment for a curry feast. They are deliciously soothing, offering an often-appreciated cooling effect when consumed with those spicy curries.

250g (1 cup) Greek yoghurt
400ml (scant ¾ cups) full-fat (whole) milk
250ml (1 cup) tinned (canned) mango pulp or the equivalent ripe cut mango pieces
2 tbsp sugar
½ tsp cardamom powder (optional)
Handful of ice cubes
3 tbsp pistachio nuts, lightly crushed
Whipped cream, to garnish
A pinch of saffron, to garnish

Place the yoghurt, milk, mango, sugar and cardamom powder (if using) in a blender and blend until super-smooth. Add the ice cubes and blend until crushed.

Divide into two glasses and sprinkle some pistachio nuts over the top. Garnish with a squirt of whipped cream and top with a few more pistachios and saffron.

Mulligatawny soup

POSH BOMBAY MIX
SERVES 4 AS A SNACK

Delicious served with drinks before a meal, you simply have to try this posh Bombay mix (shown on page 13). This one really packs a punch! Use the Bombay mix of your choice. You'll find the best selection at Asian grocers, but it is also available in supermarkets. If eating gluten-free is important, be sure to check the bag, as some can contain gluten.

PREP TIME: 10 MINS

A few large handfuls of your Bombay mix of choice
1–2 green chillies, finely chopped
3 tbsp finely chopped coriander (cilantro) stems
¼ red onion, finely chopped
½ tomato, deseeded and diced
½ tbsp mustard oil
½ tsp chaat masala (see page 168)
1 tbsp lemon juice

Using a cocktail mixer or any container with a firm-fitting lid, add your favourite Bombay mix along with the rest of the ingredients. Close the lid and shake hard. Eat immediately or the Bombay mix will get soggy.

TAJAH BADAM
SERVES 4–6 AS A SNACK

I love bringing out this tasty snack of spicy Bangladeshi almonds when we have friends over. It is always devoured and only take a few minutes to throw together. It is pictured on page 13.

PREP TIME: 5 MINS
COOKING TIME: 2 MINS

1 tbsp rapeseed (canola) oil
250g (3 cups) flaked (slivered) almonds
4 long green chillies, finely sliced lengthways
Pinch of ground turmeric
Juice of 1 lime
Salt, to taste
3 tbsp chopped coriander (cilantro), to serve

Heat the oil in a large frying pan. Add the almonds and toast for about 1 minute until lightly browned. Add the chillies and turmeric and stir to combine.

Serve on a warmed plate with the lime juice squeezed over the top and season with salt. Garnish with the coriander (cilantro).

STREET
FOOD

Street food is hugely popular in the Indian subcontinent, as it is all over the world. People have busy lives nowadays, so it's nice to be able to quickly pick up food that is both delicious and convenient.

It might be called 'street food', but the very fact that it is so good has meant that the same meals can now be found on the menus of many fashionable restaurants in the West. Street-food restaurants are springing up all over the place, and it's little wonder why they are so trendy.

So although these crowd-pleasing recipes are tasty enough to get people queuing up in the streets, you will no doubt recognize and see them on the menus of today's must-try Indian restaurants. They not only make excellent snacks but stand up to the best and most exciting meals.

KEEMA PAU

SERVES 4 OR MORE AS PART OF A MULTI-COURSE MEAL

My friend Roxanne Bamboat is a travel blogger from Mumbai. She writes the fantastic blog The Tiny Taster, and I highly recommend looking it up and reading about her travels. When I was researching recipes for my book *The Curry Guy Veggie*, I flew out to Mumbai with my a friend of mine and, luckily, Roxanne just happened to be in town to show us the sights and introduce us to some of the best food that Mumbai has on offer. Roxanne is from the Parsi community, a group that fled oppression in Iran for India sometime between the 8th and 10th centuries, where they became, and still are, an important part of society in Mumbai. One memorable stop was breakfast at the oldest Iranian café in Mumbai: Kayani & Co, which is popular with many celebrities and Bollywood stars. She ordered keema pau (pav) for us and it was so good. Keema pau is very popular street food, but if you ever find yourself at Kayani & Co, it is also one of the best breakfasts you'll ever eat.

PREP TIME: 10 MINS
COOKING TIME: 20 MINS

500g (1lb 2oz) minced (ground) lamb
5 tbsp rapeseed (canola) oil
2.5cm (1in) piece of cinnamon stick
3 green cardamom pods, bruised
500g (1lb 2oz) onion, finely chopped
2 tbsp garlic and ginger paste (see page 172)
½ tsp ground turmeric
1 generous tbsp garam masala (see page 167)
Generous handful of coriander (cilantro) leaves
4 green bird's eye chillies
70g (¼ cup) fresh or frozen peas
1 tbsp dried fenugreek leaves (kasoori methi)
Salt, to taste
2 limes, quartered
Soft hamburger buns

Mix the minced lamb with 500ml (2 cups) of water and break it up with your hands until the mixture is about the same consistency as porridge. This will help achieve a smooth keema without any lumps. Set aside.

In a large pan or wok, heat the rapeseed (canola) oil over a medium–high heat. When visibly hot, stir in the cinnamon and cardamom pods and let the flavour of these spices infuse into the oil for about 30 seconds. Add the onion and fry, stirring occasionally for about 10 minutes, or until the onion turns light brown. Stir in the garlic and ginger paste and fry for an additional 30 seconds, then tip in the meat/water mixture. Cook on high for about 5 minutes to cook the meat through, stirring regularly to prevent any meat lumps.

Add the turmeric and garam masala and stir well to combine and simmer while you prepare the coriander (cilantro) and chillies. Blend the coriander and chillies with about 70ml (¼ cup) of water into a smooth paste, then pour it over the keema. Stir well and cover the pan. Continue cooking for a further 5 minutes. Add the peas, cover and continue cooking for another 5 minutes. This is a dry curry, so there is no need to add more water unless it is looking a little too dry.

To finish, add the dried fenugreek leaves (kasoori methi) by rubbing the leaves between your fingers and continue cooking until the oil separates from the meat mixture. Season with salt.

Pour onto a warm serving plate and serve with the lime wedges and hamburger buns, which can be broken up to scoop up the keema.

TIP
Toasting the hamburger buns in a little butter is a nice and delicious touch.

PUNJABI CHOLE
SERVES 4 OR MORE AS PART OF A MULTI-COURSE MEAL

You might think that cooking chickpeas with teabags is a bit strange. Chickpeas are naturally quite dry, even after simmering for a long time, as they don't naturally retain much moisture. Cooking them with teabags helps retain the moisture, which is important for Punjabi chole. The sauce does not taste at all like tea, but the teabags do give the curry its distinctive deep brown colour. This is delicious street food at its best that is usually served with freshly made bhatura (see page 314). Punjabi chole bhatura is street food that simply must be tried!

PREP TIME: 10 MINS, PLUS
   OVERNIGHT SOAKING
COOKING TIME: 5 MINS

300g (1½ cups) dried chickpeas
   (garbanzo beans)
3 English tea teabags
½ tsp bicarbonate of soda (baking
   soda)
5cm (2in) piece of cinnamon stick
2 black or 4 green cardamom pods,
   bruised
5 cloves
4 generous tbsp ghee
½ tsp asafoetida*
1 tsp cumin seeds
2 medium red onions, blended with a
   little water to make a paste
2 tbsp garlic and ginger paste (see
   page 172)
300g tomatoes, blended
2 tbsp chole masala (see page 170 or
   shop-bought)
1 tbsp dried pomegranate seeds,
   lightly crushed (optional)
1 tsp ground coriander
1 tsp chilli powder (more or less to
   taste)
½ tsp ground turmeric
1 tsp dried fenugreek leaves (kasoori
   methi)
Salt, to taste
1 small red onion, thinly sliced into
   rings
3 tbsp finely chopped coriander
   (cilantro)
4 green bird's eye chillies, sliced
   lengthways (optional)
Fresh bhatura (see page 314), to serve

Wash and soak the dried chickpeas overnight. When ready to cook, drain the chickpeas and place them in a large saucepan. Cover with water and add the teabags, bicarbonate of soda (baking soda), cinnamon, cardamom pods and cloves. Bring to a simmer and cook for about 1 hour until the chickpeas are really soft, then drain. You should be able to easily squash one between your fingers. Set aside.

Heat the ghee in a large, high-sided frying pan over a medium–high heat. When it begins to shimmer, stir in the asafoetida and cumin seeds and let these infuse into the ghee for about 30 seconds. Add the blended onions and stir to combine. Reduce the temperature to medium and fry for about 10 minutes, or until the onions turn deep brown. Stir in the garlic and ginger paste and fry for a further 30 seconds before adding the tomatoes. Add the chole masala, pomegranate seeds (if using), ground coriander, chilli powder and turmeric. Simmer for about 5 minutes, then tip in the cooked chickpeas minus the teabags. Add the dried fenugreek leaves (kasoori methi) by rubbing the leaves between your fingers and season with salt.

Garnish with the onion rings, coriander (cilantro) and some green chillies, if liked, and serve with fresh bhatura.

NOTE

*If you are gluten-free, please check the asafoetida packaging as some brands contain wheat flour. This recipe contains very little asafoetida, so it can easily be left out without much difference in flavour.

PAV BHAJI
SERVES 4 OR MORE AS PART OF A MULTI-COURSE MEAL

I was introduced to pav bhaji by my friend and award-winning chef Syed Ahmed, of Duke Bombay Café in Darlington. I love the food that comes out of his kitchen, and this buttery pav bhaji is one of my all-time favourites. Authentic pav bhaji is cooked with a lot of butter. If you aren't keen on using the amount of butter I suggest here, you can of course reduce the quantity.

Pav bhajis are normally served with a top and bottom buttered bun with generous portions of the potato mixture and toppings. If you are serving these as part of a multi-course meal, you might want to give each person half a bun with the sauce. The bread and potato mixture, though delicious, can be quite filling.

PREP TIME: 15 MINS
COOKING TIME: 25 MINS

FOR THE VEGETABLES
2 large potatoes, peeled and finely sliced
250g (9oz) cauliflower florets
1 small carrot, peeled and diced
100g (¾ cup) fresh or frozen peas
400g (14oz) tin (can) chopped tomatoes
Salt, to taste

FOR THE MASALA
200g (¾ cup) unsalted butter
1 large red onion (about 250g/9oz), finely chopped
1 tsp cumin seeds
1 tbsp red chilli powder (more or less to taste)
½ tsp ground turmeric
4 fat garlic cloves, grated
2.5cm (1in) piece of ginger, peeled and grated
1 red (bell) pepper, finely chopped
1 tbsp garam masala (see page 167)
Salt, to taste

TO SERVE
Soft buns
Butter, for spreading
Coriander (cilantro) leaves, chopped
4 lemon wedges
1 red onion, finely chopped

Put the potatoes, cauliflower, carrot, peas and tomatoes in a large pot and add just enough water to cover. Bring to the boil and cover with a lid. Cook for about 20 minutes, stirring occasionally until the potatoes and vegetables are soft. Using a potato masher, mash it all up. It should be a bit wetter than mashed potato consistency – like creamy and slightly chunky potato soup – so add a drop of water if needed. Season with salt and keep warm.

Melt about 100g (7 tablespoons) of the butter in a large frying pan over a medium–high heat. Toss in the onion and cumin seeds and fry until the onion is soft. Add the chilli powder, turmeric, garlic, ginger and red (bell) pepper and fry for a further minute or so. Stir in the garam masala and season with salt. Whisk this mixture into the mashed vegetables. Top with the remaining butter and allow to melt.

To serve, cut the buns in half and butter them generously on both sides. Place them buttered-side down in a hot frying pan to brown. Place the toasted buns on warmed plates with a good helping of the bhaji. Sprinkle with coriander (cilantro) and serve with lemon wedges and red onion on the side.

BHEL PURI

Bhel puri can be made with many different ingredients, but the key ingredient is kurmure (puffed rice), which can be found in most Indian/Asian shops. This delicious snack food originates from Mumbai but is now popular all over India – so much so, it's made its way to restaurants and street-food stalls here in the UK. It's so good, it's addictive, and it's super-easy to make too. You want to mix the ingredients up just before serving. Once you get the idea behind bhel puri, you can adjust the recipe depending on how much you want to make and what you feel like adding. Bhel puri is traditionally served in rolled-up newspapers, but a simple bowl will do.

PREP TIME: 10 MINS
COOKING TIME: 20 MINS

1 potato, unpeeled
100g (5 cups) kurmure (puffed rice)
1 red onion, finely chopped
3 green chillies, finely chopped
125ml (½ cup) mint and coriander
   sauce (½ recipe quantity on page
   335, or shop-bought)
6 tbsp tamarind sauce (see page 336
   or shop-bought)
20g (½ cup) fine sev
5 tbsp roasted peanuts
5 tbsp Bombay mix (optional)
5 papdi or other crispy biscuit, broken
   into pieces (optional)
Juice of 1 lemon
3 tbsp finely chopped coriander
   (cilantro)
Salt, to taste

Bring a saucepan of water to a boil. When ready, add the potato and boil until fork-tender. The cooking time will vary depending on the size of the potato, so it's ready when it's ready. Transfer to a chopping board to cool, then peel and cut into small cubes.

In a large bowl, mix the kurmure, onion, green chillies and potato together. Add the mint and coriander sauce along with the tamarind sauce. Try to coat all the rice with the sauces. Now stir in the remaining ingredients, season with salt and serve.

NOTE

Many other ingredients are popular additions to bhel puri. Try finely diced mango or pomegranate seeds for a good sweet touch, or broken potato crisps.

HARA BHARA KEBAB BURGER

MAKES 8 BURGER-SIZE KEBABS

Hara bhara kebabs not only look great but they're also delicious and good for you. These can be eaten on their own with a little mint and coriander sauce (see page 335) or mango pickle (page 331), or used as a filling for the kathi roll (page 67). I like to add small, hot hara bhara kebabs to tomato-based curries, or substitute them for the paneer in my butter paneer recipe (see page 144). Be sure to add them at the end of cooking, though, so that they don't fall apart. You really can't beat a good burger, so that's how I've done them here.

PREP TIME: 15 MINS, PLUS
   CHILLING TIME
COOKING TIME: 25 MINS

1 large potato, about 350g (12oz), cut into 6 pieces
225g (8oz) spinach
5 tbsp rapeseed (canola) oil
3 green cardamom pods, lightly smashed
2.5cm (1in) piece of cinnamon stick
2 cloves
1 tsp cumin seeds
1 tsp coriander seeds
1 small onion, finely chopped
30g (¼ cup) peas
100g (3½oz) mint, finely chopped
100g (3½oz) coriander (cilantro), finely chopped
2–3 green chillies, finely chopped
5 garlic cloves, finely chopped
2.5cm (1in) piece of ginger, peeled and finely chopped
125g (4½oz) paneer cheese, grated
2 tbsp gram (chickpea) flour, plus extra if needed
1 tsp chaat masala (see page 168)
Juice of 1 lime
Salt, to taste

Bring a pan of water to the boil and cook the potato for about 10 minutes until soft. Use a slotted spoon to fish out the potato chunks, then mash them lightly with a fork.

Now blanch the spinach in the same water for about 30 seconds. Remove it from the water and squeeze as much of the water out as you can, then finely chop it.

Heat a frying pan over a medium heat and add 2 tablespoons of the oil. When visibly hot, stir in the cardamom pods, cinnamon, cloves, and cumin and coriander seeds. Move the spices around in the oil for about 45 seconds, then remove the cardamom pods and cinnamon.

Add the onion and fry for about 5 minutes until translucent and soft. Stir in the blanched spinach, mashed potato, peas, mint, coriander (cilantro), chillies, garlic and ginger and cook for a further 3 minutes. Allow to cool.

Place these ingredients with the paneer, gram flour and chaat masala in a food processor or large pestle and mortar and blend to a thick paste. Add the lime juice and season with salt, if needed.

Form this paste into eight large patties (or you could make more smaller ones, if you wish). If you find that it is too wet, you could add a little more gram flour. Place the patties in the fridge for about 15 minutes before frying.

When ready to cook, heat the remaining oil in a frying pan and fry the patties for about 3 minutes per side, or until lightly browned and heated through.

NOTE
You can substitute about 150g (5½ oz) of defrosted shop-bought frozen spinach for the fresh spinach if you wish. There is no need to blanch this as it was done before freezing.

MAKE IT VEGAN
You could leave the cheese out or use a non-dairy cheese of your choice. Why not top it all with some meltable dairy-free cheese?

VADA PAV
MAKES 8

These mildly spiced, deep-fried potato burgers are a delicious way to use up leftover mashed potatoes. The mashed potato is first fried with a few complementary spices and herbs, and then formed into large balls that are dipped into a seasoned gram-flour batter. Everything, right up to making the sandwich, can be done ahead of time. At busy restaurants and street stalls, the potato vada are formed and fried earlier in the day and heated through again in hot oil before serving. This is really convenient if you are serving a group of friends. When I tried these at food stalls in India there was always a plate of roasted chillies you could help yourself to for topping your vada pav, making them as mild or spicy as you want. If you really want to treat yourself, spread lots of butter on the buns before grilling!

PREP TIME: 10 MINS
COOKING TIME: 25 MINS

4 potatoes (about 800g/1lb 12oz), peeled and diced
3 tbsp rapeseed (canola) oil
1 tsp black mustard seeds
½ tsp ground turmeric
3 green chillies, finely chopped, plus extra to garnish
1 tbsp finely chopped ginger
1 tsp chilli powder
10 curry leaves, roughly chopped
Salt, to taste
3 tbsp finely chopped coriander (cilantro)
Rapeseed (canola) oil, for deep-frying

FOR THE BATTER
120g (1 cup) sifted gram (chickpea) flour, plus extra if needed
½ tsp salt
½ tsp chilli powder
½ tsp ground turmeric

TO FINISH
4 soft hamburger buns
Ghee, butter or oil, for browning the buns
Mint and coriander sauce (see page 335)
Tamarind sauce (see page 336) (optional)
Roasted green chillies

Boil the potatoes in water for about 10 minutes until fork-tender. Drain and mash.

Heat the oil in a large frying pan over a medium–high heat. Add the mustard seeds. When they begin to pop (after about 30 seconds), stir in the turmeric, green chillies, ginger, chilli powder and curry leaves. Move this all around in the pan to flavour the oil, then add the mashed potatoes and mix well. Season with salt and add the coriander (cilantro). Allow to cool slightly, then form into eight lemon-size balls.

Whisk the batter ingredients together, adding enough water slowly to make a thick and smooth batter. The batter should cling to, and coat, the vada. If you find it is too thin, sift in a little more flour.

Heat the oil for deep-frying in a large pan. The oil should be deep enough to cover the vada. You are ready to start deep-frying when a piece of potato sizzles immediately when dropped into the hot oil. If you have an oil thermometer, aim for 200°C (390°F). Carefully lower the vada into the oil and fry until crispy brown – about 3–5 minutes should do. Depending on the size of your pan, you may need to cook these in small batches of three or four.

While the vada are frying, brown the buns in another pan in some ghee, butter or oil. When toasted to your liking, spread the mint and coriander sauce over the bun halves. Place a vada on top of the bottom bun and top with tamarind sauce (if using) and one or more roasted chillies if you like it spicy. Add the top bun and serve.

PANEER KATHI ROLL
MAKES 4

This is a different way of making paneer kathi rolls. Usually the paneer is cubed and then wrapped in a chapatti. This is very good, but I like the paneer grated, as I saw them doing it at Zindiya Streatery & Bar in Birmingham. The cheese is heated through and mixed well with all the other ingredients, making the plain old paneer kathi roll a luxurious and mouthwatering wrap.

PREP TIME: 10 MINS, PLUS
    OVERNIGHT SOAKING THE
    DHAL
COOKING TIME: 10 MINS

4 chapattis or parathas (shop-bought
    or homemade), warmed
Mint and coriander sauce (see page
    335)
Tamarind sauce (see page 336)

FOR THE SALAD
4 tbsp washed moong dhal, soaked in
    water overnight
150g (5½oz) red cabbage, finely
    shredded
150g (5½oz) white cabbage, finely
    shredded
1 red onion, diced
1 carrot, grated
2 tbsp extra virgin olive oil
Juice of 1–2 limes
Salt and freshly ground black pepper,
    to taste

FOR THE FILLING
2 tbsp rapeseed (canola) oil
1 tsp black mustard seeds
2 Kashmiri dried red chillies, broken
    into 3 pieces and deseeded
1 onion, finely chopped
½ tsp ground turmeric
200g (7oz) paneer cheese, grated

Start by mixing the salad. Toss all the ingredients in a large bowl and season to taste. Cover and place in the fridge until ready to use.

For the filling, heat the oil in a large frying pan over a medium–high heat. When visibly hot, add the mustard seeds. When they begin to pop (after about 30 seconds), add the Kashmiri chillies, followed by the onion. Allow the onion to fry until translucent and lightly browned – about 5 minutes should do it. Now stir the turmeric into the oil, then add the paneer and stir it around until it is heated through.

Divide the cheese mixture between four warmed chapattis. Top with equal amounts of the salad and top with the mint and coriander and tamarind sauces. Wrap tightly, then cut each kathi in half diagonally. Serve immediately.

MAKE IT VEGAN

These wraps are delicious even without the paneer. You could simply leave the paneer out or choose your favourite dairy-free cheese. I have used both non-dairy grated mozzarella and Cheddar with good results.

MUMBAI TOASTIE
SERVES 2

If you haven't tried the famous Mumbai toastie yet, it's time you did. These are so good. Buttered fluffy white bread topped with seasoned potatoes, vegetables and the essential mint and coriander sauce... this is a sandwich you would expect from the exciting city that is Mumbai. These are often served as a simple sandwich, but for me, it's the buttered and toasted version that gets it! If you've made some of my potato curry (see page 154) and have leftovers, you could use it on these toasties if you wish.

PREP TIME: 10 MINS
COOKING TIME: 20 MINS

FOR THE POTATO FILLING
2–3 tbsp ghee or vegetable ghee
1 tsp cumin seeds
10 curry leaves
1 onion, finely chopped
2–3 green chillies, sliced into rings
½ tsp ground turmeric
1 tsp chilli powder (optional)
1 tbsp garlic and ginger paste (see page 172)
2 potatoes, peeled and cut into cubes
Salt and freshly ground black pepper, to taste
3 tbsp finely chopped coriander (cilantro)

TO ASSEMBLE
150ml (generous ½ cup) mint and coriander sauce (page 335), but without the yoghurt
4 pieces of white bread
4 slices of Cheddar cheese
8 slices of tomato
8 slices of cucumber
8 slices of red (bell) pepper
8 slices of red onion
Butter, for frying

To make the potato filling, heat the ghee in a large pan over a medium–high heat. When hot, add the cumin seeds and curry leaves. Temper these in the hot oil for about 30 seconds, then add the onion. Fry for about 5 minutes until fragrant and soft, then add the chillies, turmeric, chilli powder (if using) and garlic and ginger paste. Stir this all up well and tip in the cubed potatoes. Add just enough water to cover, and simmer until the potatoes are fork-tender and quite dry – about 10 minutes should do. Season with salt and black pepper and stir in the coriander (cilantro). Set aside to cool slightly.

When ready to make the toastie, spread the mint and coriander sauce all over each slice of bread. Top two of the slices of the bread with the potato mixture, spreading it evenly all over the bread. Then stack each of these slices with two pieces of cheese, four tomato slices, four cucumber slices, four red (bell) pepper slices and four slices of red onion. Place the final two pieces of bread on top.

Heat a large frying pan over a medium–high heat. Add 2 generous tablespoons of butter and fry the sandwiches in the butter. When nicely browned, carefully flip them over and fry the other side until browned. Serve immediately.

MAKE IT VEGAN
Use vegetable ghee instead of the butter, and use a good vegan meltable cheese instead of Cheddar. Omit the mayonnaise.

PANI PURI

SERVES 6–12

I've loved pani puri for years, but it wasn't until I met Pratik Master, owner of the excellent restaurant Lilu in Leicester, that it dawned on me how easily these delicious flavour bombs could be served at home. Pratik prepared a plate of puri shells with a variety of easy-to-make fillings and we sat, snacked and chatted for hours.

Making the small puri shells is difficult, so I would suggest that you purchase them ready-made at an Asian grocers or online. Good-quality black and green pani (water) can also be purchased, but I have included recipes for them on page 337 if you want to make your own. The recipe also calls for fine sev or boondi. Fine sev is a fine, hair-like, crispy fried gram flour topping, and boondi is also a fried gram topping but looks like little balls. Both are available at Asian shops. Try to find them if you can, as they are both a nice, crunchy addition to pani puri, but you can leave them out if you must.

You can really get creative with pani puri. Try them with fried potatoes or perhaps a spoonful of yoghurt sauce (see page 338). The sky's the limit. Get everything prepared ahead of time and let your friends go wild on filling their puris.

PREP TIME: 15 MINS
COOKING TIME: 20 MINS (FOR THE POTATO)

150g (5½oz) room-temperature boiled potato, grated or cut into very small pieces
400g (14oz) tin (can) chickpeas (garbanzo beans), drained and rinsed
30 small puri shells

LITTLE EXTRAS FOR SERVING
Salt
Chilli powder
Ground cumin
2 lemons, cut into wedges
Amchoor (dried mango powder)
200g (¾ cup) plain yoghurt, whisked
Chaat masala (see page 168)
Finely chopped coriander (cilantro)
Pomegranate seeds
Tamarind sauce (see page 336 or shop-bought)
Green pani (see page 337 or shop-bought)
Black pani (see page 337 or shop-bought)
Fine sev or boondi

This is more of a fun assembly line than a recipe. Place the boiled potatoes (grated or cut) in a serving bowl. Do the same with the chickpeas. Prepare bowls of the other ingredients and/or come up with a few sides of your own. This can all be done ahead of time.

When ready, let the pani puri party commence! Present the puri shells with all the toppings and there's nothing more to do than say 'dig in'! Tell people to gently break open the top of the puri shells with their finger and try them with different fillings. Some might like them with just chickpeas, chilli powder, chaat masala, yoghurt and pomegranate seeds. Others might fill them with a bit of everything before topping the tiny puri shell with the green or black pani (water) and a good sprinkling of sev or boondi and popping them into their mouth. Don't add anything to the puri shells beforehand or the shells will get soggy.

MAKE IT VEGAN
Don't top with the yoghurt. The pani puri will still taste amazing.

SAMOSA CHAAT

Crispy samosas right out of the hot oil take this popular chaat to a whole new level. You could use any samosas, even shop-bought, but why miss out on the fun of making them yourself? This is an excellent way to use up leftover samosas. However, your samosa chaat will be better if you make the samosas just before serving.

Samosa chaat is so popular in India and it is now being seen on many more Indian restaurant menus in the West as well. In fact, this easy recipe has become a must at my cooking classes. People just love it! Samosa chaat might be seen more often on Western menus these days, but it's still not one that jumps off the page and says 'try me!' Once tried, however, there's no going back. This simple recipe is one of my all-time favourites.

PREP TIME: 5 MINS, PLUS
    MAKING THE SAMOSAS IF
    USING HOMEMADE
COOKING TIME: 10 MINS

8 hot samosas (see pages 18–21 or shop-bought)
400g (14oz) tin (can) chickpeas (garbanzo beans), drained and rinsed
1 large red onion, finely chopped
3 tbsp mint and coriander sauce (see page 335)
3 tbsp yoghurt sauce (see page 338)
3 tbsp tamarind sauce (see page 336)
2 large handfuls of fine sev or similar*

Place two hot samosas in the centre of each of four serving plates. (If using shop-bought or leftover samosas, you could microwave them until hot, or better, place them in an oven preheated to 200°C (400°F/Gas 6) for about 10 minutes.) You could leave the samosas whole or break them up a bit.

Cover the samosas with the chickpeas and onion. Top with mint and coriander sauce, yoghurt sauce and tamarind sauce. To finish, cover generously with fine sev.

FINE SEV SUBSTITUTES

*Fine sev is used a lot to top and garnish chaats. It's made from gram (chickpea) flour and looks a lot like tiny pieces of angel hair pasta. You can purchase it at many Asian shops and also online to add a nice crunch to your chaats. If you can't find it, you could use another crispy gram flour-fried noodle or puffed balls of gram flour called bundi, which is easier to find.

MAKE IT VEGAN

Substitute homemade dairy-free yoghurt and you're in for a treat.

AUTHENTIC CURRIES

In this chapter you will find some of my favourite authentic curries from India, Pakistan, Sri Lanka and Bangladesh. I developed these recipes so that you could experience these dishes the way they are served in the Indian subcontinent.

You'll notice how each recipe starts with a bit of oil and then other base ingredients are added to the pan to make the sauce. These sauce-making steps are all but eliminated when making curry house-style curries (see pages 182–235). In those recipes, a base sauce is used instead of having to prepare a base for each curry.

For a bit of fun, you could try substituting curry house-style base sauce in these recipes. Forget frying those onions and just use a base sauce. Likewise, you might like to try some of these authentic sauce-making techniques in the curry-house recipes. They won't be the same as those you are served at curry houses, but they still work with more authentic cooking techniques. You really can't go wrong and it is a great way of getting to know different cooking styles.

CHICKEN XACUTI
SERVES 4 OR MORE AS PART OF A MULTI-COURSE MEAL

Chicken xacuti is one of Goa's most famous curries. It is known for its spiciness and its subtle flavour of nutmeg, poppy seeds, coconut and star anise. Xacuti is usually cooked with skinless chicken on the bone, which is what I've done here. Lamb on the bone is also a popular main ingredient. The curry is normally served with plain rice or semolina fried potatoes like the recipe on page 320. Those potatoes are fantastic and I highly recommend giving them a try with your xacuti.

PREP TIME: 10 MINS, PLUS
    SOAKING TIME
COOKING TIME: 25 MINS

FOR THE XACUTI MASALA
6 Kashmiri dried red chillies, chopped
    (seeds removed for a milder curry)
75g (1 cup) dried coconut flakes
1 tbsp cumin seeds
1 tbsp coriander seeds
1 tsp ajwain (carom) seeds
1 tbsp fennel seeds
1 tbsp black poppy seeds
7 cloves
1 tbsp (about 35) black peppercorns
5cm (2in) piece of cinnamon stick
4 star anise
½ tsp ground turmeric
8 garlic cloves, finely chopped
5cm (2in) piece of ginger, peeled and
    finely chopped

FOR THE CURRY
8 skinless chicken thighs on the bone
2 tsp rapeseed (canola) oil
1 tsp black mustard seeds
10 fresh or frozen curry leaves
2 onions, finely chopped
2 green bird's eye chillies, finely
    chopped
500ml (2 cups) chicken stock or water
1½ tbsp tamarind paste or
    concentrate
¼ tsp ground nutmeg
20g (¼ cup) coriander (cilantro),
    finely chopped
Salt, to taste

Start by making the xacuti masala. In a dry frying pan, toast the Kashmiri chillies for about 1 minute, turning regularly until fragrant. Place in a bowl of warm water to soak for about 30 minutes. Now toast the coconut flakes until lightly browned and set aside. Toast the cumin, coriander, ajwain (carom) seeds, fennel and poppy seeds, the cloves, peppercorns, cinnamon stick and star anise over a medium–high heat until fragrant and warm to the touch. Transfer to a bowl and allow to cool.

When the chillies are soft, drain them, reserving the soaking water, then blend them with the coconut flakes and the rest of the masala ingredients, along with a little of the chilli soaking water to make a paste, but taste the water first: if it is bitter, use fresh water instead.

Pour the paste over the chicken in a large bowl and mix well to coat. You can start cooking the curry now, but if you would like to marinate the chicken for a couple of hours or overnight, it will be even better.

When ready to cook, heat the oil in a large frying pan or wok over a high heat. When bubbles begin to form on the bottom of the pan, add the mustard seeds. When they begin to pop (after about 30 seconds), reduce the heat to medium–high and stir in the curry leaves and let them flavour the oil for about 30 seconds. You'll know when the oil is perfectly flavoured because it will smell so nice. Add the onions and fry for about 5 minutes until soft, lightly browned and translucent. Stir in the chillies, then the chicken and all of the marinade. Stir well to coat the chicken in the onion mixture. Add the stock or water and simmer for about 15 minutes until the chicken is tender and cooked through.

Stir in the tamarind paste or concentrate and nutmeg, then give it a taste. For a sourer flavour, add more tamarind. Nutmeg can taste quite strong to some, but add more if you like. To serve, stir in the coriander (cilantro) and season with salt.

CHICKEN ZAFRANI
SERVES 4 OR MORE AS PART OF A MULTI-COURSE MEAL

This delicious curry has a rich flavour that's all its own. I like it with chillies, often more than called for in the recipe, but if you leave them out it is a great curry for kids and those who prefer milder curries. You can get away with only marinating the chicken for about 30 minutes, but if you marinate the meat for about 24 hours, it will be even better. The marinade is used to make the sauce. This makes cooking the dish a lot easier as you just have to take the marinated chicken out of the fridge and cook it. You can literally get home from work and cook this one up in under 30 minutes.

PREP TIME: 15 MINS, PLUS
   MARINATING TIME
COOKING TIME: 30 MINS

800g (1lb 12oz) skinless chicken
   thighs – on or off the bone
3 tbsp ghee or rapeseed (canola) oil
1 x 5cm (2in) cinnamon stick
5 green cardamom pods, lightly
   smashed
2 star anise
Pinch of saffron
2 tbsp double (heavy) cream
½ tsp dried fenugreek leaves (kasoori
   methi)
Salt, to taste

FOR THE FIRST MARINADE
2 tbsp garlic and ginger paste (see
   page 172)
Juice of 1 lemon
½ tsp salt

FOR THE SECOND MARINADE
Rapeseed (canola) oil, for shallow-
   frying
3 onions, thinly sliced
12 skinned almonds, soaked in water
   for 20 minutes
12 cashew nuts, soaked in water for
   20 minutes
½ tsp ground turmeric
1 tbsp ground cumin
1 tbsp ground coriander
1 tsp Kashmiri chilli powder
250g (1 cup) plain yoghurt
2 green bird's eye chillies, finely
   chopped

Place the chicken thighs in a large mixing bowl and add all of the first marinade ingredients. Mix well to combine and marinate while you make the second marinade.

For the next marinade, heat about 10cm (4in) of oil in a large saucepan or wok. When visibly hot, add the onions and fry for 7–10 minutes until golden brown. Transfer to paper towel to soak up any excess oil.

Place the fried onions in a spice grinder or food processor and grind to a smooth onion paste. You can add a drop of water to assist with blending if needed. Now add the soaked almonds and cashew nuts, turmeric, cumin, coriander and chilli powder and blend again until smooth.

Whisk this paste together with the yoghurt and finely chopped chillies. Do not blend the yoghurt or it will become runny. Pour this over the chicken and rub this marinade into the meat. Leave to marinate for at least 30 minutes or overnight – the longer the better.

When ready to cook, melt the ghee or oil in a large saucepan with a tight-fitting lid over a medium–high heat. Add the cinnamon stick, cardamom pods and star anise. If you don't like whole spices in your curries, be sure to count them in and then count them back out again at the end of cooking. Let these spices infuse into the ghee for about 30 seconds, then tip in the chicken pieces along with all the marinade.

Cover and simmer over a low heat for about 25 minutes, or until the chicken is cooked through. You can add a drop of water if the curry is looking thirsty but the chicken will release moisture to make the sauce. When the chicken is cooked through, stir in the saffron and cream and cook for a further 3 minutes, then add the dried fenugreek leaves (kasoori methi) by rubbing the leaves between your fingers into the sauce. Season with salt and serve.

NOTE

This chicken zafrani, like all authentic curries, can be adjusted to your personal preference. Feel free to cut the chicken thighs into bite-size pieces. If you prefer more sauce, add a little water or stock and cook it down until you are happy with the consistency. If you like creamy curries, adding more cream, though not authentic, will do the job!

BUTTER CHICKEN

SERVES 4 OR MORE AS PART OF A MULTI-COURSE MEAL

In 1947, Kundan Lal Gujral opened the first tandoori restaurant, called Moti Mahal, in Delhi, India. Although tandoor-style ovens had already been used for thousands of years, he was the first to have large tandoors manufactured for use in a restaurant. The restaurant served delicious marinated chicken, meat and vegetables, all charred to perfection in a tandoor. Not one to waste, Gujral came up with the idea of using the leftover marinades in a curry, and butter chicken (murgh makhani) was born. For the chicken, use tandoori chicken tikka (see page 259) or tandoori chicken legs (see page 31). Reserve the marinade for the sauce.

PREP TIME: 10 MINS
COOKING TIME: 30 MINS

4 tbsp rapeseed (canola) oil or seasoned oil (see page 8)
2.5cm (1in) piece of cinnamon stick or cassia bark
2 star anise
6 green cardamom pods, lightly bruised
2 Indian bay leaves (cassia leaves)
2 onions, finely chopped
1 carrot, grated
1 tsp salt, plus extra, to taste
2 tbsp garlic and ginger paste (see page 172)
2 x 400g (14oz) tins (cans) chopped tomatoes
1 tsp paprika
1 tbsp ground cumin
1 tbsp ground coriander
1 tsp ground turmeric
1.5kg (3lb 5oz) grilled tandoori chicken (see page 259 or 31) and the reserved marinade
300ml (1¼ cups) double (heavy) cream
3 tbsp butter, chilled
Freshly ground black pepper, to taste
1 tbsp garam masala (see page 167)

Heat the oil in a large saucepan over a medium–high heat. When hot, toss in the cinnamon stick, star anise, cardamom pods and bay leaves, and stir them in the oil for about 30 seconds.

Add the onions and carrot, and fry for about 15 minutes, stirring occasionally, so that the onions turn soft and translucent but not browned. Sprinkle 1 teaspoon of salt over the top to help release some of the moisture from the onions. Now add the garlic and ginger paste and fry for 30 seconds, followed by the tomatoes.

Add the paprika and ground cumin, coriander and turmeric, and simmer for about 3 minutes. At this stage you have a choice. You can either leave the sauce as it is or take the whole spices out and blend it to a smooth sauce. I'll leave that one to you. I usually leave it as is.

Reduce the heat to medium and place the grilled chicken pieces in the sauce to heat through. To finish, whisk in the cream and reserved marinade from preparing the chicken, and turn the heat back up to medium–high. Add the chilled butter, 1 tablespoon at a time, and check for seasoning, adding more salt if needed. Sprinkle with the garam masala and serve.

CHICKEN LABABDAR

SERVES 4 OR MORE AS PART OF A MULTI-COURSE MEAL

Chicken lababdar is very similar to butter chicken and, for that matter, chicken tikka masala. I like to serve my lababdar curries a bit spicier than the others by adding more Kashmiri chilli powder and fresh chillies. Lababdar curries are a lot less fussy than butter chicken as the chicken isn't marinated and is cooked from raw in the sauce. I use chicken on the bone in this recipe, which is the authentic way of cooking it. The bones add flavour, but you could use boneless cubed chicken thighs or breasts if that is more appealing to you.

PREP TIME: 15 MINS, PLUS
    SOAKING TIME
COOKING TIME: 30 MINS

3 tbsp rapeseed (canola) oil
3 green cardamom pods, smashed
2.5cm (1in) piece of cinnamon stick
1 blade of mace
1 medium red onion, finely chopped
½ tsp salt
2 green chillies, finely chopped
4 tbsp garlic and ginger paste (see page 172)
½ tsp ground turmeric
1 tsp Kashmiri chilli powder, or more to taste
1 tbsp ground coriander
1½ tsp ground cumin
250ml (1 cup) tomato purée (see page 172)
Sugar, to taste (optional)
1.5kg (3lb 5oz) whole skinless chicken, cut into 8–10 pieces
10 cashew nuts
3 green bird's eye chillies
½ tsp dried fenugreek leaves (kasoori methi)
3 tbsp finely chopped coriander (cilantro)
3 tbsp single (light) cream
1 generous tbsp cold butter
Salt, to taste

Heat the oil over a medium–high heat in a large frying pan or wok. Add the cardamom pods, cinnamon and mace and allow these spices to infuse into the oil for about 30 seconds. Add the onion and salt and fry for about 8 minutes, or until the onion is golden brown. Stir in the green chillies and garlic and ginger paste and fry for about 45 seconds, stirring continuously.

Add the turmeric, Kashmiri chilli powder, ground coriander and cumin and stir to combine before adding the tomato purée. Taste the sauce – if you like a sweeter sauce, add sugar to taste, but I rarely do as I find the tomatoes sweet enough. Add the chicken pieces and brown them for about 2 minutes, then add 250ml (1 cup) of water. Cover the pan and simmer for about 12 minutes, or until the chicken is just cooked through.

Meanwhile, blend the cashew nuts and green bird's eye chillies with 70ml (¼ cup) of water into a smooth, thin paste. Pour the paste over the chicken while it's cooking.

After 12 minutes, remove the chicken and whole spices from the pan. Then remove the sauce and blend until smooth in a blender or using a hand-held blender. Pour this back into the pan and, over a medium heat, add the dried fenugreek leaves (kasoori methi) by rubbing the leaves between your fingers into the sauce, as well as the coriander (cilantro) and cream. Return the chicken to the pan and simmer until cooked through and hot. Stir in the butter until it melts into the sauce. Season with salt and serve.

CHICKEN AND COCONUT CURRY

SERVES 4 OR MORE AS PART OF A MULTI-COURSE MEAL

If you like spicy curries, this one is for you. The soaked and blended Kashmiri chillies give this curry an eye-catching red hue. If you are not a spicy curry fan, you could remove the seeds from the chillies so that you still get the glow but without all the heat.

PREP TIME: 10 MINS, PLUS
   SOAKING TIME
COOKING TIME: 15 MINS

12 Kashmiri dried red chillies
1 tsp cumin seeds
1 tsp coriander seeds
2 tsp sesame seeds
10 black peppercorns
4 cloves
3.5cm (1½in) piece of cinnamon stick
Seeds from 4 green cardamom pods
2 onions, roughly chopped
2 tbsp garlic and ginger paste (see
   page 172)
3 tbsp rapeseed (canola) oil
1 tsp ground turmeric
2 tomatoes, diced
1kg (2lb 3oz) skinless chicken thighs
2 x 400ml (14fl oz) tins (cans) thick
   coconut milk
1 tsp tamarind concentrate
Salt, to taste
½ tsp garam masala
3 tbsp finely chopped coriander
   (cilantro)

Soak the Kashmiri chillies in cold water for 20 minutes. While the chillies are soaking, place the cumin seeds, coriander seeds, sesame seeds, peppercorns, cloves, cinnamon and cardamom seeds in a small dry frying pan and toast them over a medium heat until warm and fragrant but not yet smoking. Transfer to a spice grinder and grind to a fine powder. Add the soaked Kashmiri chillies, onions and garlic and ginger paste and blend to a paste. If needed, you can add a drop of water to assist blending.

Now heat the oil in a large frying pan or wok over a medium–high heat. When hot, add the spice paste and the turmeric and let it sizzle in the oil for about 3 minutes, stirring continuously. Add the tomatoes and stir well to combine. Add the chicken to the pan and fry for about 5 minutes until browned. Pour in the coconut milk and simmer, covered, until the chicken is cooked through. Stir in the tamarind concentrate and season with salt.

To serve, sprinkle with the garam masala and garnish with the coriander (cilantro).

CHICKEN ALEESA
SERVES 6 OR MORE AS PART OF A MULTI-COURSE MEAL

During one of our visits to the beautiful state of Kerala, my wife Caroline and I were invited to breakfast at the home of Chef Shihabudeen V. M. and his family. This was no ordinary breakfast! In fact, it was one of the most amazing home-cooked meals we had ever experienced. Shihabudeen and his wife Ruvaida cooked up an incredible feast with no fewer than seven different dishes, and this delicious aleesa was one of them. Its origins are in the Middle East, but it is a very popular dish with the Muslim community in Kerala, especially during Ramadan. Caroline and I loved it so much I just had to get the recipe and, thankfully, Shihabudeen was happy to send it to me.

PREP TIME: 10 MINS, PLUS
  SOAKING TIME
COOKING TIME: 1 HOUR
  20 MINS

3 star anise
5 cloves
3 green cardamom pods, smashed
2.5cm (1in) piece of cinnamon stick
225g (1 cup) bulgur, soaked in water for 2 hours
1 large skinless chicken leg with thigh (about 350g/12½oz)
Flaked almonds or cashew nuts, to garnish (optional)
6 tbsp ghee
50g (2oz) shallots, thinly sliced
2 tsp ground turmeric
Salt, to taste

Tie the star anise, cloves, cardamom pods and cinnamon in a clean cloth. Place the tied spices in a large pot with the soaked bulgur and chicken leg. Cover with water and cover the pot with a lid. Bring to a boil, then simmer for about 40 minutes until the chicken is falling off the bone and the bulgur is nice and soft.

Meanwhile, toast the almonds or cashew nuts in the ghee until lightly browned, then transfer to a bowl to use as a garnish. This is optional.

In the same ghee, sauté the shallots until lightly browned and stir in the turmeric. You can remove some of the shallots to use as a garnish as well.

Remove the meat from the chicken bones and place it with the cooked bulgur in the pan with the browned shallots.

Cover with water and simmer for another 30–40 minutes until the chicken and bulgur are like mush – the finished dish should have the texture of cooked oatmeal. You can use a potato masher to mash it all up really well.

Season with salt and garnish with the nuts and shallots, if you like.

CHICKEN BHUNA

SERVES 4 OR MORE AS PART OF A MULTI-COURSE MEAL

Curry-house bhunas are similar to authentic bhunas in that they have a thick sauce, perfect for mopping up with hot naans or chapattis. That is where their similarity ends. You can find my curry house-style lamb bhuna on page 214; like all curry house-style recipes, it can be made with any meat or other main ingredient of your choice. Authentic bhuna is a style of cooking where the meat is cooked in its own juices and just a little water until the meat is really tender and covered in a thick sauce that is deliciously flavoured by the meat and other ingredients. You could use another meat such as beef or lamb in this recipe, but the cooking time will be longer and you will need to add a little more water; the exact amount of water depends on how long it takes for the meat to become tender. No rushing things! It's ready when it's ready.

PREP TIME: 15 MINS
COOKING TIME: 30 MINS

4 tbsp rapeseed (canola) oil
2.5cm (1in) piece of cinnamon stick
2 Indian bay leaves (cassia leaves)
    (optional)
10 black peppercorns
5 cloves
5 green cardamom pods, lightly
    smashed
2 medium onions, finely chopped
1 tsp sugar
2 tbsp garlic and ginger paste (see
    page 172)
1 tsp Kashmiri chilli powder (more or
    less to taste)
½ tsp ground turmeric
1 tbsp ground cumin
1 tbsp ground coriander
3 medium tomatoes, diced
1kg (2lb 3oz) whole skinless chicken,
    cut into 8 pieces
250ml (1 cup) hot water, plus extra if
    needed
3 green bird's eye chillies, sliced
    lengthways
½ tsp garam masala
Salt, to taste

Heat the oil in a large saucepan that has a lid. When the oil is bubbly hot, add the cinnamon stick, bay leaves, black peppercorns, cloves and cardamom pods. Stir the spices for about 40 seconds to infuse their flavours into the oil. Add the onions and sugar and fry for 8–10 minutes until they turn a caramelized brown. Add the garlic and ginger paste, Kashmiri chilli powder, turmeric, cumin and coriander. Give it all a good stir to combine, then add the tomatoes and chicken.

Brown the chicken for about 2 minutes, then pour in the hot water, reduce the heat to medium and cover the pan. Simmer, covered, for 10 minutes, then give it a stir. Only add a drop more water if it is looking dry. The idea here is not so much to simmer the chicken in a lot of liquid but just to have enough water in the pan to cook the chicken through without frying it. Cover the pan again and simmer for another 10 minutes, stirring from time to time and adding more water as needed. By this time, you should have a sauce that is so thick it coats the meat. When the oil rises to the top, your curry is ready! Throw in the chillies and garam masala and season with salt.

TAWA CHICKEN WING FRY

SERVES 4 OR MORE AS PART OF A MULTI-COURSE MEAL

If you're looking for a delicious chicken dish that only takes minutes to make, this is the one! Traditionally it's cooked on a tawa (a flat, round pan with no sides that dips down slightly in the centre), but you could of course use any pan and other cuts of chicken. Thigh works really well here, but I like to use cheaper cuts of meat like wings when I can. You can purchase skinless chicken wings at Asian grocers, and I suggest you do so as skinning wings is a really big job. Chicken wings are so tasty and I love picking them up to devour every last bit of meat and sauce!

PREP TIME: 5 MINS
COOKING TIME: 10 MINS

3 tbsp rapeseed (canola) oil or
    rendered chicken fat (shop-bought
    or homemade – see page 88)
1kg (2lb 3oz) skinless chicken wings,
    whole or cut in half
1 tsp salt, or to taste
2 tbsp garlic and ginger paste (see
    page 172)
1 tsp ground turmeric
1 tbsp ground coriander
1 tbsp tandoori masala (see page 168)
1 tsp Kashmiri chilli powder (more or
    less to taste)
200ml (generous ¾ cup) water or
    spice stock (see page 167)
1 large tomato, diced
Large handful of coriander (cilantro),
    finely chopped
15 fresh or frozen curry leaves
Juice of 1 lemon

Heat the oil in a large tawa or frying pan over a medium–high heat. Add the chicken pieces and give them a good stir to coat them in the oil. Season with salt, add the garlic and ginger paste and stir some more to combine. Fry for about 30 seconds, then sprinkle over the turmeric, ground coriander, tandoori masala and chilli powder, and stir it all up again.

Add the water or spice stock and tomato, stirring continuously, then add half the coriander (cilantro) and the curry leaves. With this recipe it is really important to continue stirring so that the chicken cooks evenly. Fry until the water has almost evaporated but the chicken still looks nice and moist in a thick gravy.

To serve, squeeze the lemon juice over the top and garnish with the remaining coriander. Check for seasoning, adding more salt or chilli powder if needed.

CHICKEN MASALA CURRY

SERVES 8 OR MORE AS PART OF A MULTI-COURSE MEAL

This authentic Punjabi curry is such a good recipe to have as part of your repertoire. If you've ever ordered the 'chicken curry' off the menu at a home-style restaurant, there is a good chance it was just like this. Although this chicken curry is delicious served as described, you can do so much more with it if you want to get creative. You could add a few handfuls of freshly chopped or frozen spinach leaves and transform this into a mouthwatering chicken saag curry. Why not try adding some thick coconut milk or whisked plain yoghurt? You'll get two different and equally tasty curries! If you like your curries spicy, add a few finely chopped green bird's eye chillies and/or a couple of teaspoons of Mr Naga chilli paste – this is used at most curry houses and is available at Asian grocers and online. This will definitely turn up the heat.

PREP TIME: 10 MINS
COOKING TIME: 30 MINS

3 tbsp rapeseed (canola) oil
1 tsp cumin seeds
1 tsp coriander seeds
1 Indian bay leaf (cassia leaf)
4 onions, finely chopped
1 tbsp ground cumin
1 tbsp ground coriander
2 tbsp garlic and ginger paste (see page 172)
1 tsp red chilli powder (more or less to taste)
1 tsp ground turmeric
4 tennis ball-size tomatoes, finely chopped
1 tsp salt
100ml (scant ½ cup) tomato purée (see page 172) or plain passata (sieved tomatoes)
1.6kg (3lb 8oz) skinless chicken thighs, bone-in
1–2 tsp garam masala (see page 167)

In a large saucepan that has a lid, heat the oil over a medium–high heat. When hot, add the cumin seeds, coriander seeds and bay leaf and temper in the oil for about 30 seconds. Pour in the chopped onions. Fry for about 5 minutes until the onions are soft and translucent. Stir in the ground cumin and coriander, garlic and ginger paste, chilli powder and turmeric followed by the chopped tomatoes and allow to sizzle over a medium heat for about 5 minutes. Add the salt to this mixture and it will help the onion release moisture into the sauce. The onions and tomatoes will begin to break down, turning into a thick sauce.

Stir in the tomato purée or passata (sieved tomatoes) and sizzle for about 30 seconds, then add the chicken. Stir it all up nicely and pour in just enough water to cover the chicken. Cover the curry and let it simmer for about 10 minutes. The sauce will become nice and thick and will stick to the chicken pieces as they cook.

Remove the lid and stir, adding a drop more water if you prefer a thinner sauce or turning up the heat if it is too runny. You'll know the curry is ready when the oil comes to the top. Simply skim it off.

Stir in 1 teaspoon of the garam masala and taste. Add more salt if needed. I usually use about 2 teaspoons of garam masala.

CHICKEN NAMKEEN

SERVES 6 OR MORE AS PART OF A MULTI-COURSE MEAL

Chicken namkeen is delicious as the dish is cooked in chicken fat. You can purchase rendered chicken fat at some speciality shops and farm shops, but I usually render my own. Rendering your own chicken fat is easy: purchase two 1.5kg (3lb 5oz) chickens and remove the fat from the carcasses and the skin and cut it into small 2.5cm (1in) pieces. Fry the fat over a medium heat in a non-stick pan for 5 minutes. This will release some fat. Cover the skin and fat with 500ml (2 cups) of water and simmer, covered, for 1 hour. Lift the lid and turn the crispy fat over and fry the other side for a further 20 minutes, uncovered. By now, all the water will have evaporated and you will be left with enough fat for this curry. Use one of the chickens for the curry and use the other for another recipe.

PREP TIME: 15 MINS
COOKING TIME: 30 MINS

250ml (1 cup) rendered chicken fat
1.5kg (3lb 5oz) whole chicken, cut
    into 20 pieces
400g (14oz) tin (can) plum tomatoes
6 green bird's eye chillies, slit down
    the middle
1 tsp freshly ground black pepper
Salt, to taste
5cm (2in) piece of ginger, peeled and
    julienned

Heat a large high-sided frying pan over a high heat and pour in the rendered chicken fat. Add the chicken and fry, covered, for about 20 minutes, stirring regularly so that it cooks evenly. Once all the chicken pieces are cooked through and a bit crispy, pour all but about 4 tablespoons of the oil out of the pan. You can freeze this fat for the next time you make a namkeen.

Tip in the tomatoes and the green chillies – remove the seeds if you don't like really spicy curries. Continue cooking and stirring until the sauce thickens to your preferred consistency.

Season with the black pepper and salt and garnish with the ginger.

DUCK HAAS PATHA KOBI

SERVES 4 OR MORE AS PART OF A MULTI-COURSE MEAL

If you like duck, you've simply got to try this authentic Bangladeshi duck curry! The first time I tried it, the duck breasts were marinated in a well-known commercial brand of balti masala. It was really good but I prefer the simple marinade below. These ingredients really bring out the flavour of the duck without competing with it.

PREP TIME: 10 MINS
COOKING TIME: 20 MINS

4 duck breasts
1 tbsp vegetable oil
1 tbsp garam masala (see page 167) or tandoori masala (see page 168)
Pinch of chilli powder
2 tbsp garlic and ginger paste (see page 172)
Spring onions (scallions), chopped, to serve

FOR THE CABBAGE
3 tbsp vegetable oil
1 tbsp panch phoran
2 tbsp garlic slivers
Salt, to taste
1 tbsp garlic and ginger paste (see page 172)
1 heaped tsp dried chilli (hot pepper) flakes, or to taste
200ml (generous ¾ cup) plain passata (sieved tomatoes) or blended chopped tomatoes
½ Savoy cabbage, shredded

FOR THE WHOLE GARAM MASALA
2 star anise
10 black peppercorns
1 tsp cumin seeds
1 tsp coriander seeds
2.5cm (1in) piece of cinnamon stick

Prepare the duck breast by removing the skin and rubbing the flesh with the oil, garam masala or tandoori masala, chilli powder and the garlic and ginger paste. Set aside to marinate while you prepare the rest of the dish.

Cut each duck skin into 3 pieces and place in a saucepan with 250ml (1 cup) of water and all of the whole garam masala ingredients. Simmer the water until reduced to about 5 tablespoons, then strain and put the reduction to one side to marinate.

For the cabbage, heat the 3 tablespoons of oil in a saucepan over a medium–high heat. Add the panch phoran and fry for about 30 seconds. Now add the garlic slivers and a little salt and fry until the garlic turns light brown. Be careful not to burn it. Stir in the garlic and ginger paste, dried chilli (hot pepper) flakes and the passata (sieved tomatoes), followed by the shredded cabbage. You want to just cook the cabbage through so that it still has a bit of crunch to it. Add the duck skin reduction and stir it all up well. Keep warm.

Meanwhile, sear the duck breasts in a dry frying pan over a high heat. I prefer my duck slightly pink inside so I cook the breasts for about 2 minutes per side. You can cook for longer if you prefer the meat cooked through.

To serve, slice the duck breasts thinly. Divide the cabbage mixture onto four plates and top each plate with one thinly sliced duck breast. Season with salt and sprinkle with the chopped spring onions (scallions) to serve.

FIERY HOT 7-INGREDIENT LAMB CURRY

SERVES 4 OR MORE AS PART OF A MULTI-COURSE MEAL

Look at the ingredients list of most Indian recipes and it's no wonder so many people find cooking Indian food a bit daunting. This authentic Rajasthani recipe, with its list of only seven ingredients, is therefore quite unique but is in no way lacking in magnificent flavour. The meat breaks down and becomes so juicy and tender in the ghee. Be warned... this curry is really spicy. If you are not a spicy curry fan, you could use a mild paprika instead of the dried chillies and/or chilli powder.

I have to admit I was rather sceptical about using so much ghee, and it might be a bit scary for some, but believe me... it is amazing. The ghee is needed as, when flavoured with the lamb, it actually becomes the sauce. Dip hot naans into the curry or spoon it over hot rice. You're in for an incredible eating experience. Due to the amount of ghee used, stir well before serving and ensure the sauce is really hot. I like to serve this over warm rice with a twist of lime juice, kachumber salad (see page 326) and mint and coriander sauce (see page 335).

PREP TIME: 10 MINS
COOKING TIME: 45–60 MINS

12 large garlic cloves, peeled
A big scoop of ghee (about 330g/
    1½ cups)*
1kg (2lb 3oz) lamb on the bone, cut
    into 5cm (2in) pieces
20 Kashmiri dried red chillies
2 tbsp Kashmiri chilli powder, or to
    taste
2 tbsp coriander seeds
Salt, to taste

Slice 8 of the garlic cloves in half lengthways and lightly smash. Blend or pound the remaining cloves into a paste. Set aside.

Heat the ghee over a medium–high heat. When bubbly hot, stir in the lamb, chillies, chilli powder, coriander seeds, smashed garlic and garlic paste. Give it all a good stir and simmer for 45 minutes, only adding a little water if the mixture is sticking to the pan. Stir regularly and cook until the lamb is succulent and tender. Don't rush this. If after 45 minutes it is not tender, continue cooking until it is. Season with salt.

NOTE
*Using lots of ghee is the traditional way of cooking this curry. If you would prefer a healthier option, choose another recipe! There are plenty of curries in this book that are far less fatty; I recommend giving this one a go just as it's meant to be.

CHANA GOSHT

SERVES 4 OR MORE AS PART OF A MULTI-COURSE MEAL

Chana gosht is a favourite staff curry behind the scenes at many restaurants. One of the best I've tried was at Lahore Kebab House in Shoreditch when I was researching recipes for my first book. I didn't get the recipe from them at the time but wished that I had. This recipe came about by surprise. I was preparing shami kebabs, which are made with the same ingredients. It wasn't until I tried the reduced mixture I was cooking, before blending it all up for the shamis, that I realized that the flavour was so close to that curry I enjoyed so much at Lahore! I make this curry all the time now. In the recipe, you pan-fry the lamb chops, which works well. I also like this curry with grilled lamb chops, cooked over hot coals on the barbecue. It adds an amazing smoky, charred flavour.

PREP TIME: 20 MINS, PLUS
    MARINATING TIME
COOKING TIME: 1 HOUR
    15 MINS

3 tbsp ground coriander
2 tbsp ground cumin
1 tsp freshly ground black pepper
1 tsp red chilli powder
1 tsp ground turmeric
1 tbsp paprika
5 tbsp rapeseed (canola) oil
1kg (2lb 3oz) lamb chops
2 large onions, finely chopped
4 green chillies, finely chopped
3 tbsp garlic and ginger paste (see
    page 172)
400g (14oz) tin (can) chopped
    tomatoes, or chopped fresh
    tomatoes
150g (1 cup) chana dhal, soaked for
    20 minutes
Salt, to taste
1 tsp garam masala (see page 167), to
    sprinkle
3 tbsp chopped coriander (cilantro),
    to garnish

Stir all of the ground spices together. Mix 1 tablespoon of the oil with 1 heaped tablespoon of the ground spice mixture and rub this into the meat. For best results, let the meat marinate in the spices for 2 hours. When ready to cook, heat 2 tablespoons of oil in a large frying pan over a medium–high heat and brown the meat for about 2 minutes on each side. You may need to do this in batches.

Transfer the meat to a plate and pour the rest of the oil into the pan. Fry the onions and chillies over a medium–high heat until the onions are soft and translucent, about 5 minutes. Now add the garlic and ginger paste and the rest of the ground spices. Stir this all up and add the meat, tomatoes, chana dhal and just enough water to cover.

Simmer the curry until the chana dhal is soft and the meat is super-tender. This will take about 1 hour. You may need to add a little water during the cooking process. This is normally a drier curry, so when your lentils are soft, continue to simmer until you have a thick sauce. Season with salt and sprinkle with the garam masala.

Serve garnished with the coriander (cilantro).

TIP

Watch those lentils! They have a tendency to stick to the pan, so add a little more water and stir occasionally when necessary.

LAMB MASALA CURRY

SERVES 8 OR MORE AS PART OF A MULTI-COURSE MEAL

MyLahore is a family-run restaurant chain that seems to be doing everything right. While researching for *The Curry Guy Easy* book, I paid their Bradford branch a visit and had a lamb curry that was about as close to perfection as it gets. The curry I tried was their lamb rogan josh, which I loved, but I was much more interested in the lamb masala curry that was used to make it. The meat was so tender and the flavour was exceptional. I asked the shift manager, Ateeq Bhatti, if I could have the recipe for the meat curry and he was happy to oblige! The recipe I received, however, was to cook about 15kg (33lb) of meat, so it was on an industrial scale, as you might expect from a successful restaurant. I've simplified the recipe and reduced the quantities for you here.

PREP TIME: 10 MINS
COOKING TIME: 1 HOUR

200ml (generous ¾ cup) rapeseed (canola) oil
1 bay leaf
5cm (2in) piece of cinnamon stick
3 black cardamom pods (or 6 green pods), bruised
1½ tsp cumin seeds
1½ tsp coriander seeds
2 star anise
3 large onions, finely chopped
4 tbsp garlic and ginger paste (see page 172)
4 tomatoes, diced
1 tsp ground turmeric
1½ tbsp bassar curry masala (optional)
1 tbsp chilli powder
1.5kg (3lb 5oz) lamb leg or shoulder, cut into bite-size pieces
2 tbsp plain yoghurt (optional)
Salt, to taste

Heat the oil in a large saucepan over a medium–high heat. When the oil is visibly hot, add the bay leaf, cinnamon, cardamom pods, cumin and coriander seeds and the star anise, and temper the spices in the oil for about 30 seconds. Add the chopped onions and fry for 5–7 minutes until soft and lightly browned. Stir in the garlic and ginger paste and fry for a further 30 seconds.

Now stir in the tomatoes, turmeric, bassar (if using) and chilli powder. Add the meat and brown for a few minutes, then pour in just enough water to cover. Simmer the lamb for 40 minutes–1 hour until it is good and tender. Don't rush this! If after 1 hour the meat is not tender enough, cook it longer. The curry is ready when the meat is tender and the oil rises to the top. (I usually skim off the oil.)

To finish, stir in the yoghurt, 1 tablespoon at a time. It will hardly be noticeable in the sauce, but it thickens and adds flavour to it. Season with salt and serve.

NOTE

If you can't find bassar, you might want to add a little more chilli powder, but I suggest adding it at the end of cooking, to taste. Bassar curry masala contains mustard oil and should always be cooked before consuming.

LAMB DHANSAK

SERVES 4 OR MORE AS PART OF A MULTI-COURSE MEAL

Dhansak curries are very popular at curry houses all over the UK, but like so many of the curries we know and love here, our dhansaks are totally different to what would be called a dhansak in India. Authentic dhansaks have both Persian and Gujarati influences. The Parsis brought with them the idea of cooking meat, vegetables and lentils together into a thick stew when they fled Iran. The Gujaratis added more spices to the rather mild Iranian version. These special dhansaks are normally served at family dinners on a Sunday and big events like weddings, and are usually made with goat or mutton on the bone and served with brown rice.

PREP TIME: 10 MINS, PLUS
    SOAKING TIME
COOKING TIME: 50 MINS

50g (¼ cup) each of masoor, chana
    and toor lentils
3 generous tbsp ghee
10 black peppercorns
1 tsp cumin seeds
2.5cm (1in) piece of cinnamon stick
2 medium onions, finely chopped
2 tbsp garlic and ginger paste (see
    page 172)
2 garlic cloves, thinly sliced
2 green chillies, finely chopped
500g (1lb 2oz) cubed lamb or mutton,
    on or off the bone
1 tsp Kashmiri chilli powder
½ tsp ground turmeric
2 tbsp garam masala (see page 167)
2 medium tomatoes, diced
2 tbsp tamarind paste
4 baby aubergines (eggplants), peeled
    and cut into 1cm (½in) rounds
100g (3½oz) butternut squash or
    pumpkin, cut into 1cm (½in) cubes
100g (3½oz) potato, peeled and cut
    into 1cm (½in) cubes
3 tbsp finely chopped coriander
    (cilantro)
3 tbsp finely chopped mint leaves
2 tbsp dried fenugreek leaves (kasoori
    methi)
Salt, to taste
Chopped coriander (cilantro), to
    garnish

Soak the lentils together in cold water for about 30 minutes. When ready to cook, melt the ghee in a large pan or wok over a medium–high heat. Add the peppercorns, cumin seeds and cinnamon stick and infuse the spices into the ghee for about 40 seconds. Add the onions and fry for 5–7 minutes until lightly browned. Stir in the garlic and ginger paste, sliced garlic and the chillies and stir it all up to combine and sizzle for about 30 seconds.

Add the lamb and brown it for about 2 minutes. Stir in the chilli powder, turmeric and 1½ tablespoons of the garam masala. Stir these spices in, then add the tomatoes, tamarind paste, aubergines (eggplants), squash and potato. Add just enough water to cover – about 1 litre (4¼ cups) – and simmer for 50 minutes, or until the lamb is really tender and the vegetables and lentils have all broken down into a thick sauce. Lentils can stick to the bottom of the pan, so be sure to top up the water if necessary.

To finish, stir in the coriander (cilantro) and mint, then add the dried fenugreek leaves (kasoori methi) by rubbing the leaves between your fingers into the sauce. Stir it all up, season with salt and garnish with a colourful layer of coriander (cilantro).

KACCHI LAMB BIRYANI

SERVES 6–8

Order a biryani at a curry house and you are much more likely to be served something like the restaurant-style biryani on page 234. I first tried an authentic kacchi biryani back in 2013 at Sheba on Brick Lane in London, which they cook up for special occasions. This is my take on their delicious and hugely popular dish.

PREP TIME: 25 MINS, PLUS MARINATING TIME
COOKING TIME: 50 MINS

3 onions, finely sliced and fried (see page 173), plus about 250ml (1 cup) of the reserved cooking oil
1 leg of lamb, cut through the bone into 12 or more pieces*
2 tbsp sea salt
Whole garam masala (5cm/2in piece of cinnamon stick, 10 peppercorns, 1 bay leaf, 1 tbsp cumin seeds)
500g (1lb 2oz) good-quality basmati rice
60g (2oz) coriander (cilantro) leaves, finely chopped
20g (¾ oz) mint leaves, finely chopped
6 tbsp melted ghee
Pinch of saffron threads infused in 300ml (1¼ cups) hot milk
1 tbsp rose water
½ tsp ground cumin
Dried rose petals (optional)
180g (1½ cups) plain (all-purpose) flour
Raita of your choice, to serve

FOR THE MARINADE

2 tbsp garlic and ginger paste (see page 172)
420g (scant 1¾ cups) plain yoghurt
Juice of 2 lemons
2 fresh green chillies, roughly chopped
1 tbsp ground cumin
1 tbsp garam masala (see page 167)
½ tsp ground turmeric
1 tsp ground cinnamon
¼ tsp ground mace
½ tsp chilli powder
30g (1oz) coriander (cilantro) leaves, finely chopped
10g (⅓oz) mint leaves, finely chopped

Mix the marinade ingredients in a bowl with a quarter of the fried onions and 200ml (generous ¾ cup) of cooled reserved cooking oil. Add the lamb and rub the marinade into it. Cover and marinate overnight in the fridge.

When ready to cook, bring 1.5 litres (6¼ cups) water to a boil in a large pan. Add the salt, whole garam masala and rice, and simmer for 6 minutes. After the 6 minutes, remove half the rice from the water with a strainer and place in a small bowl. Cook the remaining rice for another minute and remove to a second bowl.

Now spoon about 3 tablespoons of the reserved onion oil into a large, heavy-based saucepan and tip in the marinated meat along with all of the marinade. Spread the first batch of rice, including any whole spices, over the lamb. Cover with half the remaining fried onions and half the chopped coriander (cilantro) and mint.

Add the second bowl of rice on top and then the remaining fried onions and herbs. Spoon the melted ghee over the top layer, followed by the saffron-infused milk, the rose water and a sprinkle of ground cumin. Scatter some dried rose petals on top (if using).

Mix the flour with enough water to make a soft dough. Run it around the top of the pan and secure the lid tightly on top. Heat the biryani over a high heat for about 2 minutes. When you hear it simmering, reduce the heat to very low and cook for about 40 minutes. Don't be tempted to lift the lid.

After 40 minutes, your kitchen will smell amazing. Take your biryani to the table and unseal the lid. Lift it and enjoy the amazing aroma. Stir the meat from the bottom into the rice about three or four times and serve with your favourite raita.

TIP
*Ask your butcher to cut your leg of lamb into pieces.

LAMB NIHARI
SERVES 4 OR MORE AS PART OF A MULTI-COURSE MEAL

This recipe was sent to me by my friend Usman Butt – executive chef of Imran's in Birmingham's Balti Triangle. If you're a lamb curry fan, this is one you've simply got to try. The sauce is quite mild and has a delicious flavour that when teamed with the tender lamb shanks is about as good as it gets.

Lamb nihari is a fantastic all-round option for entertaining. Your guests can add chopped green chillies, lemon juice, julienned ginger and coriander (cilantro) to taste at the table. If you want the curry to be fiery hot, add loads of chillies, or simply go for some of the less spicy options to produce the perfect curry for you.

PREP TIME: 20 MINS
COOKING TIME: 3½ HOURS

4 lamb shanks (about 2kg/4lb 6oz in total)
½ tsp salt, plus extra to taste
125ml (½ cup) rapeseed (canola) oil or seasoned oil (see page 8)
1 whole nutmeg, crushed into small pieces
1 blade of mace
2 tbsp fennel seeds
3 Indian bay leaves (cassia leaves), shredded
2.5cm (1in) piece of cinnamon stick or cassia bark, broken into small pieces
1 tsp black peppercorns
1 tsp nigella seeds (black onion seeds)
1 tsp cloves
2 tsp cumin seeds
1 tsp paprika
1 tsp hot chilli powder
1 tsp ground ginger
40g (3 tbsp) unsalted butter
1 onion, sliced into rings
2 generous tsp chapatti flour

GARNISHES FOR THE TABLE
5cm (2in) piece of ginger, peeled and julienned
2–3 hot fresh green chillies, finely sliced
Handful of coriander (cilantro) leaves
Lemon wedges

Place the lamb shanks on a plate and rub them all over with ½ teaspoon of salt and 1 teaspoon of the oil. Set aside while you prepare the spice masala.

This is a raw spice masala so no need to roast the spices first. Put the nutmeg, mace, fennel seeds, bay leaves, cinnamon, peppercorns, nigella seeds, cloves and cumin seeds in a spice grinder and grind to a fine powder. Stir in the paprika, chilli powder and ground ginger.

Melt the butter in a large saucepan with a tight-fitting lid over a medium heat. Add the onion rings and fry for about 5 minutes until soft, translucent and lightly browned. Transfer to a plate with a slotted spoon and set aside.

Now pour the remaining oil into the saucepan and brown the lamb shanks for about 2 minutes.

Add the ground spices and browned onions and pour in 1.2 litres (5 cups) warm water.

Arrange the lamb shanks in the saucepan, cover and simmer over a low heat for 3 hours, basting and turning the shanks every 30 minutes. After 3 hours, carefully lift out the shanks into a large, warmed serving bowl. Skim off as much excess oil from the cooking liquid as possible and discard.

Mix the chapatti flour with 4 teaspoons water to make a smooth paste. Whisk the paste into the sauce and simmer for 5–6 minutes to thicken. Season with salt and pour the sauce over the meat in the serving bowl. Serve the garnishes in little bowls on the table to add to the lamb nihari as you like.

QUICK STIR-FRIED LAMB
SERVES 2 OR MORE AS PART OF A MULTI-COURSE MEAL

Like many of my recipes, I found this one by chance. I was in Tooting, London, with my wife one evening and we happened upon a restaurant called Vijaya Krishna. We both ordered the Alleppey lamb roast off the menu and absolutely loved it. I asked for the recipe and thankfully the chef Shabaz Ali was happy to invite me back to the kitchen the next day. This is my interpretation of their excellent dish. It is a dry curry and definitely worth a try!

To make it, you need to start with small pieces (tikka) of pre-cooked lamb. I often simmer the lamb tikka in base sauce until cooked and tender. The lamb-flavoured base sauce is then delicious used in other lamb curries. Dry the meat before frying. This is a great way to use up leftover lamb roast from Sunday dinner too. The most important part of getting this dish right is to ensure that, however you cook your lamb, it is good and tender before adding it to the pan. The recipe serves two, but it can easily be scaled up to serve more.

PREP TIME: 10 MINS
COOKING TIME: 10 MINS

3 tbsp rapeseed (canola) oil
1 large onion, finely chopped
2 green chillies, finely chopped
20 fresh or frozen curry leaves
1 generous tbsp garlic and ginger paste (see page 172)
400–500g (14–1lb 2oz) pre-cooked lamb (leg or shoulder) (see page 177)
1 tbsp mixed powder (see page 169) or curry powder (see page 171)
½ tsp chilli powder
1 tbsp freshly ground black pepper (or to taste)
1–2 tbsp dark soy sauce
Salt, to taste
3 tbsp finely chopped coriander (cilantro) leaves
Lemon wedges

Heat the oil in a large frying pan over a high heat. When visibly hot, add the chopped onion and fry for about 5 minutes until lightly browned. Stir in the fresh green chillies and the curry leaves and fry for a further 30 seconds until fragrant. Add the garlic and ginger paste and fry for another 30 seconds.

Add the lamb tikka and fry over a high heat until heated through and crisp. Stir in the mixed powder or curry powder, chilli powder, black pepper and soy sauce and season with a little salt, if needed.

To serve, garnish with the chopped coriander (cilantro) and the lemon wedges, which can be squeezed over the top at the table.

PAKISTANI DRY MEAT CURRY

SERVES 4 OR MORE AS PART OF A MULTI-COURSE MEAL

Have you ever tried a good Pakistani dry meat curry? Done correctly, this has to be one of my favourite curries. The lamb is marinated and then simmered in water and the marinade until fall-apart tender. Then comes the fantastic final cooking, which is all explained below. I'm getting hungry just thinking about it! For my version of this now-famous curry, I used marinated, diced leg of lamb. If you have the leg bone from the leg, throw that in with the meat too as it adds a nice flavour. In Pakistan and at authentic Pakistani restaurants, the lamb meat, usually shoulder, is cooked in small pieces on the bone. You could do this too – it's messier to eat but so good! Pakistani dry meat curry is delicious served with naans or chapattis.

PREP TIME: 20 MINUTES, PLUS
   MARINATING TIME
COOKING TIME: 1½ HOURS

900g (2lb) lean lamb leg meat, cut
   into bite-size pieces
175ml (¾ cup) ghee
3 medium white onions, thinly sliced
2 tbsp garam masala (see page 167)
2 tsp Kashmiri chilli powder
1 tbsp dried fenugreek leaves (kasoori
   methi)
Salt, to taste
4 tbsp finely chopped coriander
   (cilantro), to garnish
3 limes, quartered, to serve

FOR THE MARINADE
70ml (¼ cup) white vinegar
125g (½ cup) Greek yoghurt
1½ tsp gram (chickpea) flour
2 tbsp garlic and ginger paste (see
   page 172)
8 green bird's eye chillies, blended to
   a paste with a drop of water
2 tbsp mustard oil

Whisk all the marinade ingredients together in a large mixing bowl until creamy smooth. Add the meat and mix well with your hands to ensure it is nicely coated and marinate for 3 hours or overnight – the longer the better.

When ready to start cooking, bring 1 litre (4½ cups) of water to the boil and add the lamb chunks with all the marinade and stir well. Reduce the heat and simmer for about 1 hour, or until the lamb is really tender. You might need to add a little more water during cooking, but the idea is to end up with tender lamb chunks and about 250ml (1 cup) of cooking stock. Tip the cooked meat and remaining liquid into a bowl.

Now, using the same pan, melt the ghee over a high heat and add the onions. Fry for about 15 minutes, or until the onions are a deep brown. Using a slotted spoon, transfer half the onions to a separate bowl. If you want to make this recipe the traditional way, leave all the ghee in the pan. If you want to go for the healthier option, pour out all but about 2 tablespoons of the ghee. This ghee can be stored in the fridge and used in other curries.

Reduce the heat to medium–high and stir in the garam masala and chilli powder and return half the fried onions to the pan. Now add the meat and remaining broth to the pan and cook until the broth has almost all evaporated. Turn up the heat to high and flash-fry the meat until it is crispy and the ghee is beginning to separate from the other ingredients. Add the dried fenugreek leaves (kasoori methi) by rubbing the leaves between your fingers into the pan and season with salt. When you are testing the meat for seasoning, it is very easy to continue snacking on it, so try not to do that if you are serving a crowd. Garnish with the coriander (cilantro) and serve with lime wedges.

KASHMIRI MUTTON ROGAN JOSH
SERVES 4 OR MORE AS PART OF A MULTI-COURSE MEAL

You will find the hugely popular curry-house way to make a rogan josh on page 218. There are many authentic recipes for this famous curry and this one is different in that no garlic or onions are used in the sauce. As much as I love garlic, it really isn't missed in this, one of my favourite rogan josh recipes. Rogan josh is known for its bright red colour, which is accomplished here with paprika and rattanjot. You could leave the rattanjot out as it doesn't add much flavour, but it sure gives the dish a nice, appealing natural red glow! Rattanjot can be difficult to find but if you google it you'll find it online.

PREP TIME: 15 MINS, PLUS
    MARINATING TIME
COOKING TIME: 1 HOUR
    10 MINS

1kg (2lb 3oz) diced mutton or lamb
    on the bone
200ml (generous ¾ cup) rapeseed
    (canola) oil*
1 tsp rattanjot (optional)
2.5cm (1in) piece of cinnamon stick
3 whole black cardamom pods, lightly
    smashed
4 whole green cardamom pods,
    lightly smashed
5 cloves
5 dried Indian bay leaves (cassia
    leaves)
½ tsp asafoetida**
1 tsp ground ginger
1½–2 tbsp paprika
200g (7oz) tomato purée (see page
    172)
Salt, to taste
Naans or chapattis, to serve

FOR THE MARINADE
5cm (2in) piece of cinnamon stick
Seeds from 6 green cardamom pods
10 black peppercorns
1 tbsp fennel seeds
500g (2 cups) plain yoghurt
½ tsp Kashmiri chilli powder

To make the marinade, toast the cinnamon, cardamom seeds, peppercorns and fennel seeds in a dry frying pan over a medium heat. When the spices become fragrant (after about 2 minutes) and warm to the touch but not yet smoking, transfer them to a plate to cool slightly. Grind them into a fine powder using a spice grinder or pestle and mortar. Whisk the yoghurt until it is creamy smooth, then whisk in the ground spices along with the Kashmiri chilli powder.

Place the meat in a large mixing bowl and rub the marinade into it with your hands. Cover and marinate for at least 2 hours or overnight – the longer the better.

When ready to cook, heat the oil in a large saucepan or wok over a medium heat. When visibly hot but not smoking, stir in the rattanjot (if using), the cinnamon, cardamom pods, cloves, bay leaves and asafoetida and let these spices infuse into the oil for about 45 seconds. Stir in the ground ginger and paprika followed by the meat. Give it all a good stir to combine and coat the meat with the oil.

Now add 250ml (1 cup) of water and cover the pan with a lid. Simmer over a medium heat for 45 minutes until the meat is nice and tender. Stir in the tomato purée and cook for a further 15 minutes, or until the texture of the meat is to your liking and the oil separates from the sauce. Season with salt and serve with naans or chapattis.

NOTES

*Using lots of oil is the traditional way of cooking this curry. If you would rather go for a healthier option, use about 2 tablespoons of oil and add just enough water to cover and simmer the meat. There are plenty of curries in this book that use less oil though, so I recommend giving this one a go just as it's written so that you can experience it the way it's meant to be.

**If you are gluten-free, please check the asafoetida packaging as some brands contain wheat flour.

RAILWAY MUTTON (LAMB) CURRY

SERVES 4 OR MORE AS PART OF A MULTI-COURSE MEAL

Railway mutton curry is a lot like a traditional British stew. The original curry was served in the first-class cars of the Indian railways and stems back to the British Raj. The story goes that a British officer was served a lamb curry and found it to be too spicy so asked for the curry to be milder. The chef added some yoghurt and coconut milk to the sauce to cool it down and the officer loved it. Over time, this curry became much milder, with only a little chilli powder added; you could always add more to taste. Most of our curry house-style curries were developed here in the UK for the British palate. This famous curry was developed for the British as well, but most definitely has its origin in India. Although you could definitely cook the meat in the curry sauce, I cook it separately, as it would have been cooked back in the days when this curry was popular on Indian trains. The cooked meat would then have been used in a variety of curries served on the train, from mild to fiery hot, with the cooking stock used to flavour the curries. You might like to double or triple the meat part of the recipe and use the additional pre-cooked meat in one of the curry house-style curries in this book (see pages 182–235).

PREP TIME: 15 MINS
COOKING TIME: 2 HOURS

1kg (2lb 3oz) mutton or lamb
   shoulder on the bone, cut into
   bite-size pieces
5 tbsp (¼ cup) mustard oil
5 cardamom pods, bruised
3 Kashmiri dried red chillies
4 cloves
2.5cm (1in) piece of cinnamon stick
20 fresh or frozen curry leaves
2 medium red onions, finely chopped
2 tbsp garlic and ginger paste (see
   page 172)
½ tsp Kashmiri chilli powder
½ tsp ground turmeric
1 tbsp ground coriander
1 tbsp cumin
300g (10½ oz) chopped tomatoes
3 green chillies, finely chopped
3 potatoes, peeled and quartered
1 generous tsp tamarind concentrate
200ml (generous ¾ cup) thick
   coconut milk
1 tsp dried fenugreek leaves (kasoori
   methi)
Salt, to taste
Chopped coriander (cilantro), to
   garnish (optional)

Place the meat in a saucepan and add just enough water to cover. Bring to a simmer and cook for about 90 minutes, or until super-tender. Add a drop of water if necessary to keep the meat covered while cooking.

Meanwhile, heat the mustard oil in a large saucepan. When visibly hot, add the cardamom pods, Kashmiri chillies, cloves and cinnamon stick and let these spices infuse into the oil for about 30 seconds. Add the curry leaves and let them fry with the spices for another 30 seconds before adding the onions. Fry for about 5 minutes until the onions are soft and translucent, then the stir in the garlic and ginger paste and fry for a further 30 seconds.

Now add the ground spices and tomatoes, stir well and add the green chillies – this is your base for the curry. When the meat is almost cooked to perfection, add the potatoes and cook until tender. This should take about 15 minutes. Then add the meat and potatoes to the curry sauce, with about 500ml (2 cups) of the cooking stock. Simmer until you are happy with the consistency. This curry can be either really soupy or thick, depending on your preference. Stir in the tamarind concentrate and coconut milk. You're almost done now.

To finish, add the dried fenugreek leaves (kasoori methi) by rubbing the leaves between your fingers into the sauce. Season with salt and garnish with some chopped coriander (cilantro) if you like.

PORK VINDALOO

SERVES 4 OR MORE AS PART OF A MULTI-COURSE MEAL

Goa was the birthplace of vindaloo curry. In the 15th century, the Portuguese controlled what is now Goa and brought with them their Portuguese recipes and ingredients from the new world – the Americas. The name 'vindaloo' is believed to have come from the Portuguese dish *carne de vinho e alho*, or meat with wine and garlic. The Goans couldn't pronounce *vinho e alho* and ended up calling it vindaloo. The name stuck.

One thing the Goans changed when making *vinho e alho*, or vindaloo, was that they added a lot of chillies and spices indigenous to the area. They loved spicy chillies, which had only recently made their way to the Indian subcontinent via the Portuguese.

I learned this recipe from Chef Vivek Kashiwale, who has now moved on from the small restaurant near Leeds where I met him to share his culinary expertise in Dubai. I feel pretty lucky to have learned this delicious and authentic Goan pork vindaloo from him.

PREP TIME: 20 MINS, PLUS
MARINATING TIME
COOKING TIME: 1½ HOURS

800g (1lb 12oz) pork leg, diced
3–4 tbsp coconut oil or rapeseed (canola) oil
1 head of garlic, cloves cut into thin slivers*
1 tsp brown mustard seeds
10 fresh curry leaves
2 onions, finely chopped
2 tomatoes, finely chopped
1 tsp chilli powder
2 bay leaves
Salt, to taste
Squeeze of lemon, to serve

FOR THE MARINADE
1 tsp chilli powder
1½ tbsp ground cumin
1½ tbsp ground coriander
½ tsp ground fenugreek
½ tsp ground cloves
1 tbsp ground black pepper
½ tsp ground turmeric
¾ tsp ground cinnamon
½ tsp ground cardamom
4 green chillies, finely chopped
5 tbsp red wine vinegar
2 tbsp soft brown sugar
1 tbsp tamarind concentrate (or another 2 tbsp of vinegar)
3 tbsp garlic and ginger paste (see page 172)

*If you don't want to finely slice all that garlic, you could substitute a large handful of dried garlic flakes. Just simmer them in the sauce until tender.

Start with the marinade. Place all the marinade ingredients in a large glass bowl and stir into a smooth paste. Add the pork and mix well to combine. Cover and leave the pork to marinate in the fridge for 30 minutes or overnight.

When ready to cook, heat the oil in a saucepan over a low heat. Add the garlic slivers and allow to cook gently for about 20 minutes. It is important not to burn the garlic, so watch carefully. It should be soft and translucent but not browned. Transfer the garlic from the saucepan to a plate and set aside, leaving as much of the oil in the pan as possible.

Turn up the heat to high and add a little more oil, if required. When visibly hot, stir in the mustard seeds. When they begin to pop (after about 30 seconds), add the curry leaves and sauté for 30 seconds before adding the chopped onions. Reduce the heat to medium–high and fry for about 5 minutes until the onions are soft and translucent.

Add the chopped tomatoes, chilli powder, bay leaves and the pork with all its marinade to the pan, then pour in just enough water to cover. Leave to simmer for about 1 hour, or until the pork is very tender. You may need to add a drop more water while simmering.

To finish, stir in the slivered garlic you sautéed earlier and season with salt. Squeeze the lemon juice over the top and serve.

CHILLI PORK BUNNY CHOW
SERVES 6 OR MORE AS PART OF A MULTI-COURSE MEAL

OK then... there's bunny chow, that famous curry dish from South Africa, and then there's this bunny chow, which I learned from the then-head chef at Scarfs Bar at the Rosewood London. My friend Palash Mitra has since moved on to chef at other restaurants around the world, but I bet he still makes this amazing bunny chow. It's simply too good to leave off the menu. For best results, be sure to source some good French sourdough rolls. Any crusty rolls will do, but when I'm making a curry like this, I like to use the best I can find. I usually serve this with a simple green salad or sometimes I cook up some vegetable bhajis and serve them on the side on top of crisp chicory leaves.

PREP TIME: 15 MINS, PLUS
MARINATING TIME
COOKING TIME: 1¾ HOURS

1.5kg (3lb 5oz) pork belly, deboned and diced
2 tbsp vegetable oil
4 dried chillies
10 curry leaves
2 green chillies, slit
4 medium red onions, cut into 1cm (½ in) slices
Salt, to taste
Juice of ½ lime
6 crusty sourdough rolls, hollowed out

FOR THE MARINADE
10 kokum berries, soaked in 100ml (scant ½ cup) hot water (use the water in the marinade)
2 tbsp garlic and ginger paste (see page 172)
1 tsp ground turmeric
2 tsp salt
8–10 peppercorns
3 bay leaves
2 star anise
4 tbsp honey
3 tbsp dark soy sauce

Marinate the pork in the marinade ingredients overnight. Transfer the pork to a heavy-based cooking pot and add just enough water to cover. Cook over a low–medium heat for 1½ hours, or until the pork is fall-apart tender. Don't rush this! Drain the pork and reserve the liquid.

Heat the oil in a saucepan or wok and add the dried chillies. Let them sizzle until they become a couple of tones darker (about 30 seconds), but be careful not to blacken them. Now add the curry leaves and fry for 30 seconds, or until they are crisp, shiny and fragrant. Stir in the green chillies and the red onions and sauté for about 5 minutes until they are soft and translucent.

Transfer the diced pre-cooked pork to this base masala and stir-fry, stirring constantly for 3–4 minutes to caramelize. If the meat feels dry, add 1–2 tablespoon of the reserved cooking liquid and cook until the liquid has almost evaporated but the meat is deliciously juicy. The pork will acquire a shiny glaze. Check for seasoning and finish with a squeeze of lime.

Divide the meat mixture between six hollowed-out sourdough rolls and you are ready to enjoy one of my favourite meals.

SRI LANKAN PORK CURRY

SERVES 6 OR MORE AS PART OF A MULTI-COURSE MEAL

I first learned this pork curry recipe on a visit to Sri Lanka, where the chef at one of my hotels very kindly walked me through the cooking process. He made a special Sri Lankan curry powder that took hours to roast before being ground into a fine powder. I have changed the ingredients and method slightly for ease using my own curry powder blend, but I think I've still kept it very authentically Sri Lankan. The most important thing with this recipe is to use the freshest ingredients you can get your hands on and ensure the pork is very tender. Get that right and the other ingredients finish the job for you with very little effort. Any good-quality curry powder can be used if you don't want to make your own.

PREP TIME: 15 MINS
COOKING TIME: 1 HOUR

3 tbsp rapeseed (canola) oil or coconut oil
1 tsp black mustard seeds
5cm (2in) piece of cinnamon stick
1 tbsp cumin seeds
20 curry leaves
2 large red onions, finely chopped
2 tsp red chilli powder (or to taste)
3 tbsp curry powder (see page 171)
1 tsp ground turmeric
2 tbsp garlic and ginger paste (see page 172)
1 green chillies, cut into thin rings (or more to taste)
1 tbsp tomato paste
1 generous tbsp tamarind pulp
400ml (14fl oz) tin (can) thick coconut milk
900g (2lb) pork leg, cut into large chunks
About 500ml (2 cups) water or chicken stock, to cover
Salt and freshly ground black pepper, to taste
1 tsp garam masala (see page 167)

Heat the oil over a medium–high heat in a wok or large saucepan. When hot, add the black mustard seeds. When they begin to crackle (after about 30 seconds), add the cinnamon stick, cumin seeds and curry leaves and fry for a further 30 seconds until fragrant.

Add the onions and fry for about 5 minutes until soft and translucent, then pour in the ground spices and the garlic and ginger paste. Add the green chillies and tomato paste, followed by the tamarind pulp and coconut milk. Mix well and add the pork with just enough water or stock to cover. Simmer for about 40 minutes, or until the pork is fork-tender.

Season with salt and black pepper and sprinkle with the garam masala to serve.

BANGLADESHI SHATKORA BEEF
SERVES 4 OR MORE AS PART OF A MULTI-COURSE MEAL

Whenever I go out to a Bangladeshi-run curry house, I look for their shatkora curries. I absolutely love the intensely tangy shatkora fruit. These are available frozen from Asian grocers, and when in season they can often be purchased fresh. If you have trouble finding them, you could substitute shatkora pickle or, if all else fails, quartered limes, but the flavour will not be the same.

This is a popular beef curry that, when prepared like this, is usually made in bulk and promoted as a house special. Not only does the beef need to cook until tender, but the shatkora require a long simmer so that they are not tough, and also to release their flavour into the sauce. Only the rind of the fruit is used, because the pulp is terribly bitter. If you have a couple beef marrow bones, throw them into the dish as it simmers.

This recipe was inspired by a visit to Omar's, a small curry house in Hatfield Peverel. It may be small but the curries I enjoyed there are right up there with the best!

PREP TIME: 15 MINS
COOKING TIME: 1 HOUR

3 tbsp rapeseed (canola) oil or seasoned oil (see page 8)
2 black cardamom pods, lightly bruised
1 large onion, finely chopped
2 tbsp garlic and ginger paste (see page 172)
3 tbsp tomato purée (see page 172)
1 tsp ground turmeric
1 tsp ground cumin
1 tsp ground coriander
1 tsp medium chilli powder
1 tsp paprika
800g (1lb 12oz) beef topside, cut into bite-size pieces (see note)
750ml (3¼ cups) spice stock (see page 167), plus a little extra if required
¼ shatkora, outer rind only, cut into small pieces
1 tsp garam masala (see page 167)
Salt, to taste
Chopped coriander (cilantro) leaves, to finish

Heat the oil in a large frying pan over a medium–high heat. When hot, toss in the cardamom pods and, after about 30 seconds, add the onion and fry for 5–7 minutes until soft, translucent and lightly browned.

Now add the garlic and ginger paste and fry for a further minute, stirring. Add the tomato purée and the ground spices, and cook for another minute. Add the beef and about 250ml (1 cup) of the spice stock. Boil it all for about 5 minutes, then add the remaining spice stock and the shatkora rind.

Reduce the heat and simmer for 45 minutes–1 hour, or until the sauce reduces to a fairly thick consistency and the meat is tender. Add more spice stock if needed.

To serve, add the garam masala, season with salt and top with the coriander (cilantro).

NOTE

In the UK, most people prefer their curries cooked with meat off the bone, but this recipe is sometimes made using beef ribs. If you like ribs, give them a go. You'll love the beefy ribs in this sauce.

KASHMIRI MEATBALL CURRY
SERVES 4 OR MORE AS PART OF A MULTI-COURSE MEAL

I made this famous Kashmiri meatball curry (lamb rista) the traditional way once. It took forever to make as the meat is pounded with a mallet until it looks like putty. I won't be doing that again soon! Here I have simplified the recipe by using a food processor. The meatballs are delicious in this spicy sauce. In addition to the amazing flavour, the meatballs (rista) have a spongy texture that I really love. This recipe is usually made with mutton, but here I used lamb. Other minced (ground) meat such as venison, chicken or turkey work well too.

PREP TIME: 20 MINS
COOK TIME: 1½ HOURS

1 good pinch of saffron
4 Kashmiri dried red chillies
1 cinnamon stick
6 green cardamom pods, bruised
1 tsp black peppercorns
1 tsp ground turmeric
6 tbsp rapeseed (canola) oil or ghee
5cm (2in) piece of cinnamon stick
4 green cardamom pods, bruised
1 blade of mace
4 tbsp garlic and ginger paste (see page 172)
2 tsp ground fennel
1 tsp ground cumin
2 tsp ground coriander
1½ tsp Kashmiri chilli powder
2 tbsp paprika
½ tsp ground cloves
6 tbsp onion paste (see page 173)
125g (½ cup) plain yoghurt (optional)
Salt and freshly ground black pepper, to taste
Rice, naans or chapattis, to serve

FOR THE MEATBALLS (RISTA)
900g (2lb) minced (ground) fatty lamb
2 tsp garam masala (see page 167)
1 tbsp baking powder
1 tbsp cornflour (cornstarch)
2 tsp salt
2 tsp ground fennel
1 tbsp paprika

Place the saffron in a glass or bowl and cover with 70ml (¼ cup) of hot water. Set aside to soak.

To make the meatballs, put the lamb in a food processor with the rest of the meatball ingredients. Blend for a few minutes until the meat is like a smooth paste.

Wet your hands with water and take a small golf ball-size piece of the meat and roll it into a ball. Do this very lightly by rolling it between your wet hands to get the ball as round and smooth as possible. Repeat with the remaining meat; you should have about 12–14 balls.

Pour 1 litre (4½ cups) of water in a saucepan and bring to the boil. Add the Kashmiri chillies, cinnamon, cardamom pods, peppercorns and turmeric. Then add the meatballs one at a time. Reduce the heat to medium and simmer, covered, for 1 hour 10 minutes. After this time, uncover and turn off the heat.

Now make the sauce. Heat the oil in a large frying pan or wok over a medium heat. When the oil begins to shimmer, add the cinnamon stick, cardamom pods and mace. Let these spices infuse into the oil for about 30 seconds, then add the garlic and ginger paste and fry for about 30 seconds to cook off the rawness. Now add the ground spices followed by the onion paste and the yoghurt (if using).

Stir this well, then add about 500ml (2 cups) of the cooking liquid from the meatballs, along with the saffron water and the meatballs. Simmer until you are happy with the consistency. If you prefer a runnier sauce, you could add more cooking stock; for a thicker sauce, just cook it down.

Season with salt and black pepper. You could also add more chilli powder if you prefer a spicier curry. Serve with rice, naans or chapattis.

SALMON KOFTA BHUNA
SERVES 4 OR MORE AS PART OF A MULTI-COURSE MEAL

This recipe was sent to me by my friend Milon Miah, head chef at Spice Island in Barnard Castle. The recipe was taught to Milon by his mother, but he claims to have modernized it a bit. I've never tried the original but have to say his version, which he makes with chital (a freshwater Bangladeshi fish) is truly delicious. I'm not the only one who thinks so. Milon recently won first place with this dish on the reality TV show *The Chef*. The ingredients are all very simple but they work so well together. All you need is a little plain white rice and you've got yourself a masterpiece meal in minutes.

PREP TIME: 15 MINS
COOKING TIME: 15 MINS

2 tbsp rapeseed (canola) oil, plus extra for shallow-frying
2 onions, finely chopped
½ each of green and red (bell) peppers, diced
3 garlic cloves, finely chopped
3 spring onions (scallions), roughly chopped
2 green chillies, finely chopped
3 tbsp finely chopped coriander (cilantro) leaves
1 tsp ground turmeric
1 tsp chilli powder
1 tbsp mixed powder (see page 169) or curry powder (see page 171)
20 cherry tomatoes, halved
Salt, to taste
Lemon or lime wedges, to serve

FOR THE KOFTAS
500g (1lb 2oz) salmon fillet or chital fish
1 tsp mixed powder (see page 169) or curry powder (see page 171)
½ tsp ground turmeric
1 tsp chilli powder
3 tbsp finely chopped coriander (cilantro) leaves
2 spring onions (scallions), thinly sliced
½ tsp salt, or to taste

To make the koftas, place the salmon or chital in a food processor and blitz until you have a thick paste. Add the rest of the kofta ingredients and mix well. Set aside.

Heat the rapeseed (canola) oil in a large pan over a medium–high heat. When visibly hot, stir in the chopped onions and diced peppers and fry until the onions are soft and translucent, about 5 minutes. Stir in the garlic, spring onions (scallions), chillies, coriander (cilantro) and the ground spices and stir it all up well. Add just enough water to cover and simmer until the water has almost evaporated.

Meanwhile, form the fish paste into about 12 small, flat koftas. In a large frying pan, pour in oil to the depth of about 2.5cm (1in) and heat over a medium–high heat. When hot, add the koftas and fry for about 2 minutes on one side. Flip over and fry for another 2 minutes, or until cooked through.

Place the tomatoes and koftas on top of the simmering sauce for about 2 minutes until the tomatoes are warmed through. Season with salt.

To serve, divide the sauce mixture equally between four warmed plates. Place three koftas on each and serve with wedges of lemon or lime.

SKEWERED HALIBUT CURRY

SERVES 4–6

Don't let the fact that there are a lot of ingredients in this one scare you off! This is one of my favourite seafood recipes and it's actually quite easy to make.

PREP TIME: 20 MINS, PLUS
    MARINATING TIME
COOKING TIME: 30 MINS

1 tbsp rapeseed (canola) oil
1kg (2lb 2oz) meaty fish, such as
    halibut or cod, cut into 5cm (2in)
    cubes
1 red onion, quartered
1 tsp ground cardamom
1½ tsp ground cinnamon
1 tbsp ground turmeric
1 tbsp chilli powder (more or less to
    taste)
1 tbsp garam masala (see page 167)
1 tbsp dried red chilli (hot pepper)
    flakes
1 tsp salt (more or less to taste)
Handful of green chillies
Salt and freshly ground black pepper,
    to taste
Juice of 1 or more limes
Rice, to serve

FOR THE SAUCE
1 tbsp rapeseed (canola) oil
1 stick of cinnamon
3 cloves
3 green cardamom pods
20 fresh curry leaves
1 red onion, roughly chopped
2 tbsp finely chopped lemongrass
5cm (2in) piece of ginger, peeled and
    finely sliced
6 garlic cloves, roughly chopped
3 green chillies, roughly chopped (or
    to taste)
2 tomatoes, roughly chopped
1 tsp finely ground black pepper
1 tsp red chilli powder
1 tsp ground turmeric
400ml (14fl oz) tin (can) thick
    coconut milk

Preheat the oven to 180°C (350°F/Gas 4).

Start by marinating the fish and onion. Pour the oil over the cubed fish and red onion, then add the ground spices and chilli flakes and season with salt. Mix it all up and allow to marinate for 10 minutes (and not more than 30 minutes).

Meanwhile, prepare the sauce. Pour the oil into a large pan set over a medium–high heat. When it begins to bubble, add the cinnamon stick, cloves and cardamom pods. Fry for about 30 seconds to allow the oil to take on the flavour of the spices, then add the curry leaves, onion, lemongrass and ginger. Cook this until the onion becomes translucent and soft (about 5 minutes), then add the garlic and green chillies. Let this sizzle for about 1 minute, then pour in the chopped tomatoes. Stir this all up nicely to combine and add black pepper, chilli powder and turmeric. Turn up the heat slightly and add the coconut milk. Bring it to a simmer and allow it to thicken slightly.

Skewer the cubed fish, red onion and green chillies and place in a roasting pan. Cover the fish with the sauce and cook for about 15 minutes, or until the fish is cooked through. Season with salt and perhaps a little more black pepper. Squeeze the lime juice over the top. Serve with plain white rice.

MALABAR FISH CURRY

SERVES 4 OR MORE AS PART OF A MULTI-COURSE MEAL

I think that one of the most valuable things I've learned during my visits to southern coastal India is the low-fat way they cook up amazing seafood curries. Hardly any oil is required as many of the aromatic ingredients are simply boiled in water to produce a delicious sauce. Although you can use tamarind concentrate instead of kokum for this recipe, it is traditionally made with kokum and that's the way I like it most.

PREP TIME: 10 MINS
COOKING TIME: 20 MINS

150g (1½ cups) fresh or frozen grated coconut
½ tsp ground turmeric
1 tbsp Kashmiri chilli powder
2 tbsp minced ginger
1 green chilli, finely chopped
3 kokum peels or 2 tsp tamarind concentrate
500g (1lb 2oz) cod or other meaty fish like halibut or ling, cut into medium chunks
1 tbsp rapeseed (canola) oil
1 tsp black mustard seeds
10 curry leaves
3 shallots, thinly sliced
Salt, to taste

Blend the coconut and turmeric into a fine paste or powder and set aside.

Bring 500ml (2 cups) of water to the boil in a pot, preferably a clay pot if you have one. Add the coconut mixture, chilli powder, ginger, green chilli and kokum or tamarind concentrate and simmer for about 15 minutes. Add the fish and simmer with the pan covered for a further 7 minutes, or until the fish is just cooked through. Be careful not to overcook the fish or it will fall apart.

Meanwhile, heat the oil in a small frying pan over a medium–high heat. When visibly hot, add the mustard seeds and when they begin to crackle (after about 30 seconds), reduce the heat to medium and stir in the curry leaves and shallots and fry until the shallots are soft and lightly browned. Pour over the curry. You can leave it as a garnish or stir the infused oil into the curry. Check for seasoning and season with salt if needed.

KOLKATA (CALCUTTA) PRAWNS
SERVES 4 OR MORE AS PART OF A MULTI-COURSE MEAL

Kolkata-style prawn (shrimp) curries are making their way onto many curry-house menus. This recipe was inspired by a visit to my local curry house, Raj Bari in Yarm. I didn't see the chefs making the dish while I was there, but they were nice enough to let me know what went into it. I returned home and decided to make the curry all over again for my family. It was that good!

PREP TIME: 10 MINS
COOKING TIME: 15 MINS

500g (1lb 2oz) raw tiger prawns
  (shrimp), peeled and deveined
½ tsp ground turmeric
2 tbsp ghee or mustard oil
1 tsp black mustard seeds
3 green cardamom pods, lightly
  bruised
4 cloves
5cm (2in) piece of cinnamon stick
1 bay leaf
20 fresh curry leaves
2 shallots, finely chopped
2 tbsp garlic and ginger paste (see
  page 172)
1 fresh green chilli, halved lengthways
  and deseeded
½ tsp paprika
2 tbsp coconut flour
400ml (14fl oz) tin (can) thick coconut
  milk
Pinch of saffron threads
1 tsp garam masala (see page 167)
Salt, to taste
1 tbsp finely chopped coriander
  (cilantro)

Sprinkle the prawns (shrimp) with the turmeric and mix well.

Heat the ghee or oil in a large frying pan or wok over a medium–high heat. When hot, toss in the mustard seeds. When they begin to pop (after about 30 seconds), reduce the heat to medium and add the rest of the whole spices, bay leaf and curry leaves. Fry for 30 seconds, then add the shallots and sauté for about 5 minutes until translucent and soft.

Add the garlic and ginger paste and the fresh chilli, and stir to combine. Add the prawns and paprika and fry, stirring regularly, until the prawns begin to turn pink. Stir in the coconut flour, coconut milk and saffron and simmer for a further few minutes so that the sauce thickens slightly and the prawns cook through. To serve, stir in the garam masala and season with salt. Top with the coriander (cilantro).

ANA CHINGRI
(PRAWN WITH PINEAPPLE)
SERVES 4 OR MORE AS PART OF A MULTI-COURSE MEAL

This is a flavour combo not to be missed. The spicy pineapple chutney teamed with the prawn (shrimp) curry just plain gets it. I like to serve ana chingri in the hollowed-out pineapples, just as Chef Eshan 'Mo' Miah suggested I do. I'm not one to pass up good advice and I've been serving this curry in pineapples ever since. Feel free to use bowls though.

PREP TIME: 15 MINS
COOKING TIME: 15 MINS

6 garlic cloves, unpeeled
1 pineapple
½ tsp roasted cumin seeds (see page 163)
Salt, to taste
4 fresh green chillies, very finely chopped
4 tbsp finely chopped coriander (cilantro), plus extra to serve
2 tbsp rapeseed (canola) oil
1 tsp mustard seeds
½ onion, finely chopped
1 tbsp garlic paste*
2 Indian bay leaves (cassia leaves)
1 tsp ground cumin
1 tsp ground chilli powder
½ tsp ground turmeric
1 tomato, chopped
2 tbsp tomato purée (see page 172)
500g (1lb 2oz) raw prawns (shrimp), shelled and deveined
Juice of 1 lime
Homemade naans or chapattis (see pages 304–10), to serve

*To make this, blend 1–2 cloves of garlic with just enough water to make a smooth paste.

Roast the garlic cloves directly over a gas hob flame on a skewer or in a dry frying pan, turning them as they roast, until blackened all over. Set aside to cool.

Using a large, sharp knife, cut the pineapple in half lengthways and scoop out most of the flesh from the centre. Place the scooped-out pineapple in a blender, add the cumin seeds and ½ teaspoon of salt, and squeeze the roasted garlic cloves out of their skins into the blender. Blend to a paste, then transfer to a bowl.

Add the fresh chillies and chopped coriander (cilantro) to the pineapple paste and mix well. Reserve 2 tablespoons for the curry and store the rest in the fridge until ready to serve.

Heat the oil in a large saucepan over a high heat and add the mustard seeds. They will begin to pop after about 30 seconds. When they do, reduce the heat to medium–high and add the onion along with a pinch of salt. Fry for about 5 minutes until translucent and soft, then stir in the garlic paste and fry for a further 30 seconds.

Add 4 tablespoons of water, the bay leaves, cumin, chilli powder, turmeric and the reserved 2 tablespoons of pineapple paste. Cook for a further 2 minutes, then add the chopped tomato and tomato purée.

Throw in the prawns (shrimp) and stir into the sauce until cooked through. Check for seasoning and spoon into the hollowed-out pineapples. Top with chopped coriander (cilantro) and a squeeze of lime juice, and serve with the spicy pineapple paste, and some homemade naans or chapattis.

SRI LANKAN JAFFNA CRAB CURRY

SERVES 4 OR MORE AS PART OF A MULTI-COURSE MEAL

If you are a crab fan, this is a good one. Any crabs will do. You could try the frozen imported crabs from Asian shops, but I find that the brown crabs we get here in the UK are perfect for almost any crab dish. They may not be as visually beautiful as other varieties, but I love the flavour and using crabs that are locally sourced.

PREP TIME: 20 MINS, PLUS
  PREPARING AND COOKING
  THE CRABS
COOKING TIME: 25 MINS

3 tbsp fresh or frozen grated coconut
2 tbsp rapeseed (canola) oil
1 tsp black mustard seeds
1 tsp cumin seeds
1 tsp fennel seeds
20 fresh or frozen curry leaves
2 onions, finely chopped
4–8 green chillies, finely chopped
1 tbsp finely chopped ginger
3 tbsp garam masala (see page 167)
1 tsp ground coriander
Pinch of ground turmeric
3 tomatoes, diced (optional)
3 cloves garlic, finely chopped
2 x 400ml (14fl oz) tins (cans) light
  coconut milk
4 cooked crabs, cleaned, quartered
  and shells cracked
Juice of 2 limes
4 tbsp finely chopped coriander
  (cilantro), stalks included
Salt and freshly ground black pepper,
  to taste

In a dry frying pan over a medium heat, toast the coconut until lightly browned, then set aside.

Heat the oil in a large wok or frying pan over a medium–high heat until visibly hot. Toss in the mustard seeds and when they begin to pop in the hot oil (after about 30 seconds), reduce the heat to medium and stir in the cumin seeds, fennel seeds and curry leaves.

Add the onions, chillies and ginger and sizzle for a few minutes until the onions become translucent and soft. Then add the garam masala, ground coriander and turmeric. Stir this all up and add the tomatoes (if using), garlic and toasted coconut.

Make sure the onions are nicely coated in the spices, then add the coconut milk, 200ml (generous ¾ cup) of water and the crabs. Bring to a simmer, cover and cook until the sauce is reduced by half. Be sure to stir regularly.

Just before serving, squeeze the lime juice into the sauce and sprinkle in the chopped coriander (cilantro). Check for seasoning and add salt and black pepper if needed.

BOMBAY ALOO

SERVES 4 OR MORE AS PART OF A MULTI-COURSE MEAL

Monday nights are always curry nights at my house. On Sundays, we usually cook up a roast Sunday dinner with all the fixings, so I always make extra roast potatoes for this curry. You could do the same in place of the pre-cooked stewed potatoes used here, although the cooking stock is nice added to this sauce.

Bombay aloo can be served either quite saucy or dry, and as I usually serve this curry as a side dish, my sauce is on the dry side. If serving as a vegetarian main course, you might want to add more liquid.

PREP TIME: 10 MINS, PLUS
    MAKING THE BASE SAUCE
    AND COOKING THE
    POTATOES
COOKING TIME: 15 MINS

4 tbsp ghee, rapeseed (canola) oil or
    seasoned oil (see page 8)
1 tsp cumin seeds
1 onion, finely chopped
2 tbsp garlic and ginger paste (see
    page 172)
7 tbsp tomato purée (see page 172)
300ml (1¼ cups) base curry sauce
    (page 164 or 166), heated (or more
    for a saucier dish – see
    introduction)
600g (1lb 5oz) pre-cooked stewed
    potatoes (see page 179), cut into
    bite-size chunks, plus 100ml
    (scant ½ cup) of the cooking stock
    or water
1 tbsp mixed powder (see page 169)
1 tsp chilli powder
2 tomatoes, quartered
Salt, to taste
1 tsp dried fenugreek leaves (kasoori
    methi)
½ tsp garam masala (see page 167)
3 tbsp finely chopped coriander
    (cilantro)

Heat the ghee or oil in a pan over a medium–high heat, then add the cumin seeds. When they become fragrant, stir in the onion and fry for about 5 minutes until soft and translucent. Stir in the garlic and ginger paste and enjoy that garlicky aroma.

Now stir in the tomato purée, base sauce and potato cooking stock or water, and bring to a simmer. There is no need to stir unless it is obviously catching on the pan. Scrape any caramelized sauce on the sides of the pan back in, then add the pre-cooked potatoes, mixed powder and chilli powder.

Continue to simmer while spooning the sauce over the potatoes. When well coated, add the tomatoes and cook for a further 2 minutes.

Season with salt and sprinkle with the dried fenugreek leaves (kasoori methi) and garam masala. Top with the chopped coriander (cilantro) to serve.

MALAI KOFTA CURRY

SERVES 4 OR MORE AS PART OF A MULTI-COURSE MEAL

I promise, you won't miss the meat when you make these koftas. Served in the mildly spiced, creamy sauce, they are real crowd pleasers! The koftas could also be made smaller and flattened into patties so you don't need to cook with as much oil.

PREP TIME: 20 MINS
COOKING TIME: 40 MINS

4 tbsp rapeseed (canola) oil or vegetable oil, plus extra for deep-frying
½ tsp ground turmeric
1 tsp chilli powder
1 tbsp ground cumin
1 tbsp ground coriander
10 almonds
10 cashew nuts
2 onions, finely chopped
2 green chillies, finely chopped
2 tbsp garlic and ginger paste (see page 172)
400g (14oz) tin (can) chopped tomatoes
200ml (generous ¾ cup) single (light) cream, plus extra to serve
Salt, to taste
Garam masala (see page 167), to serve

FOR THE KOFTAS

250g (9oz) peeled potatoes
1 tbsp rice flour
1 tbsp plain (all-purpose) flour (or an additional 1 tbsp rice flour if gluten-free)
200g (7oz) paneer cheese, grated
½ tsp ground turmeric
1 tsp chilli powder
Large handful of baby spinach leaves, washed and roughly chopped
4 tbsp finely chopped coriander (cilantro) leaves
½ Salt, to taste

Start by making your koftas. Par-cook the potatoes for 5 minutes until almost cooked through – it should be easy to stick a fork in but there should still be some resistance. Remove the potatoes from the water and allow to cool, and then grate them. Squeeze as much moisture as possible from the grated potatoes and mix with the rice and plain (all-purpose) flours. Let stand for about 5 minutes.

Mix the grated paneer, turmeric, chilli powder, the chopped spinach and coriander (cilantro) into the grated potato, then add the salt. Form into koftas slightly larger than golf balls and set aside while you make your sauce.

Heat the oil in a large saucepan over a medium–high heat. When visibly hot, stir in the turmeric, chilli powder, cumin, ground coriander, almonds and cashew nuts. Temper this all in the oil for about 30 seconds, then add the chopped onions. Fry for about 5 minutes until soft and translucent.

Add the green chillies and the garlic and ginger paste and fry for a further minute, then add the tomatoes. Simmer for about 5 minutes, then blend to a smooth sauce using a hand-held or countertop blender. Return this to the pan and add about 400ml (scant 1¾ cups) of water and simmer down for about 15 minutes. Stir in the cream and continue to simmer until you are happy with the consistency. Season with salt and keep warm.

You can fry your koftas while the sauce is simmering if time is an issue. To cook the koftas, heat about 10cm (4in) of rapeseed or vegetable oil in a saucepan – you need enough oil in your pan to just cover the koftas, so add more if required. The oil is hot enough for frying when a small piece broken off one of the koftas sizzles and rises to the top immediately when thrown in. Carefully place your koftas in the oil and fry until crispy brown on the exterior. About 5 minutes should do the trick. Don't overcrowd your pan. Do this in batches if necessary.

Place the fried koftas on paper towel to soak up excess oil and then place in a large serving bowl or individual bowls and cover with the sauce. Sprinkle with garam masala and a drizzle of cream to serve.

MANCHURIAN GOBI
SERVES 4 OR MORE AS PART OF A MULTI-COURSE MEAL

Put simply, cauliflower never tasted so good. The double-frying technique makes it easier to prepare ahead and gets those cauliflower nuggets extra crispy.

PREP TIME: 15 MINS, PLUS
MARINATING TIME
COOKING TIME: 20 MINS

About 750g (1lb 10oz) cauliflower,
broken into florets
1 tsp ground turmeric
Rapeseed (canola) oil, for frying
2 tbsp finely chopped coriander
(cilantro) leaves

FOR THE MARINADE

2 tbsp garlic and ginger paste (see
page 172)
1 tsp red chilli powder
2 tsp ground black pepper
Salt, to taste

FOR THE BATTER

125g (1 cup) plain (all-purpose) flour
30g (¼ cup) cornflour (cornstarch)
40g (¼ cup) rice flour, or more
cornflour

FOR THE SAUCE

2 tbsp rapeseed (canola) oil or sesame
oil
2 red onions, finely chopped
5 garlic cloves, thinly sliced
2.5cm (1in) piece of ginger, peeled
and finely chopped
3 green chillies, finely chopped
125ml (½ cup) plain passata (sieved
tomatoes), or blended chopped
tomatoes
2–3 tbsp hot sauce of your choice
1 tbsp light soy sauce
1 tbsp white wine vinegar or coconut
vinegar
1 heaped tbsp sugar (optional)
4 spring onions (scallions), sliced,
plus extra to serve

Bring 1 litre (4½ cups) of lightly salted water to a rapid boil, then turn off the heat. Add the cauliflower and turmeric and let the cauliflower cook in the hot water for about 3 minutes. Drain and transfer the par-cooked cauliflower to a sheet or two of paper towel to dry. The turmeric can stain so don't use one of your best tea (dish) towels.

Once dry, mix together the marinade ingredients and rub the marinade all over the cauliflower. Let rest for about 20 minutes, or longer. This can all be done ahead of time.

When ready to cook, make the batter. Mix the batter ingredients well in a mixing bowl and add just enough water to make a thick batter. It should be pourable but it needs to be thick enough to coat the cauliflower. Add the cauliflower florets to the batter so that they are all nicely coated.

Now heat about 10cm (4in) of rapeseed (canola) oil in a large pan over a medium–high heat. The oil is hot enough when a small piece of battered cauliflower sizzles immediately when dropped in the oil. Fry the battered cauliflower for about 3 minutes until lightly browned. I usually do this in batches so that I don't overcrowd the pan. Transfer the cooked cauliflower to paper towel to cool while you cook the rest of the cauliflower. Now turn up the heat to high and fry the cauliflower again for another 2–3 minutes until crispy and golden brown. This double frying makes the cauliflower nice and crispy.

To make the sauce, heat the 2 tablespoons of rapeseed (canola) oil in a large frying pan over a medium–high heat and sauté the chopped onion for about 5 minutes until soft and translucent. Add the chopped garlic, ginger and chillies and fry for a further 30 seconds. Now pour in the passata (sieved tomatoes) or blended tomatoes, hot sauce, soy sauce, vinegar and sugar (if using). Allow to simmer for about 2 minutes, then stir in the chopped spring onions and the cauliflower. Mix well so that the cauliflower is evenly coated with the sauce.

To serve, check for seasoning and sprinkle with a little more chopped spring onions and the coriander (cilantro) to serve.

JACKFRUIT DUMPLING CURRY

SERVES 4 OR MORE AS PART OF A MULTI-COURSE MEAL

I first tried this delicious vegetarian curry at Baluchi at LaLit London. I loved it and asked my chef friend Jomon Kuriakose to send me the recipe. His recipe was slightly different in that it was prepared on a restaurant scale, but I have adapted it for the home cook. I really like the flavour and meaty texture of jackfruit. It goes so well with the other dumpling ingredients. To save time, you could let the sauce simmer while you prepare the dumplings. Sometimes I simplify this curry by making sauce and then just adding small pieces of jackfruit. I like to serve this with steamed basmati rice (see page 314).

PREP TIME: 20 MINS, PLUS
 SOAKING THE CASHEW NUTS
COOKING TIME: 50 MINS

Rapeseed (canola) oil, for frying
Rice, to serve
Fried onions (see page 173) and
 coriander (cilantro), to garnish

FOR THE DUMPLINGS
2 large (about 250g/9oz) potatoes
250g (9oz) grated jackfruit (tinned or
 fresh)
1 tbsp rice flour
1 tbsp cornflour (cornstarch)
 (optional)
200g (7oz) paneer cheese, grated
2.5cm (1in) piece of ginger, peeled
 and minced
2 green chillies, finely chopped
3 tbsp finely chopped coriander
 (cilantro) leaves
1 tsp salt

FOR THE SAUCE
5 medium onions, roughly chopped
2.5cm (1in) piece of ginger, peeled
 and crushed
2 garlic cloves
2 green chillies, finely chopped
3 green cardamom pods, smashed
1 Indian bay leaf (cassia leaf)
100g (3½oz) cashew nuts, soaked in
 water overnight
100ml (scant ½ cup) double (heavy)
 cream
1 tsp white pepper
1 level tsp salt
75g (5 tbsp) cold butter

Start by making the dumplings. Par-cook the potatoes for about 10 minutes, or until almost cooked through. You should easily be able to stick a fork in, but there should be some resistance. Remove the potatoes from the water and allow to cool, then grate them. Add the jackfruit and squeeze as much moisture as possible out of this mixture.

Add the remaining dumpling ingredients and knead until you have a smooth dough-like mixture, then divide into 12 equal-size balls. Heat about 10cm (4in) of rapeseed (canola) oil in a large saucepan or wok. When bubbly hot, add one of the balls and ensure it doesn't fall apart. If it does, add a little more cornflour (cornstarch). This should solve the problem.

Fry the dumplings until they turn a light brown (you might want to do this in batches). Transfer to paper towel to soak up excess oil and set aside.

To make the sauce, simmer the onions in 125ml (½ cup) of water with the ginger, garlic, green chillies, green cardamom pods and bay leaf. When the onions begin to turn translucent (after about 10 minutes), add the soaked cashew nuts and simmer over a low heat for 30 minutes. If it looks like it is getting a bit dry, add a little more water.

Blend the sauce and pass it through a fine sieve to get a smooth sauce consistency. Add some or all of the double cream and season with the white pepper and salt. Add the fried jackfruit dumplings and simmer in the sauce until heated through.

Add the butter, allowing it to melt into the sauce. Serve on warm plates with rice and garnish with fried onions and coriander (cilantro).

CREAMY VEGETABLE KORMA

SERVES 4 OR MORE AS PART OF A MULTI-COURSE MEAL

This might look similar to the mild kormas you find at curry houses but British kormas are kormas in name only. This authentic dish is on the spicy side but the spice level can be adjusted to taste.

PREP TIME: 10 MINS
COOKING TIME: 20 MINS

1 potato (about 185g/6½oz), cut into small cubes
12 cauliflower and/or broccoli florets
75g (½ cup) peas
75g (½ cup) sweetcorn
1 carrot, peeled and finely chopped
15 green beans, roughly chopped
1 small red (bell) pepper, roughly chopped
Pinch of saffron (optional)
3 tbsp warm milk (optional)
3 tbsp ghee, clarified butter or rapeseed (canola) oil
5cm (2in) piece of cinnamon stick
3 green cardamom pods, bruised
15 fresh curry leaves
2 onions, finely chopped
1 tbsp garlic and ginger paste (see page 172)
3 tomatoes, diced
½ tsp ground turmeric
125ml (½ cup) double (heavy) cream or whisked plain yoghurt
Salt, to taste
3 tbsp finely chopped coriander (cilantro) or whole leaves, to serve
1 tsp garam masala (see page 167), to sprinkle

FOR THE KORMA PASTE

2 tbsp chana dhal
1 tbsp cumin seeds
1 tbsp coriander seeds
200ml (generous ¾ cup) thick coconut milk or creamed coconut
30 cashew nuts
2 tbsp sesame seeds
4 cloves
2 green chillies, roughly chopped
2 dried red chillies
1 tbsp sugar
10 black peppercorns

Parboil your cubed potato until almost cooked through – about 5 minutes. Then add the rest of the vegetables and simmer them with the potato until just cooked through but still quite fresh-looking, about 2 minutes. Drain and set aside.

To make the korma paste, lightly toast the lentils in a dry frying pan for 1½–2 minutes until light brown, then transfer to a plate to cool. Roast the cumin and coriander seeds in the same way. They are ready when fragrant. If they begin to smoke, get them off the heat. Place the lentils, cumin seeds and coriander seeds in a spice grinder with the other paste ingredients and grind to a smooth, thick paste.

When you're ready to make the curry, soak the saffron in 3 tablespoons of warm milk (if using) and set aside. Heat the ghee, butter or oil in a large saucepan that has a lid. When visibly hot, add the cinnamon stick and cardamom pods and temper these spices in the oil for about 30 seconds before adding the curry leaves. Temper the leaves for another 30 seconds, then add the chopped onions. Fry the onions until soft and lightly browned, about 5 minutes, and then stir in the garlic and ginger paste.

Add the chopped tomatoes and turmeric and let this mixture all cook for another 2 minutes before adding your prepared korma paste. Toss in the par-cooked vegetables and about 250ml (1 cup) of water to cover. Stir well and place the lid on the top. Cook, covered, for about 2 minutes until the sauce has thickened and the vegetables are fully cooked. If you prefer a thicker sauce, remove the pan lid for 1 minute, or until you are happy with the consistency.

Pour in the cream or yoghurt and the saffron-infused milk (if using) and cook for another minute with the lid on.

To finish, season with salt, garnish with the coriander (cilantro) and sprinkle the garam masala over the top.

MAKE IT VEGAN

Substitute more thick coconut milk for the cream or try substituting vegan coconut yoghurt or non-dairy cream.

BLACK-EYED BEAN CURRY

SERVES 4 OR MORE AS PART OF A MULTI-COURSE MEAL

I learned this recipe at a brilliant restaurant in Newcastle called Ury. I was invited there one afternoon to watch the head chef prepare this bean curry. Talk about gorgeous! This one is so easy to make but the flavours are still complex and work so well together.

PREP TIME: 10 MINS
COOKING TIME: 20 MINS

2 tbsp coconut oil or rapeseed
   (canola) oil
1 tsp brown mustard seeds
1 tsp fenugreek seeds
20 fresh or frozen curry leaves
2 onions, sliced and cut into 2.5cm
   (1in) pieces
2 green chillies, split lengthways
6 garlic cloves, sliced
2.5cm (1in) piece of ginger, peeled
   and julienned
1 tsp ground turmeric
½ tsp chilli powder
1 tsp ground coriander
3 tomatoes, diced, or 300–400g
   (10½ –14oz) tinned (canned)
   chopped tomatoes
600g (1lb 5oz) cooked or tinned
   (canned) black-eyed beans, drained
   and rinsed
200g (¾ cup) plain yoghurt
4 tbsp finely chopped coriander
   (cilantro), to serve
Yoghurt sauce (see page 338) or plain
   yoghurt, to serve (optional)

Heat the oil in a wok or large frying pan over a medium–high heat. When hot, stir in the mustard seeds. They will begin to pop after about 30 seconds. When they do, stir in the fenugreek seeds and curry leaves and temper in the oil for about 30 seconds.

Add the chopped onions and sliced green chillies and stir it all into the oil. You want to cook the onions for about 10 minutes until they are good and soft and lightly browned. Stir in the garlic and ginger. Sprinkle in the turmeric, chilli powder and ground coriander. Add the diced tomatoes or, if you prefer a deeper colour, try adding some tinned (canned) tomatoes. Give it all a good stir, then add the black-eyed beans. I normally soak and cook dried beans but tinned are a lot more convenient and work really well.

To finish, stir in the yoghurt 1 tablespoon at a time.

Serve immediately, garnished with coriander (cilantro) and a little more yoghurt or yoghurt sauce if you like.

MAKE IT VEGAN
Substitute 200ml (generous ¾ cup) thick coconut milk, or vegan coconut yoghurt, for the dairy yoghurt.

CHANA

SERVES 4 OR MORE AS PART OF A MULTI-COURSE MEAL

If you ever find yourself in the Northern Quarter of Manchester, you'll find some fantastic home-style curry cafés that you've simply got to try. These are no-nonsense restaurants and/or takeaways that look like old greasy spoons but are immaculate, and the food is out of this world. You can still get a curry and rice for a fiver! One of my favourites is Al-Faisal Tandoori.

I first visited Al-Faisal Tandoori back in 1998 and little has changed. They still have the green tables with chairs that are attached and water and glasses are on every table. They are only open until 8pm and there is no alcohol on the menu but it is the perfect place for a lunch or early dinner. The food is cooked fresh daily. This simple recipe was given to me on the day I visited by Tariq Malik. I love it!

PREP TIME: 10 MINS, PLUS
PREPARING THE CHICKPEAS
COOKING TIME: 1¼ HOURS

4 tbsp rapeseed (canola) oil
2 tbsp garlic and ginger paste (see page 172)
250g (1½ cups) dried chickpeas (garbanzo beans), soaked in water overnight, then drained
½ tsp bicarbonate of soda (baking soda)
1 heaped tbsp cumin seeds
½ tsp ajwain (carom) seeds
½ tsp chilli powder
1 onion, finely chopped
Salt, to taste
Chopped green chillies and coriander (cilantro), to serve

Heat 1 tablespoon of the oil in a saucepan over a medium–high heat until visibly hot. Stir in the garlic and ginger paste and fry for about 1 minute. Now add the prepared chickpeas and bicarbonate of soda (baking soda) and cover with water. Simmer for about 70 minutes, adding a little more water when necessary, until the chickpeas are tender. This is quite a thick curry, so when the chickpeas are close to fork-tender cook down the water to a minimum.

In a separate frying pan, heat the remaining oil over a medium–high heat and temper the cumin seeds and ajwain (carom) seeds in the oil for about 40 seconds. Add the chilli powder and chopped onion and fry until the onion is lightly browned and soft – about 7 minutes. Pour this over your finished chickpeas and give it all a good stir.

Season with salt and serve with chopped green chillies and coriander (cilantro), which can be added to taste at the table.

MAKE THIS CURRY EVEN EASIER
I prefer the texture of slowly simmered dried chickpeas, which is how this is made at Al-Faisal Tandoori. I have, however, made this recipe using two 400g (14oz) tins (cans) of chickpeas with excellent results.

VEGETABLE STUFFED PAPAD ROLL CURRY

SERVES 4 OR MORE AS PART OF A MULTI-COURSE MEAL

The papad rolls can be a bit fussy to make. Don't worry! Just do your best. They tend to come out fine in the end. You could use cutlery but I like to pick up the papad rolls and dip them into the sauce by hand. It's messy, mind! If you want to prepare ahead, you could make the sauce up to three days in advance, but frying the papad rolls and adding the extra cheese is best done just before serving. You can wrap anything you like into the papads – reduced potato curry (see page 154), for example.

PREP TIME: 20 MINS
COOKING TIME: 20 MINS

1 onion, roughly chopped
3 tbsp rapeseed (canola) oil
2 green chillies, finely chopped
1 tsp garam masala (see page 167) or curry powder (see page 171)
½ tsp ground turmeric
1 tsp chilli powder
1 tbsp garlic and ginger paste (see page 172)
400g (14oz) tinned (canned) chopped tomatoes, blended
2 tbsp single (light) cream
1 tbsp unsalted butter
Salt, to taste
3 tbsp finely chopped coriander (cilantro), plus extra to serve

FOR THE PAPAD ROLLS
2 tbsp rapeseed (canola) oil, plus extra for shallow-frying
1 tsp cumin seeds
1 tsp fennel seeds
1 tbsp garlic and ginger paste (see page 172)
100g (3½oz) grated cauliflower
60g (2oz) grated carrot
60g (2oz) grated cabbage
50g (1/3 cup) finely chopped green beans
200g (7oz) paneer cheese, grated
6–10 papads

Start by making the curry sauce. Put the onion in a blender or food processor and blend to a paste with just a little water.

Heat the oil in a large frying pan over a medium–high heat. When hot, pour in the blended onion and let it brown for about 3 minutes before adding the chillies, garam masala or curry powder, turmeric and chilli powder. Continue frying for another minute. The sauce should turn quite brown. Add the garlic and ginger paste and mix it all up well. Stir in the blended tomatoes and cream, then whisk in the butter until melted and emulsified into the sauce. Season with salt and keep warm.

To make the papad rolls, heat the oil in a large frying pan. When visibly hot, toss in the cumin and fennel seeds. Temper them in the oil for about 20 seconds, until they become fragrant, then stir in the garlic and ginger paste and let it sizzle for a further 20 seconds. Pour in the grated vegetables and finely chopped green beans and fry until tender – 2 minutes should do the trick. Add most of the grated paneer, then turn the heat off and let the mixture cool slightly.

Fill a deep plate or casserole with water and place a few papads in it. It is best if they aren't touching. Soak them for about 3 minutes, then carefully remove one from the water bath. Place it on a clean surface and then scoop about 2–3 tablespoons of the vegetable and paneer mixture just under the centre. Fold the sides in and then roll it up like a burrito or tight cylinder shape. Allow to dry a little while you do the same with the remaining papads.

Shallow-fry the papad rolls in oil until crispy all over. You will need to do this in batches, so keep them warm while you fry the remaining papads. Stir the reserved grated paneer into the sauce or sprinkle it on top. Place your papad rolls in the sauce so they are sticking out and garnish with coriander (cilantro).

MAKE IT VEGAN
Non-dairy butter or ghee and cream can be substituted. You could also use dairy-free cheese instead of the paneer or simply leave it out.

BUTTER PANEER

Butter paneer just plain gets it! This one is so good simply served with plain white rice. The sauce isn't only good with paneer. Try making small hara bhara kebabs (see page 63) and deep-frying them before adding them to the sauce. Just wonderful!

PREP TIME: 15 MINS, PLUS
   MARINATING TIME
COOKING TIME: 20 MINS

400g (14oz) paneer cheese, cut into
   2.5cm (1in) cubes
2 x 400g (14oz) tins (cans) chopped
   tomatoes
2 tbsp garlic and ginger paste (see
   page 172)
4 green cardamom pods
2 cloves
1 bay leaf
1 tbsp chilli powder
2 tbsp rapeseed (canola) oil
2 green chillies, split lengthways
   (optional)
80g (5½ tbsp) butter, diced
75ml (5 tbsp) single (light) cream
Salt, to taste
1½ tbsp sugar, to taste (optional)

FOR THE MARINADE
1 tbsp rapeseed (canola) oil
2 tbsp garlic and ginger paste (see
   page 172)
1½ tsp salt
Juice of 1 lemon
2 tsp red chilli powder
120g (½ cup) Greek yoghurt
¼ tsp garam masala (see page 167)

TO SERVE
¼ tsp garam masala (see page 167)
2 tsp dried fenugreek leaves (kasoori
   methi), crushed
3 tbsp chopped coriander (cilantro)

Mix the marinade ingredients and marinate the cubed paneer for about 20 minutes.

Meanwhile, place the tomatoes, garlic and ginger paste, cardamom pods, cloves, bay leaf and chilli powder in a blender and blend until smooth. Pour this through a sieve, pressing the sauce through into an awaiting saucepan. Discard any solids that don't make it through the sieve. Bring the sauce to a low simmer and continue cooking while you prepare the paneer.

Heat the oil in a large frying pan over a medium–high heat. When visibly hot, add the paneer cubes, leaving as much of the marinade in the bowl as possible. Fry the paneer on one side and then flip over to sear the opposite side. The paneer can now be used in the curry, but if time permits, go ahead and fry every side of the paneer cubes until lightly browned and crisp. Set aside.

Returning to your simmering sauce, add the chillies (if using) and stir in the butter 1 tablespoon at a time, whisking until it is emulsified into the sauce. Stir in the cream and season with salt. Taste the sauce. If you prefer a sweeter sauce, add about 1½ tablespoons of sugar, or to taste.

To serve, whisk the reserved marinade into the sauce, 1 tablespoon at a time. Add the paneer and dust the top with the garam masala and crushed dried fenugreek leaves (kasoori methi) and sprinkle with chopped coriander (cilantro).

SAAG PANEER
SERVES 4 OR MORE AS PART OF A MULTI-COURSE MEAL

It's so often the case that the best recipes are the simplest. You don't need to slave over the hob all day to make a delicious meal. Back in 2015, I visited Thali on Old Brompton Road in London. I was there to review the restaurant and they brought out a meal that was beyond amazing.

One of the side dishes they served that evening was this saag paneer. This wasn't a dish I would normally order, but I loved it! So much so, I asked them for the recipe. This is my play on their amazing recipe. You will need a big pan for this one as there is so much spinach, but it does reduce down a lot during cooking. You could also use frozen spinach for this recipe, which is a lot easier.

PREP TIME: 10 MINS, PLUS
   OPTIONAL MARINATING TIME
COOKING TIME: 20 MINS

250g (9oz) paneer cheese, cubed
5 tbsp rapeseed (canola) oil
800g (1lb 12oz) fresh baby spinach
   leaves, or 450g (1lb) frozen spinach
1 tsp cumin seeds
1 tsp red chilli powder (more or less to
   taste) (optional)
1 tsp ground turmeric
4 fat garlic cloves, finely chopped
2 tbsp plain yoghurt
Salt, to taste
3 tbsp single (light) cream (optional)

FOR THE MARINADE
½ tsp ground turmeric
½ tsp chilli powder
½ tsp salt
1 tsp rapeseed (canola) oil

With a fork, make a few holes in each paneer cube and then mix well with the marinade ingredients. You can fry these immediately but the paneer does benefit from a longer marinating time. I often marinate paneer overnight.

Fry the paneer in about 3 tablespoons of the oil in a frying pan set over a medium–high heat until nicely browned. Set aside while you cook the spinach.

Pour 285ml (generous 1 cup) of water into a large saucepan and bring to the boil. Add the spinach and simmer until the water has evaporated. Allow the spinach to cool, then blitz to a thick paste in a food processor. Set aside.

Now heat the remaining oil in a large frying pan over a medium–high heat. When visibly hot, add the cumin seeds and stir them around in the oil for about 30 seconds, then add the chilli powder and turmeric. Stir in the garlic and fry until it turns a light golden brown. Be careful not to burn the garlic or it will turn bitter.

Add the blended spinach to the pan and stir in the yoghurt, 1 tablespoon at a time. Stir in the fried paneer and heat through. Season with salt and serve immediately. I like to stir in about 3 tablespoons of single (light) cream to finish the dish off. This is optional but very nice.

CHILLI PANEER STIR-FRY

SERVES 2 OR MORE AS PART OF A MULTI-COURSE MEAL

This is a lip-smacking way to serve paneer. The sauce is sweet, savoury and just as spicy as you like it. Use your favourite hot sauce for this one. You can use less if you really don't like your sauces spicy hot. I like to roll the seared, soft paneer with the fried veggies and sauce into chapattis. Of course, it's also good served as a saucy curry over plain white rice.

PREP TIME: 10 MINS
COOKING TIME: 10 MINS

3 tbsp rapeseed (canola) oil
200g (7oz) paneer cheese, cubed
200g (7oz) mixed coloured (bell)
    peppers, roughly chopped
3 spring onions (scallions), roughly
    chopped
Plain rice or rotis, to serve

FOR THE SAUCE
250ml (1 cup) tomato ketchup
3 tbsp hot sauce of your choice
5 garlic cloves, finely chopped
2.5cm (1in) piece of ginger, peeled
    and finely chopped
2 tbsp light soy sauce or coconut
    aminos
1 tbsp cornflour (cornstarch)
1 tsp freshly ground black pepper
1 tsp white pepper
Salt, to taste

Start by preparing the sauce. Whisk together all of the sauce ingredients up to and including the white pepper. Season to taste with salt and set aside.

Heat the oil in a large frying pan over a medium–high heat. When visibly hot, add the cubed paneer to the pan and brown on two sides. Stir in the peppers and spring onions (scallions) and fry until cooked through but still crisp, about 1–2 minutes.

Now add the prepared sauce and stir it all up nicely. Check for seasoning and serve hot with plain rice or wrapped into hot rotis.

MUTTAR PANEER
SERVES 4 OR MORE AS PART OF A MULTI-COURSE MEAL

This is an authentic Punjabi muttar paneer recipe but with a British twist. In this version, the sauce is blended until silky smooth. We do like our smooth sauces here in the UK. It's worth noting that this sauce is not limited to paneer and peas. It goes well with so many other main ingredients. Prawns (shrimp), chicken, bite-size pieces of seekh kebab... If you think it sounds good, it will be.

PREP TIME: 10 MINS, PLUS
    MARINATING TIME
COOKING TIME: 15 MINS

1kg (2lb 3oz) paneer cheese, cut into 4cm (1½in) cubes
1 tbsp rapeseed (canola) oil
2 tbsp garlic and ginger paste (see page 172)
1 tsp salt
Juice of 1 lemon
2 tsp chilli powder
5 tbsp Greek yoghurt, whisked
½ tsp garam masala (see page 167)

FOR THE SAUCE
3 tbsp rapeseed (canola) oil or seasoned oil (see page 8)
4 green cardamom pods, lightly bruised
2 cloves
1 bay leaf
2 large onions, finely chopped
3 tbsp garlic and ginger paste (see page 172)
1.2kg (2lb 10oz) tomatoes, halved
2 tbsp raw cashew paste (see page 173)
1 tbsp chilli powder, or to taste
2 fresh green chillies, quartered
150g (1 cup) frozen peas
5 tbsp single (light) cream
½ tsp garam masala (see page 167)
80g (⅓ cup) cold butter, diced
Juice of 1 lemon
Salt, to taste
2 tsp dried fenugreek leaves (kasoori methi), crushed

Put the paneer in a bowl with the oil, garlic and ginger paste, salt, lemon juice and chilli powder, and mix gently to coat. Set aside for about 15 minutes, then stir in the whisked yoghurt and garam masala. Leave to marinate while you prepare the tomato sauce.

In a large saucepan, heat the oil until hot. Toss in the cardamom pods, cloves and bay leaf, and sizzle for 30 seconds. Add the onions and fry for a further 3 minutes until soft and translucent but not browned. Stir in the garlic and ginger paste.

Fry for another 30 seconds, stirring, then add the tomatoes, 125ml (½ cup) of water and the cashew paste. Let this come to a simmer and cook until the onions and tomatoes break down into a thick sauce, about 5 minutes. Using a jug or hand-held blender, blend until super-smooth, about 3–4 minutes.

Return the sauce to the pan and stir in the chilli powder and green chillies. Let this all come to a mild bubble, then add the paneer cubes and peas, and heat through for about 2 minutes (if you cook the cheese too long, it will begin to disintegrate into the sauce, so watch carefully).

To finish, swirl in the cream and garam masala, then stir in the cold butter one piece at a time. Stir in the lemon juice and season with salt. Top with the dried fenugreek leaves (kasoori methi) and serve.

TIP
My pan-fried paneer (see page 180) and grilled paneer (page 298) can be substituted for the raw marinated paneer with equally tasty results.

DUM ALOO

SERVES 2 OR MORE AS PART OF A MULTI-COURSE MEAL

I first tried dum aloo at a friend's wedding. The catering company made it with small new potatoes and I loved it. It wasn't until years later that I tried it again. That time I was on a stag do somewhere in London. It's all a bit of a blur now, but I can remember that curry as if it was yesterday. A huge karahi was brought to our table filled with deep-fried whole potatoes in a thick red sauce. This is my version of that dish. I just wish I could remember where I had it.

PREP TIME: 20 MINS, PLUS
    SOAKING TIME
COOKING TIME: 25 MINS

5–6 medium roasting potatoes,
    peeled
2 tbsp rapeseed (canola) oil, plus
    extra for deep-frying
8–12 Kashmiri dried red chillies,
    soaked in 250ml (1 cup) water for
    30 minutes
1 tbsp tandoori masala (see page 168)
½ tsp ground ginger (optional)
250g (1 cup) plain yoghurt
2.5cm (1in) piece of cinnamon stick
½ tsp asafoetida*
1 tsp chilli powder, plus extra to taste
1 bay leaf
5 cardamom pods, bruised
1 tbsp fennel seeds
½ tsp ground turmeric
½ tsp ground cloves
1 tsp ground cumin
1 tsp ground coriander
Salt and freshly ground black pepper,
    to taste

TO SERVE
3 tbsp finely chopped coriander
    (cilantro)
½ tsp garam masala (see page 167)
Juice of ½ lemon

Par-cook the whole potatoes in boiling water until about 80% cooked through – 15–20 minutes. They should be soft enough to easily stick a fork in but hard enough that you wouldn't want to start eating them.

For deep-frying, heat about 10cm (4in) of oil – enough to cover the potatoes. When hot (if you have an oil thermometer, aim for 190°C/375°F), carefully place the par-cooked potatoes in the oil and fry for about 3 minutes until crispy and brown. Set aside.

Now pour your soaked chillies and the soaking water into a blender and add the tandoori masala and ground ginger and blend until smooth. Stir this into the yoghurt in a large mixing bowl. Set aside.

To cook the curry, heat the 2 tablespoons of rapeseed (canola) oil in a large wok or frying pan over a medium–high heat. Stir in the cinnamon stick, asafoetida, chilli powder, bay leaf, cardamom pods, fennel seeds, turmeric, cloves, cumin and ground coriander and fry it all, stirring continuously, for about 1 minute.

Now pour in the yoghurt mixture and whisk. The oil will rise to the top as it is added, so you need to whisk briskly to emulsify it into the sauce. Once you've achieved a smooth, red, emulsified sauce, season with salt and try it. I usually add more chilli powder at this point too as the potatoes can stand up to a spicier sauce.

In go the fried potatoes! Stir them into the sauce, then cover the pan to simmer for about 10 minutes. It's really hard to overcook a potato, so just let them simmer in the sauce and become fall-apart gorgeous. When they are cooked to perfection, you should be able to cut into them with a fork and take a sneaky bite or two. Just don't rush things. Your curry is ready when the potatoes are super-soft and the sauce has thickened. Check for seasoning.

To serve, sprinkle with coriander (cilantro) and garam masala and add a twist or two of lemon juice.

NOTE
*If you are gluten-free, please check the asafoetida packaging as some brands contain wheat flour.

MAKE IT VEGAN
Substitute soy or coconut yoghurt for the dairy yoghurt. The yoghurt is a sauce thickener, so whisking in about 1 generous teaspoon of cornflour (cornstarch) will help achieve a similar consistency.

POTATO CURRY
SERVES 4 OR MORE AS PART OF A MULTI-COURSE MEAL

Delicious and satisfying, potato curry is usually served for breakfast in India. It's currently served for breakfast at my house almost weekly. It's the perfect way to start the day but it's pretty good any time of day really! You've probably seen this curry on a few Indian restaurant menus. It's delicious served over rice, but the more traditional way to serve it is with fresh homemade puris (see page 311). You could cube the potatoes, but I like to serve this one the way I was taught: simply boil your potatoes and break them up by hand into the spicy sauce. This gives you less uniform, different-size chunks, which I like. If you have any left over, cook it down and spread it on a Mumbai toastie (see page 68).

PREP TIME: 10 MINS
COOKING TIME: 20 MINS

800g (1lb 12oz) medium potatoes
3 tbsp oil
2 tsp chana dhal
1 tsp white split urad dhal
1 tsp mustard seeds
1 tsp cumin seeds
10 curry leaves
Pinch of asafoetida*
1 large onion, finely chopped
2.5cm (1in) piece of ginger, peeled and finely chopped
2 tomatoes, diced
2–3 green chillies
1/3–1/2 tsp ground turmeric
1/2 tsp chilli powder
2 tsp gram (chickpea) flour, whisked in about 3 tbsp water until smooth
Salt, to taste
1/2 tsp sugar (more or less to taste) (optional)
2 tbsp chopped coriander (cilantro) leaves, to serve
Puris or rice, to serve

Bring a pan of water to a boil and add the potatoes. Cook for 15–20 minutes until they are fork-tender.

While the potatoes are cooking, heat the oil in a large saucepan over a medium–high heat until visibly hot. Stir in the chana and urad lentils and fry until lightly browned. Add the mustard seeds. When they begin to pop (after about 30 seconds), reduce the heat to medium and stir in the cumin seeds, curry leaves and asafoetida and fry for a further 30 seconds before adding the chopped onion. Fry the onion for about 5 minutes until translucent and soft, then add the ginger, diced tomatoes and chillies. Add the turmeric and chilli powder and mix it all up.

Once the potatoes are cooked, transfer them to a cutting board to cool, then peel them.

Add the potatoes to the curry by breaking them up with your hands and stir in just enough water to cover. Simmer for about 5 minutes, or until the potatoes are soft to your liking, then add the gram flour mixture and stir well. Season with salt. Some people like this curry a little sweeter, so you can add sugar to taste as well if you like, but I usually don't.

Garnish with the coriander (cilantro) leaves and serve with rice or preferably puris.

NOTE

*If you are gluten-free, please check the asafoetida packaging as some brands contain wheat flour.

BROCCOLI CURRY

SERVES 4 OR MORE AS PART OF A MULTI-COURSE MEAL

I'm pretty sure this broccoli curry was the first vegetarian curry I ever posted on my blog. In India, I've seen many similar curries that are cooked with cauliflower instead. You could do that too as it's very good. For me, however, I like the colour and flavour the broccoli adds to the dish. There really is so much going on here. From the roasted peanuts and sesame seeds to the creamy coconut milk, I just love this dish. So much so, it's now one of the curries I teach at my vegetarian cooking classes. Even those who think vegetarian curries are boring end up changing their minds very quickly when they taste this.

PREP TIME: 10 MINS
COOKING TIME: 15 MINS

500g (1lb 2oz) broccoli, cut into small
   florets
3 tbsp ghee or coconut oil
2.5cm (1in) piece of ginger, peeled
   and finely grated
70g (2½oz) grated fresh or frozen
   coconut
3 tbsp toasted sesame seeds
70g (½ cup) roasted peanuts
1 tsp red chilli powder
1 tsp ground turmeric
1 onion, finely chopped
2 green chillies, finely chopped
3 garlic cloves, finely chopped
3 tomatoes, roughly chopped
400ml (14fl oz) tin (can) thick
   coconut milk
Salt and freshly ground black pepper,
   to taste
½ tsp garam masala (see page 167)
Rice, puris or chapattis, to serve

Heat some water and steam the broccoli florets until just cooked – about 3 minutes. You should just be able to stick a fork into the side of the florets, but there should be some resistance. Set aside.

Now heat a large frying pan or wok over a medium heat and add the ghee or oil. When hot, throw in the ginger, coconut, 2 tablespoons of the sesame seeds, the peanuts, chilli powder and turmeric and cook for about 3 minutes, stirring the ingredients about the pan with a spatula.

Stir in the onion and chillies and fry for about 5 minutes until the onion is soft and translucent and just starting to brown.

Add the garlic and give it a good stir. When fragrant, add the chopped tomatoes followed by the par-cooked broccoli and coconut milk. Heat the broccoli through but try to ensure that it is tender but not at all mushy.

Season with salt and black pepper and sprinkle with the garam masala and the remaining sesame seeds. Serve immediately with rice, puris or chapattis.

SAAG ALOO

SERVES 2 AS A MAIN COURSE OR 4 AS A SIDE DISH

I make this popular vegetarian curry two ways, depending on my mood. You could blend the spinach and chillies with a little spice stock or water to make a smooth spinach purée as in the lamb saag recipe (see page 217). Alternatively, you could make it as shown with blanched, roughly cut baby spinach leaves. I like to use coconut oil for this one, which is now widely available. It adds a nice, nutty flavour to the curry.

PREP TIME: 10 MINS, PLUS
   THE TIME TO PRE-COOK
   THE POTATOES
COOKING TIME: 10 MINS

2 tbsp coconut oil, rapeseed (canola) oil or seasoned oil (see page 8)
1 tsp cumin seeds
10 fresh or frozen curry leaves
1 onion, finely chopped
1–3 green chillies, to taste
Pinch of ground turmeric
1 tsp nigella seeds (black onion seeds)
2 tbsp garlic and ginger paste (see page 172)
20 cherry tomatoes, halved
2 large pre-cooked stewed potatoes (see page 179) and 200ml (generous ½ cup) of the cooking stock plus extra if desired
200g (7oz) baby leaf spinach, blanched for 30 seconds and roughly chopped
1 tsp garam masala (see page 167)
Salt and freshly ground black pepper, to taste

Heat the oil in a large wok or frying pan over a medium–high heat. When it begins to bubble, add the cumin seeds and allow to sizzle until fragrant. About 30 seconds should do.

Now add the curry leaves followed by the chopped onion, green chillies, turmeric and nigella seeds and continue frying until the onion is soft and translucent, about 5 minutes. Stir in the garlic and ginger paste.

Add the cherry tomatoes and mix it all up well. Then, add the pre-cooked potatoes and their cooking stock and simmer for a few minutes until the sauce has thickened and the potatoes are heated through.

Stir in the chopped spinach. (If using the puréed spinach and chilli method, as detailed in the introduction, this is the time to pour it in.)

Simmer for another minute or so until you are happy with the consistency. If you prefer more sauce, add some more cooking stock or even a little base curry sauce (see page 164 or 166).

Sprinkle the garam masala over the top and season with salt and black pepper.

ONION PAKORA CURRY

SERVES 4 OR MORE AS PART OF A MULTI-COURSE MEAL

Onion pakoras, or onion bhajis as they are usually referred to in the West, aren't just served as a starter course. They are delicious in this yoghurt-based curry sauce. So next time you have a few homemade onion bhajis, give this one a try. Why wait though? Make my onion bhajis on page 24. You might just be surprised at how amazing onion bhajis can taste served in this mildly spicy sauce. If you live near an Indian snack shop, you could just purchase the onion pakoras, as I've never had a bad one.

PREP TIME: 10 MINS, PLUS
   THE TIME TO COOK THE
   ONION BHAJIS
COOKING TIME: 10 MINS

500g (2 cups) Greek yoghurt
25g (¼ cup) gram (chickpea) flour
½ tsp ground turmeric
1 tsp Kashmiri chilli powder
½ tsp ground coriander
3 tbsp rapeseed (canola) oil
1 tsp black mustard seeds
5 fenugreek seeds
½ tsp cumin seeds
2.5cm (1in) piece of cinnamon stick
15 fresh or frozen curry leaves
1 medium onion, finely chopped
1 tbsp garlic and ginger paste (see
   page 172)
12 onion bhajis (pakoras) (see
   page 24)
Salt, to taste
3 tbsp finely chopped coriander
   (cilantro), to garnish

Strain the yoghurt into a mixing bowl until creamy smooth (straining the yoghurt will help prevent it from curdling when cooked). Sift in the flour, turmeric, chilli powder and ground coriander and whisk it all in too. Add 400ml (scant 1¾ cups) of water and stir until combined into the yoghurt. Set aside.

Now heat the oil in a large frying pan over a medium–high heat. When bubbly hot, add the mustard seeds and when they begin to crackle (after about 30 seconds), stir in the fenugreek seeds, cumin seeds and the cinnamon stick. Infuse these spices into the oil until they become fragrant – 30 seconds should do the job. Be careful not to burn the spices or they will become bitter. Add the curry leaves and the onion and fry over a medium to medium–high heat for about 5 minutes until the onion is soft and translucent.

Add the garlic and ginger paste and fry for a further 30 seconds, then pour in the yoghurt mixture. Slowly bring to a simmer, then stir in the pakoras. Cook the sauce down until you are happy with the consistency. Season with salt and garnish with the coriander (cilantro).

CURRY-HOUSE PREPARATION RECIPES

Making delicious curry-house food is all about building layer upon layer of flavour. Out of all the base recipes I've included in this section, only the base sauce must be homemade to produce that instantly recognizable BIR-style curry. Everything else is commercially available – even the mixed powder can be produced using ready-made masalas and spice powders. So you can take shortcuts if you want or you could make everything from scratch, making the dishes that much nicer.

Only the best curry houses, like many of those I've mentioned, prepare everything fresh. This is especially so with spice masalas and pastes that can be expensive and time-consuming to prepare for a packed restaurant. You probably won't be cooking for that many people, so use it to your advantage and make those awesome layers of flavour go to work for you.

Even pre-cooking your meat, poultry and vegetables can add a lot of excitement to a dish. You could of course cook these from raw, but it will take longer and you'll be missing out on one or more of the things that can make British Indian restaurant cuisine so amazing. These are time-saving preparations that not only make cooking faster, but really please the palate.

THE BASE CURRY SAUCE

The starting point for any BIR-style curry is your base sauce. Visit the kitchen of a busy curry house or Indian takeaway and you are almost certain to see a large saucepan of aromatic curry sauce simmering away, being used as a base for most, if not all, of the restaurant's curries. Although they are usually quite similar, each restaurant has their own special sauce recipe.

Many connoisseurs of authentic Indian food have criticized the one-sauce-fits-all base sauce used at curry houses, but I feel this is unfair. In most restaurants, the sauce is cooked fresh daily and without it there would be much longer waiting times for your curries and higher prices, as the base sauce allows the chefs to easily cook, plate and serve many different curries.

Some people believe that using the same sauce for curries will make them taste the same, but this is far from the case. There is so much you can do to give each curry its own unique flavour.

I have provided two base sauces in this book. The first (on page 164) is an authentic sauce: it takes its time to cook but is worth every minute. The second (on page 166) is my cheat's version: it allows you to achieve tasty curries but using less time and fewer ingredients. By cooking up a big batch of base sauce, you can easily freeze portions so you can conveniently make your curries with speed and ease.

It is important to point out you DO NOT HAVE TO MAKE A BASE SAUCE to enjoy the curries in this section. You could just fry up a couple of finely chopped onions in a couple of tablespoons of rapeseed (canola) oil until soft and translucent, then follow the recipe, adding water or stock if more liquid is required. Your curry will still be delicious; you will just not get that smooth texture that makes British curries what they are.

GROUND SPICES AND SPICE BLENDS (MASALAS)

The spice blends can be roasted and ground in minutes and stored in air-tight containers in a cool, dark location, such as a cupboard, for up to two months without losing much flavour.

That spectacular aroma you get from freshly ground spices will mellow substantially faster though. When single ground ingredients, such as cumin, are called for it is always best to purchase the spices whole and then roast and grind them as required for optimum flavour. Whole spices have a longer shelf life than ground too.

To make your own spice masalas and ground single spices, it is worth getting a good spice grinder. I use a Waring spice grinder, which allows me to achieve very fine powders and has lasted me years. There are less expensive grinders that will do a good job but they usually don't last very long. You can just use a pestle and mortar; they are more work but get excellent results.

When roasting and grinding whole single spices like cumin, simply use the instructions I give for the spice blends. Do I always do that? Nope. Sometimes I cheat and purchase my spices ready-ground, and that is OK too.

PRE-COOKED MEAT, POULTRY, PANEER AND VEGETABLES

I've included some pre-cooked ingredients to use in your curries just as they do at curry houses. These save cooking time and add extra flavour.

The pre-cooked meat, poultry, paneer and vegetables, along with cooking stocks and marinades, help make the curries taste as if they have been slowly simmering for hours, even though they only took minutes to whip up. These pre-cooked ingredients can all be added to the classic British curry sauces as you like.

Also hugely popular are barbecued meats, paneer and vegetables. Chicken tikka masala (see page 186), for example, just wouldn't be the same without those nicely charred pieces of chicken, whereas stewed chicken is a good bet for a curry like chicken dhansak (see page 205). That said, these curries are all yours, so use whatever pre-cooked ingredient you like. Perhaps you would like a lamb korma instead of the featured chicken korma? Just add lamb instead and perhaps some pre-cooked lamb cooking stock.

I would like to make it clear that, although pre-cooked ingredients make these curries taste and look more authentic, you can use raw ingredients if you prefer. If you want to add raw chicken to your chicken dhansak, for example, that's fine, but it will mean a longer cooking time.

BASE CURRY SAUCE

MAKES 3 LITRES (3 US QUARTS) OR ENOUGH FOR 10–15 SERVINGS

This smooth curry sauce 'gravy', more than any other ingredient, is what gives BIR-style curries their distinctive flavour and texture. A base curry sauce is essentially just a slowly cooked onion stock with a few other veggies and spices thrown in. The sauce is quite bland in flavour but it does taste good. It needs to be bland as it is used in everything, from the mildest korma to the spiciest phall. The magic happens when this bland sauce is used in the different curries and cooked with the ingredients called for in those curries.

Base sauces at restaurants are all quite similar and rarely is an exact recipe followed. This recipe is a scaled-down version of the recipe in my first book, *The Curry Guy*. It is also different to the quick recipe on page 166. These are different recipes that both get excellent results. If you have a 3-litre (3 US-quart) stockpot, it's the perfect size for this recipe.

PREP TIME: 15 MINS
COOKING TIME: 1¼ HOURS

900g (2lb/about 7 medium) onions, roughly chopped
1 tsp salt
250ml (1 cup) rapeseed (canola) oil*
110g (3¾oz) carrots, peeled and chopped
60g (2oz) cabbage, roughly chopped
85g (3oz) red (bell) pepper, deseeded and diced
85g (3oz) green (bell) pepper, deseeded and diced
200g (1 cup) tinned (canned) chopped tomatoes, or about 4 medium fresh tomatoes, chopped
5 tbsp garlic and ginger paste (see page 172)
1½ tbsp garam masala (see page 167)
1½ tbsp ground cumin
1½ tbsp ground coriander
1½ tbsp paprika
1 tbsp ground fenugreek (optional)
½ tbsp ground turmeric

Place the onions in a 3-litre (3 US quart) stockpot over a medium heat and add the salt and oil. Give it a good stir, then add the remaining vegetables along with the garlic and ginger paste and just enough water to cover. You will simmer this for some time, so do not fill the pan to the rim. The water level should be about 5cm (2in) from the top. Bring to a simmer and then reduce the heat to low and simmer gently, covered, for about 45 minutes.

After 45 minutes, your vegetables will be much softer and the liquid will have reduced somewhat. Add the remaining ingredients and top up with water so that the water level is again about 5cm (2in) from the top. Take this as a guide; if you don't need to add water at this time, then don't.

Simmer for another 30 minutes. When the oil rises to the top and your veggies are good and soft, you're ready to blend. Skim the seasoned oil carefully off the top for use in your curries or leave it in the sauce if you like.

Using a hand-held blender, blend for about 4 minutes until the sauce is super-smooth, with no chunks and not at all grainy. This step can be done in batches in a blender. If you have a good blender, you might not need to blend as long to achieve that smooth consistency.

At this stage, the blended sauce might be quite thick. Add water until the sauce is about the same consistency as full-fat (whole) milk or stock. Sometimes I need to pour the sauce into a larger bowl to do this.

Use immediately or store in the fridge for up to 3 days, or freeze in small portions of between 500ml (2 cups) and 750ml (3¼ cups) for use later. The sauce can be frozen for up to three months.

SEASONED OIL

*Restaurants often use a lot more oil when preparing their base curry sauces. As the oil rises to the top, it can be skimmed off and used as seasoned oil in your curries, adding another delicious layer of flavour. So add more if you like.

TIPS

- Depending on the curry I am making, I often substitute some cooking stock from the chicken masala curry (see page 87), pre-cooked chicken (see page 176), pre-cooked meat (see page 177) or lamb masala curry (see page 96) for the water at the final stage (after blending the sauce).
- You can easily double up this recipe if you'd like to make more.

QUICK AND EASY BASE CURRY SAUCE (CHEAT'S METHOD)

MAKES ABOUT 1.5 LITRES (6¼ CUPS) (7–8 PORTIONS)

One of the questions I get asked most often is whether or not you have to make a **BIR** base curry sauce to achieve that famous curry-house flavour. The answer is 'yes', but you can cheat a bit. I would like to stress that a base curry sauce is essentially an authentic Indian base masala sauce, like those featured in countless Indian cookbooks, that has been developed at restaurants across the UK for speed, ease and economy. It is the liquid needed to cook the curry.

This recipe makes enough base sauce for two to three curries that serve four people. It isn't just a scaled-down version of the base sauce recipe on page 164; it is a different but similar recipe and is a good substitute for it if you are short on time. It doesn't include as many ingredients but still works exceptionally well.

If you really don't want to make a base sauce, you *can* cheat even more, as described on page 163, but you won't achieve that true curry-house taste and texture. This recipe is your best bet for a fast yet distinctively BIR curry.

PREP TIME: 10 MINS
COOKING TIME: 20 MINS

2 tbsp rapeseed (canola) oil or melted ghee
3 onions (about 600g/1lb 5oz), finely chopped
¼ red (bell) pepper, diced
1 tbsp garlic and ginger paste (see page 172)
1 large tomato, diced
½ tsp ground cumin
½ tsp ground coriander
½ tsp paprika
¼ tsp ground turmeric
¼ tsp ground fenugreek

Heat the oil over a medium–high heat in a medium saucepan. When hot, toss in the chopped onions and red (bell) pepper and sauté for about 5 minutes until the onion is soft and translucent but not browned. Add all the remaining ingredients except the water or stock, and stir it all up well. Fry for a further 30 seconds or so, then add 250ml (1 cup) of water. Turn up the heat and simmer for 5–10 minutes until the water has evaporated by half and your veggies are nice and soft.

Add another 250ml (1 cup) of water and blend this mixture – either with a hand-held blender or countertop blender – until very smooth. Depending on the blender you use, this can take a couple of minutes. Once smooth, add another 500ml (2 cups) of water. The sauce should be about the same consistency as full-fat (whole) milk, so add more or less water as needed.

TIPS
• Depending on the curry I am making, I often substitute some cooking stock from the chicken masala curry (see page 87), pre-cooked chicken (see page 176), pre-cooked meat (see page 177) or lamb masala curry (see page 96) for the water at the final stage (after blending the sauce).
• You can easily double up this recipe if you'd like to make more.

SPICE STOCK
MAKES ABOUT 750ML (3¼ CUPS)

I usually make a batch of spice stock at the same time as I make the base curry sauce. This isn't one you really need to watch closely while cooking so it's a good way of getting two jobs done at once. The aromatic strained stock can be added to curries when a little more liquid is desired to thin the sauce. So could water, for that matter, but this stock does give curries more depth.

PREP TIME: 5 MINS
COOKING TIME: 35 MINS

Handful of green cardamom pods, lightly bruised
15 Indian bay leaves (cassia leaves)
2.5cm (1in) piece of cinnamon stick or cassia bark
20 black peppercorns
Large handful of star anise
1 tsp roasted cumin seeds (see page 163)
Large bunch of coriander (cilantro), stems and leaves roughly chopped
1 or more fresh green chillies, to taste, halved lengthways (optional)

Put 1 litre (4½ cups) of water in a pan and bring to a rolling boil. Throw in the herbs and spices and stir to combine. Reduce to a simmer and cook for about 30 minutes. Strain through a fine sieve and use immediately, or store in air-tight plastic containers in the fridge for up to 3 days. It also freezes well.

GARAM MASALA
MAKES 170G (1½ CUPS)

Garam masala is a blend of warming, aromatic spices. In India, the ingredients used can vary greatly from region to region and even from family to family, and most home and professional chefs will have their own special recipe. This is one of mine, and in it I use the same spices that are popular in northern India, Bangladesh and Pakistan – essential for achieving that curry-house flavour.

Garam masala is an important part of the mixed powder (see page 169) used in most of the BIR curries in this cookbook, and is also added on its own to a lot of recipes. Sprinkling it over your finished curries is a good way to add a touch more excitement to the dish.

PREP TIME: 8 MINS
COOKING TIME: 2 MINS

6 tbsp coriander seeds
6 tbsp cumin seeds
5 tsp black peppercorns
4 tbsp fennel seeds
3 tsp cloves
7.5cm (3in) piece of cinnamon stick or cassia bark
5 dried Indian bay leaves (cassia leaves)
20 green cardamom pods, lightly bruised
2 large pieces of mace

Roast all the spices in a dry frying pan over a medium–high heat until warm to the touch and fragrant, moving them around in the pan as they roast and being careful not to burn them. If they begin to smoke, take them off the heat.

Tip the warm spices onto a plate and leave to cool, then grind to a fine powder in a spice grinder or pestle and mortar.

Store in an air-tight container in a cool, dark place and use within 2 months for optimal flavour.

CHAAT MASALA

MAKES 160G (12 GENEROUS TABLESPOONS/
SCANT 1¼ CUPS)

Chaat masala, which has a quite distinctive flavour, is usually used in small amounts, sprinkled over finished dishes and included in marinades to give them a bit more kick. Citric acid is used in a lot of commercial brands but I've chosen to use the more authentic and healthier amchoor (dried mango powder), which gives the spice blend a nice citric flavour.

Another important ingredient is the black powdered salt. I've only seen this in Asian grocers and a few gourmet spice shops. It has a strong sulphur aroma that may take some getting used to, but before long you'll probably be hooked.

PREP TIME: 8 MINS
COOKING TIME: 2 MINS

3 tbsp cumin seeds
3 tbsp coriander seeds
1 tsp chilli powder
4 tbsp amchoor (dried mango powder)
3 tbsp powdered black salt
1 tbsp freshly ground black pepper
Pinch of asafoetida*
1 tbsp dried mint (optional)
1 tbsp garlic powder
1 tsp ajwain (carom) seeds

Roast the cumin and coriander seeds in a dry frying pan over a medium heat until warm to the touch and fragrant, moving them around in the pan as they roast and being careful not to burn them. If they begin to smoke, take them off the heat. Tip onto a plate to cool.

   Grind the roasted seeds to a fine powder in a spice grinder or pestle and mortar. Add the remaining ingredients and grind some more until you have a very fine powder.

   Store in an air-tight container in a cool, dark place and use as needed, within 2 months for optimal flavour.

NOTE
*If you are gluten-free, please check the asafoetida packaging as some brands contain wheat flour.

TANDOORI MASALA

MAKES 120G (1¼ CUPS)

Most commercial tandoori masalas taste fantastic because they are loaded with salt and tangy citric acid powder. The spices used are usually quite cheap, like ground coriander and cumin, and they are made more visually appealing with the use of red food colouring.

I use a lot more spices and leave the salt and citric acid powder out. You can always add more salt to the finished dish, which gives you a lot more control over the end result. I substitute the natural tanginess of amchoor (dried mango powder) for the citric acid powder. If you would like to add red food colouring, remember that your masala will not be the bright red of commercial brands. Food colouring powder becomes redder when it is stirred into a sauce.

PREP TIME: 8 MINS
COOKING TIME: 2 MINS

3 tbsp coriander seeds
3 tbsp cumin seeds
1 tbsp black mustard seeds
5cm (2in) piece of cinnamon stick or cassia bark
Small piece of mace
3 dried Indian bay leaves (cassia leaves)
1 tbsp ground ginger
2 tbsp garlic powder
2 tbsp dried onion powder
2 tbsp amchoor (dried mango powder)
1 tbsp (or more) red food colouring powder (optional)

Roast the whole spices in a dry frying pan over a medium–high heat until warm to the touch and fragrant, moving them around in the pan as they roast and being careful not to burn them. If they begin to smoke, take them off the heat. Tip onto a plate to cool.

   Grind to a fine powder in a spice grinder or pestle and mortar and tip into a bowl. Stir in the ground ginger, garlic powder, onion powder and amchoor.

   Stir in the red food colouring powder (if using). The masala will not look overly red like the commercial brands. Store in an air-tight container in a cool, dark place and use as required, within 2 months for optimal flavour.

MIXED POWDER
MAKES 17 GENEROUS TABLESPOONS

I have to emphasize how important this recipe is. Mixed powder is really just a fancy curry house-style curry powder but it's also one of the secret ingredients that makes BIR curries what they are. You will use it in almost all of the classic curries in this book. The flavours of cumin, coriander, paprika and turmeric are in most BIR curries, and mixed powder makes it possible to add these spices all in one go, along with curry powder and garam masala. Obviously, you can adjust the flavour of your curry by adding a little more of the individual spices or masalas to taste, but adding mixed powder is usually enough to get the task of seasoning off to a good and easy start. I strongly recommend making your own mixed powder, but if that is just one step too far for you, go ahead and use a good-quality curry powder.

Mixed powder at curry houses is usually made with commercially available curry powder, garam masala and ground spices. I make my own garam masala and curry powder and have included page references to my recipes below. Roasting and grinding your own spices will get you better results but feel free to use commercially available brands.

As with the garam masala and curry powder recipes, it is a good idea to roast whole cumin and coriander seeds and then grind them to a powder for that extra flavour boost. If you only want to make a little or you want to make a lot more, simply substitute the word 'tbsp' with 'parts'.

PREP TIME: 5 MINS

3 tbsp ground cumin
3 tbsp ground coriander
4 tbsp curry powder (see page 171)
3 tbsp paprika
3 tbsp ground turmeric
1 tbsp garam masala (see page 167)

Mix all the ingredients together, store in an air-tight container in a cool, dark place, and use as needed. If you are using fresh, homemade garam masala and curry powder in your blend, your mixed powder should last for up to 2 months without losing much flavour.

CHOLE MASALA POWDER
MAKES ABOUT 250ML

Why would you want to go to the trouble of making a spice blend that is generally only used to make chole masala? Well, I want you to try the recipes in this book as they should taste and not just some quick imitation! That said, if you would like to give my Punjabi chole recipe (see page 57) a try but don't want to go to the effort of making this very tasty spice blend, you can purchase ready-made chole masala at many Asian grocers and online. Once you try the Punjabi chole masala, however, I think you'll be really happy you made a big batch of this unique spice blend. It will keep in an air-tight container for at least three months.

PREP TIME: 5 MINS
COOKING TIME: 3 MINS

3 tbsp cumin seeds
3 tbsp coriander seeds
2 tbsp dried pomegranate seeds
12 dried red chillies, seeds removed if you don't want it too spicy
½ tsp ajwain (carom) seeds
1 tsp dried fenugreek leaves (kasoori methi)
Seeds from 2 black cardamom pods or 4 green cardamom pods
3 tsp black peppercorns
10cm (4in) piece of cinnamon stick
8 cloves
2 tsp black salt
1 tsp amchoor (dried mango powder)
½ tsp dried ground ginger
1 tsp dried garlic powder

Heat a dry frying pan over a medium–high heat and toast the cumin seeds and coriander seeds together until warm to the touch and fragrant but not yet smoking. This should only take about 2 minutes. Transfer to a bowl to cool. Now add the dried pomegranate seeds, chillies, ajwain (carom) seeds, dried fenugreek leaves (kasoori methi), cardamom seeds, peppercorns, cinnamon and cloves to the pan and toast lightly for about 1 minute until fragrant but again, not yet smoking. Transfer to the bowl with the cumin and coriander. Once cooled, place in a spice grinder with the remaining ingredients and grind to a fine powder. Store in an air-tight container and use as required.

CURRY POWDER

MAKES 285G (2½ CUPS)

Commercially prepared curry powders date back to the 18th century, when spice blends were prepared by Indian merchants to sell to British army and government officials returning to Britain during the British Raj. It was a way of taking the flavours of India home with them.

Unlike garam masalas, which are blends of warming spices, curry powders usually contain other complementary ingredients, with chillies often added to produce spicier blends. This version is spicy but not overly so. If you or the people you will be cooking for don't like spicy food, you can leave the dried chillies and chilli powder out.

PREP TIME: 8 MINS
COOKING TIME: 2 MINS

6 tbsp coriander seeds
6 tbsp cumin seeds
4 tbsp black peppercorns
2 tbsp fennel seeds
2 tbsp black mustard seeds
12cm (5in) piece of cinnamon stick or cassia bark
4 Indian bay leaves (cassia leaves)
3 tbsp fenugreek seeds
3 star anise
15 cardamom pods, lightly bruised
8 Kashmiri dried red chillies (optional)
2 tbsp ground turmeric
2 tbsp hot chilli powder (optional)
1 tsp garlic powder
2 tsp dried onion powder

Roast all the whole spices, including the dried chillies (if using) in a dry frying pan over a medium–high heat until warm to the touch and fragrant but not smoking. Be sure to move the spices around in the pan so that they roast evenly. Be careful not to burn them or they will become bitter and you will have to start again.

Tip the warm spices onto a plate and leave to cool, then grind to a fine powder in a spice grinder or pestle and mortar. Add the turmeric, chilli powder (if using), garlic powder and onion powder, and stir to combine.

Store in an air-tight container in a cool, dark place and use within 2 months for optimal flavour.

PANCH PORAN
(INDIAN FIVE SPICE)

MAKES 5 TABLESPOONS

This whole spice blend is available in Asian spice shops already mixed, so you don't actually need to make your own. Panch poran does vary from region to region in the subcontinent but this is the most common blend in UK curry houses.

Some cooks prefer to use less fenugreek as the seeds can be quite bitter. You'll have to experiment with that one. Equal amounts of each ingredient are used so you can easily scale this recipe up or down.

PREP TIME: 2 MINS
COOKING TIME: 2 MINS

1 tbsp cumin seeds
1 tbsp fenugreek seeds
1 tbsp brown mustard seeds
1 tbsp fennel seeds
1 tbsp nigella seeds (black onion seeds)

For best results, roast the spices in a dry frying pan over a medium–high heat until fragrant. I usually roast them just before using.

GARLIC AND GINGER PASTE

MAKES 15 GENEROUS TABLESPOONS

This paste is used in almost every curry. It's so simple and tastes far better than any shop-bought alternative. If you want more control over how much garlic and ginger go into your dishes, make separate pastes for each using the same method.

PREP TIME: 10 MINS

150g (5½oz) garlic, roughly chopped
150g (5½oz) ginger, peeled and roughly chopped

Place the garlic and ginger in a food processor or pestle and mortar and blend with just enough water to make a smooth paste. Some chefs finely chop their garlic and ginger instead, which is a good alternative to making a paste. Store in an air-tight container in the fridge for up to 3 days and use as needed. If you're planning a curry party, go ahead and get this job ticked off early.

I often make larger batches and freeze them in ice cube trays. Frozen cubes can be transferred to air-tight plastic bags in the freezer, ready for when you get that curry craving. Be sure to let them defrost a little first.

GREEN CHILLI PASTE

MAKES ABOUT 6 GENEROUS TABLESPOONS

I purchase a lot of chillies and sometimes I need to do something with them before they go off. That isn't the only reason I make this chilli paste, however! Chilli paste is so convenient to have on hand. I often blend the chillies into a paste and then freeze the paste in ice cube trays before storing chilli cubes in freezer safe bags. Then when I need chopped chillies, as is often the case with my recipes, all I have to do is defrost and use. This is a great way of ensuring I always have the chillies I need, when I need them.

PREP TIME: 5 MINUTES

12 green bird's eye chillies
2 tbsp water

Place the chillies and water in a blender and blend to a fine paste. You may need a little more water depending on your blender. Try to keep the water to a minimum.

TOMATO PURÉE

This is a thin purée of tomatoes used in many curries for flavour and colour. Here are two ways you can make it.

METHOD 1

MAKES 4 TABLESPOONS

PREP TIME: 2 MINS

1 tbsp concentrated tomato paste
3 tbsp water

Simply mix the ingredients together to form a thinner paste. This recipe can be easily scaled up or down: just use 1 part tomato paste to 3 parts water.

METHOD 2

MAKES 425ML (1¾ CUPS)

PREP TIME: 2 MINS

400g (14oz) can plum tomatoes
Concentrated tomato paste, to taste (optional)

Blend the plum tomatoes to make a smooth purée. If you want a deeper red colour, add in a little concentrated tomato paste.

NOTE
You could also use sieved, unseasoned Italian passata.

RAW CASHEW PASTE

Raw cashew paste is used in curries to thicken the sauce and to add flavour. It is most commonly used in BIR chicken korma (see page 188) and lamb rogan josh (see page 218) but you could really add it to any curry. Why not? It's good.

PREP TIME: 5 MINUTES, PLUS SOAKING TIME

Raw cashew nuts (quantity as needed)

Soak the raw cashew nuts in cold water for about 30 minutes. Drain and place the cashew nuts in a spice grinder or blender. Add just enough fresh water to blend to a paste. That's it. You're done.

Transfer to a bowl and store in the fridge for up to 3 days.

FRIED ONIONS AND ONION PASTE

MAKES ABOUT 250ML (1 CUP)

It's no secret that fried onions taste amazing. They are an essential ingredient for dopiaza curries and biryanis and also work well in marinades. You can even blend the onions with a little water or yoghurt to form a paste that can be added to almost any curry to make it a little more interesting (see below for more on this).

Don't throw the cooking oil out. Use it in your curries – remember those layers of flavour I was talking about? Well, this onion-infused cooking oil is a good one.

PREP TIME: 10 MINS
COOKING TIME: 5–10 MINS

Rapeseed (canola) oil, for deep-frying
3 large onions, finely sliced

Heat enough oil for deep-frying in a large, heavy-based pan over a high heat. Test to see if it is hot enough by dropping a piece of onion in the oil; if it sizzles immediately and floats to the top, the oil is ready. Add the onions and fry for about 5 minutes until they turn light brown. They will continue to cook once out of the oil, so be sure to get them out when they are still light brown.

Using a wire mesh spoon, transfer the fried onions to a plate lined with paper towel to soak up the excess fat. Store in a cool, dry place in an air-tight container until ready to use. These will keep for up to a week.

TO MAKE ONION PASTE

Blend 3 fried onions with just enough water or natural plain yoghurt to make a thick paste (about 1–3 tablespoons should suffice). I usually use yoghurt, but water works too.

STIR-FRIED ONIONS AND OTHER VEGGIES

MAKES ENOUGH FOR 4–10 SERVINGS, DEPENDING ON USE

Most British Indian restaurant-style curry sauces are very smooth. Sometimes though, the curry needs just a bit more crunch – curries such a dry bhunas and spicy jalfrezis, for example. Adding a spoonful of this pre-cooked onion and pepper mixture will do just that.

In many of the curry houses I've visited, there is a tub of cooked onions and other vegetables at the ready for when they are needed. As they are already cooked, they can be added to a curry at the end of cooking. The veggies can be stored in the fridge for up to 3 days.

Is this necessary? I don't think so for the home cook, since vegetables cook very quickly anyway, as many of my recipes demonstrate. If you're cooking for a large group of people, however, you might like to have these fried veggies on hand. Add them to any curry you want even if not suggested in the recipe. If you like crunchy veggies in your curries, you really can't go wrong.

PREP TIME: 5 MINS
COOKING TIME: 10 MINS

2 tbsp rapeseed (canola) oil or seasoned oil skimmed from the base curry sauce (see page 164 or 166)
1 tsp panch poran (see page 171)
4 onions, finely sliced
1 green (bell) pepper, deseeded and thinly sliced
1 red (bell) pepper, deseeded and thinly sliced
Pinch of ground turmeric

Heat the oil in a large pan over a medium–high heat. Toss in the panch poran and sizzle for about 10 seconds before adding the onions and green and red (bell) peppers. Fry for about 10 minutes until soft but the peppers still have a nice crunch to them.

Add the turmeric and stir to combine. Tip into a bowl to cool and use as required. This same method can also be used for other vegetables.

PRE-COOKED STEWED CHICKEN AND COOKING STOCK
MAKES ENOUGH FOR ABOUT 10 SERVINGS

Pre-cooking the chicken until it is just cooked through makes cooking in most Indian restaurants not only faster, but tastier too.

The cooking stock can be added to chicken curries and gives a fantastic flavour. Simply remove the chicken pieces from the liquid and then strain it. You could also throw in a chicken carcass or two while cooking the chicken. Remove the chicken pieces (tikka) when cooked but let the sauce simmer, adding a little water if necessary until you have a beautiful, rich stock. When time permits, I let mine simmer for about 2 hours. It tastes amazing. When your stock is ready, strain it and use it to thin curry sauces when necessary or simply to give the curry more depth of flavour.

Both the chicken and the stock can be stored in the fridge for up to 3 days. They can also be frozen for up to 2 months without much loss of flavour. Always defrost both and heat the stock before using.

PREP TIME: 10 MINS
COOKING TIME: 30 MINS–
  2 HOURS, DEPENDING ON
  WHETHER YOU SIMMER
  THE CHICKEN BONES

4 tbsp rapeseed (canola) oil
5 green cardamom pods, lightly
  bruised
10 black peppercorns
2.5cm (1in) piece of cinnamon stick
  or cassia bark
1 tsp cumin seeds
1 tsp coriander seeds
3 Indian bay leaves (cassia leaves)
2 large onions, finely chopped
½ tsp sea salt
2 tbsp garlic and ginger paste (see
  page 172)
1 tsp ground turmeric
2 x 400g (14oz) tins (cans) chopped
  tomatoes
2kg (4lb 6oz) skinless, boneless
  chicken thighs or breasts, cut into
  bite-size pieces (tikka)*
Water or spice stock (see page 167), to
  cover
1 tsp garam masala (see page 167)

*Chicken breast meat is used at most
curry houses because it has a nice
texture and looks good too. Chicken
thigh meat isn't as pretty but has a lot
more flavour.

Heat the oil in a pan over a medium–high heat until small bubbles form. Add the whole spices and bay leaves, and stir continuously for about 30 seconds to release their flavours into the oil.

Add the onions and stir regularly for about 5 minutes until soft and translucent. Sprinkle the salt over the top; this will help release moisture from the onions.

Now spoon in the garlic and ginger paste, followed by the turmeric; the pan will sizzle as the paste releases its moisture. When your kitchen becomes fragrant with the magnificent aroma of garlic and ginger, tip in the tomatoes. Reduce the heat to medium and let the ingredients simmer and get to know each other for about 5 minutes. Add the chicken pieces and just enough spice stock or water to cover the chicken.

Reduce the heat and let the stock softly bubble until the chicken is just cooked through; don't overcook it. Stir in the garam masala and, using a slotted spoon, remove the chicken pieces for use in your curries, reserving the cooking stock. A little of this added to your chicken curries makes them even more delicious.

TIP

If freezer space is an issue but you want to have some stock on hand, reduce the finished stock by two-thirds. Let the remaining stock cool, and freeze in ice cube trays. Then simply toss one or two cubes into your sauces as required.

PRE-COOKED STEWED LAMB/MEAT AND COOKING STOCK

MAKES ENOUGH FOR ABOUT 10 SERVINGS

Whether the restaurant is a low-cost takeaway or an upmarket restaurant, the chefs will normally stew red meat for curries before service so that it is tender and ready to use. The reason for this is simple: if they didn't, it would take too long to serve their delicious curries.

Lamb, mutton and hoofed game require about 1–1½ hours to cook and become tender using this method. These animals are very active, so their muscly flesh is naturally tough. Beef will be tender in about 40 minutes–1 hour. Cows are quite lazy, after all.

Whatever you do, don't rush things. Stew the meat until it is good and tender. By the way, this pre-cooked lamb recipe is actually a mouthwatering curry in its own right. Lamb is the most popular red meat used in curry houses, so I've used it here, but feel free to experiment with the red meat of your choice.

PREP TIME: 10 MINS
COOKING TIME: 1–1½ HOURS,
   DEPENDING ON THE MEAT

2 tbsp rapeseed (canola) oil
6 cloves
5 black or 10 green cardamom pods, lightly bruised
10 black peppercorns
1 tbsp cumin seeds
1 tbsp coriander seeds
5cm (2in) piece of cinnamon stick or cassia bark
1 piece of mace
3 Indian bay leaves (cassia leaves)
2 large onions, finely chopped
½ tsp sea salt
2 tbsp garlic and ginger paste (see page 172)
1kg (2lb 3oz) leg of lamb, cut into 2.5cm (1in) pieces (keep the bone if you have it)
2 tbsp mild paprika
1 tsp chilli powder (optional)
1 tbsp garam masala (see page 167)
Water or spice stock (see page 167), to cover

Heat the oil in a large saucepan over a medium–high heat until hot and beginning to bubble. Add the whole spices and bay leaves and stir for about 30 seconds, until your kitchen begins to fill with the delicious aroma of the frying spices, being careful not to burn them. Add the onions and stir to coat in the oil.

Cook for about 5 minutes before adding the salt followed by the garlic and ginger paste. Fry for a further minute until the onions are soft and translucent and your kitchen smells like the best curry house in the world. This only gets better! Place the leg bone (if you have it) in the pan with the ground spices and the meat.

Brown the meat for about 2 minutes, then pour in just enough spice stock or water to cover. Simmer for 1–1½ hours until the meat is good and tender.

Allow the meat and cooking sauce to cool for use in your curries. The meat and cooking stock (remove the bone, if using) can be stored in the fridge for up to 3 days and freeze well for up to 2 months. The stock is usually strained before adding to curries.

TIP

Double this recipe and you've got a nice meal for the day you cook as well as lots of tasty pre-cooked meat for your BIR curries. If serving as a curry, be sure to season it with salt.

PRE-COOKED LAMB KEEMA
MAKES ENOUGH FOR 4–10 SERVINGS DEPENDING ON USE

You might wonder why you would want to pre-cook keema, as I did when I first started noticing the containers of prepared keema during my restaurant visits. Keema is, after all, ground meat, so it's as tender as it's going to get. This recipe takes about 30 minutes or longer to make, so you can understand why the chefs in a busy takeaway would want to get this job done before they get busy. That isn't the only reason though. Just like a slowly cooked Bolognese sauce, the flavours in this keema will develop as they cook. If you have the time, cook it longer with a little more stock as the flavour will only get better. If you aren't a big fan of biting into whole spices, be sure to count them in and remove them before using in your recipes. This keema is delicious stirred into almost any curry sauce or wrapped into samosas (see page 21). Lamb is usually used for keema meat but if you prefer you could try chicken, beef or turkey mince.

PREP TIME: 10 MINS
COOKING TIME: 30 MINS

3 tbsp rapeseed (canola) oil or seasoned oil (see page 8)
2 Indian bay leaves (cassia leaves)
7.5cm (3in) piece of cinnamon stick or cassia bark
1 tsp cumin seeds
4 green cardamom pods, lightly bruised
½ onion, finely chopped
1 tbsp garlic and ginger paste (see page 172)
1 tbsp mixed powder (see page 169)
1 tbsp garam masala (see page 167)
½ tsp ground turmeric
2 tbsp tomato purée (see page 172)
500–700g (1lb 2oz–1lb 9oz) minced (ground) lamb
About 200ml (generous ¾ cup) spice stock (see page 167) or water
1 tsp dried fenugreek leaves (kasoori methi)
3 tbsp finely chopped coriander (cilantro)
Salt, to taste

Heat the oil over a medium–high heat until small bubbles appear, then add the bay leaves, cinnamon stick, cumin seeds and cardamom pods and mix them around in the oil. After about 30 seconds the oil will become fragrant and you will hear the spices begin to crackle. When this happens, toss in the onion and give it a good stir. Fry until soft and translucent but not browned, about 5 minutes.

Add the garlic and ginger paste and let it sizzle for another minute or so, then add the ground spices and tomato purée followed by the minced meat. You'll know you're doing something right because your kitchen will smell so good.

Allow the minced meat to cook through, then pour in the spice stock or water and simmer over a low heat for about 20 minutes. You may need to add a little more water while the ingredients all get to know each other. The finished keema should be moist but not saucy, and if you'd like to cook it for longer for a more intense flavour, add more water accordingly to prevent it from drying out.

Remove the bay leaves, cinnamon stick and cardamom pods. Stir in the dried fenugreek leaves (kasoori methi) and coriander (cilantro) and season with salt. You'll probably find it tastes great, so be careful not to snack on it before making your keema curry or using it in your samosas! I find this quite difficult at times.

PRE-COOKED STEWED POTATOES

MAKES ENOUGH FOR 4–10 SERVINGS DEPENDING ON USE

This pre-cooked potato dish can be eaten on its own or used in other British Indian restaurant-style dishes. Serve it as is and it could be a delicious, authentic-style Bombay aloo, in which case I recommend cutting the potato cubes smaller. Be sure to cook the potatoes until they are soft. Nobody likes an 80% cooked, hard potato. This is exactly why you will want to make this recipe if you are intending on whipping up a potato-based curry or two. It's a good job to get done early so that all you have to do is heat them up in the curry sauce of your choice and serve. They keep for at least 3 days, covered in the fridge, and can also be frozen with their tasty cooking stock. Defrost before using.

PREP TIME: 10 MINS
COOKING TIME: 30 MINS

2 tbsp rapeseed (canola) oil or seasoned oil (see page 8)
1 tbsp ghee
1 tsp brown mustard seeds
1 tbsp cumin seeds
7.5cm (3in) piece of cinnamon stick or cassia bark
5 green cardamom pods, lightly bruised
3 large onions, finely sliced
2 tbsp garlic and ginger paste (see page 172)
400g (14oz) tin (can) chopped tomatoes
1 tbsp Kashmiri chilli powder, or to taste
1 tsp ground turmeric
500g (1lb 2oz) potatoes, peeled and each cut into 3
650ml (2¾ cups) spice stock (see page 167) or water
1 tbsp garam masala (see page 167)
Salt and freshly ground black pepper, to taste

Heat the oil and ghee over a high heat in a large saucepan, then throw in the mustard seeds. When they begin to pop (after about 30 seconds), reduce the heat to medium–high and toss in the cumin seeds, cinnamon stick and cardamom pods, and temper in the oil for a further 30 seconds. Stir in the onions and fry for about 5 minutes until soft and translucent, stirring regularly, then add the garlic and ginger paste and let it sizzle in the oil for about 1 minute. Tip in the tomatoes, chilli powder and turmeric, and stir it all up nicely.

Now add the potato pieces and cover with the spice stock or water. Cover and simmer until the potatoes are soft and cooked through, about 30 minutes. Sprinkle with the garam masala and season with salt and black pepper, giving it all a good stir. Serve the potatoes as they are immediately or remove the potato pieces and strain the stock for use in your curries. This will keep for at least 3 days in the fridge and can also be frozen. The strained cooking stock adds a nice flavour to vegetarian curries.

TIP

If serving this as a dish on its own, you might like to spice it up a bit by adding chilli powder and/or chopped green chillies to taste. Garnish with chopped coriander (cilantro).

FRIED PANEER
SERVES 4–10 DEPENDING ON USE

Paneer is often added raw to curries just before serving, as you can't cook it in a sauce long or it will begin to break up. Here is another option. The crispy exterior that the paneer gets when shallow-fried helps stop it from disintegrating in the sauce, and it's also delicious. Plain paneer doesn't have a lot of flavour, so marinating for about 30 minutes before frying will make it more interesting.

I find commercially available paneer works perfectly well for BIR curries, frying and grilling, but I also like to make my own. To do this, bring 1.5 litres (6¼ cups) of full-fat (whole) milk to a boil, whisking continuously so that it doesn't boil over. When the milk has come to a boil, reduce the heat and simmer to reduce by about 15%. Remove the milk from the heat and stir in the juice of one lemon and whisk for 5–10 minutes to separate the curds from the whey. Wrap the curds tightly in cheesecloth and hang over the sink for about 2 hours. Form the paneer into a block, pressing out any remaining whey, and you've got the 200g (7oz) of fresh paneer needed for this recipe! Your homemade paneer will keep in the fridge for up to three days.

PREP TIME: 5 MINS, PLUS
   MARINATING TIME
COOKING TIME: 10 MINS

1 tsp garlic and ginger paste (see page 172)
½ tsp chilli powder
½ tsp garam masala (see page 167)
1 tbsp Greek yoghurt
200g (7oz) paneer cheese (see above for homemade), cubed
3 tbsp rapeseed (canola) oil
Salt, to taste

Whisk the garlic and ginger paste, spices and yoghurt together in a bowl. Using a fork or toothpick, pierce the paneer cubes all over so that the marinade can penetrate. Add the paneer and leave to marinate for about 30 minutes.

When ready to fry, heat the oil in a frying pan over a medium–high heat. When it begins to bubble, remove the paneer from the marinade and add to the hot oil. Fry until browned on one side, then flip the paneer over and fry on the other side. Only frying two opposite sides is enough to help keep the cheese together while cooking in a sauce, but if you like you can brown it on all sides, as I do (it just looks better).

Transfer the browned paneer cubes to a plate lined with paper towel to absorb any excess oil, and set aside until ready to use.

BRITISH CURRY-HOUSE RECIPES

British curries are world-famous for their unique flavours and textures. They were developed over time to appeal to the British palate but are now served globally from New Delhi to New York. Over the decades they evolved into the popular curries we all expect to find on the menus of curry houses around the UK.

These BIR curries are different from authentic Indian curries in that they rely on preparing things ahead. This not only takes your dishes to a whole new delicious level but it also means you can whip up your curries at home in 20 minutes or less. The previous chapter (pages 162–81) contains all of these prep recipes, and there is also a selection of tandoori meats, paneer and vegetables in the next chapter (pages 254–303), which are delicious stirred into curries. If preparing ahead really isn't your thing, there are tips on page 163 for how to cheat. However, I really hope you make these curries as they were written. You'll be very glad you did!

I hope you enjoy making these classic BIR curries as much as I do. Here you will find recipes for the most popular versions, but you can add whatever you like to the individual sauces. You can substitute different vegetables, meat, poultry, seafood and paneer, just like when you dine out at your favourite Indian restaurant.

There are no rules. If you fancy a naga goat korma, then add some pre-cooked goat tikka and naga chillies to the korma sauce. If you want crunchy vegetables in your chicken chilli garlic, sauté your vegetables of choice in the hot oil before adding the other ingredients, like I do in the jalfrezi sauce, or add some pre-cooked vegetables (see page 175) at the end of cooking. The possibilities are endless and it can be fun to experiment. Here is a list of tips for adding each:

ADDING RED MEAT AND POULTRY

All of the classic curry recipes have been developed so that you can cook and serve your curry in about 20 minutes. To do this, you can choose from the pre-cooked tandoori or stewed meat and poultry recipes I've included in the book (see pages 259, 260 and 176–77). You aren't limited to these, though. You could add leftover pieces of meat or roast potatoes from Sunday dinner. Leftovers never tasted so good!

You could even add the meat or poultry raw to your finished base sauce. This gives a nice flavour to the sauce too. Just simmer until cooked through and tender. Chicken cooks through quite quickly, but if using raw red meat, be prepared to add some more water or base curry sauce and let the sauce simmer until the meat is tender.

ADDING SEAFOOD

Seafood cooks in no time. Simply add it raw to the simmering sauce and let it cook through. You can add full fillets of fish or tikka (bite-size pieces) – whatever you fancy. If adding as tikka, I recommend using meatier fish such as cod and halibut. Marinated raw and grilled tandoori prawns (shrimp) could also be added, which taste amazing.

ADDING PANEER

Paneer heats through in a sauce fast. Be careful not to overcook it as it tends to disintegrate. I recommend adding it just before serving the curry; 2 minutes in the hot sauce should do the job. I have included a recipe for fried paneer (see page 180), which will keep its form better in the sauce.

ADDING VEGETABLES

Vegetables can be added in a number of ways. In the jalfrezi recipe, for example, they are quickly fried when you start making the sauce. If you are cooking for a large group of veggie fanatics, you might like to try my pre-cooked vegetable recipe (see page 175), which will speed things up. Grilled, fried and steamed vegetables are also nice in the sauces. Just add them to the sauce right before serving so that you don't overcook them.

ADDING BASE CURRY SAUCE AND STOCK

The amount of base curry sauce and stock added in the following recipes is exactly as the measures I use at home. You may need to experiment. If you prefer a thicker sauce, let the base sauce and stock reduce. If you prefer more sauce or stock, add it and adjust the seasoning accordingly. You really can't go wrong.

PLANNING AHEAD

Whether you are making one of these curries or several, it is a good idea to get all the ingredients for each curry ready. I group the ingredients for each curry so that I have them at the ready before cooking. These curries are cooked fast over a high heat, so you don't want to be looking for an ingredient or chopping onions once you get stuck in!

CHICKEN CURRY

SERVES 4 OR MORE AS PART OF A MULTI-COURSE MEAL

The first time I was invited back to a curry-house kitchen to learn a recipe, it went something like this chicken curry. The chef assumed that I had no idea what a base sauce was and wanted to show me how to cook a curry house-style curry, but without the need of a base sauce. Following this example, you could cook all of the following traditional British curries without base sauce or pre-cooked ingredients. This basic mild chicken curry, like those on most curry-house menus, can easily be spiced up with more chilli powder or chopped fresh chillies to taste. You will notice that it does take longer to cook a curry in this way than if you were doing it with a base sauce and pre-cooked ingredients, but the end result is delicious.

PREP TIME: 10 MINS
COOKING TIME 25 MINS

3 tbsp rapeseed (canola) oil
2.5cm (1in) piece of cinnamon stick
Seeds from 3 green cardamom pods
2 star anise
1 tsp cumin seeds
2 onions, finely chopped
2 tbsp garlic and ginger paste (see page 172)
125ml (½ cup) tomato purée (see page 172) or plain passata (sieved tomatoes)
2 tbsp mixed powder (see page 169) or curry powder (see page 171)
2 tsp ground cumin
2 tsp ground coriander
½ tsp ground turmeric
1–2 tbsp paprika
½ tsp garam masala (see page 167)
2 medium tomatoes, diced
900g (2lb) chicken thighs or breast, cut into bite-size pieces
Pinch of dried fenugreek leaves (kasoori methi)
Salt, to taste
3 tbsp melted ghee (optional)
2 tbsp finely chopped coriander (cilantro), to garnish

Heat the oil over a medium–high heat in a large frying pan. When visibly hot, add the cinnamon stick, cardamom seeds, star anise and cumin seeds. Stir these spices around in the oil for about 30 seconds, then add the onions. Fry the onions for about 5 minutes until soft and translucent, then stir in the garlic and ginger paste and fry for a further 30 seconds. Now stir in the tomato purée and bring to a simmer. You are aiming to achieve a smooth sauce like you get when you use a prepared base sauce, so add about 250ml (1 cup) of water and simmer until the water has almost evaporated. This will help break the onions down into the sauce.

Add the ground spices and tomatoes and give it all a good stir to combine. By now, you should have a nice saucy mixture, but the onions will still need to break down some more. Add another 250ml (1 cup) of water and simmer until the water has almost evaporated. You will be left with a thick sauce and the onions will be melting into the sauce. Add the chicken and coat it well with the sauce, then cover the pan to simmer until the meat is cooked through – about 10 minutes. You will need to stir from time to time so that it cooks evenly. Remove the lid and you will have a chicken curry with a very thick sauce. It will be nice this way but if you prefer more sauce, add more water and continue to simmer until you are happy with the consistency.

To finish, rub the dried fenugreek leaves (kasoori methi) between your fingers into the sauce and season with salt. If you're not watching the calories, drizzle some ghee over the top and stir it in before serving. Garnish with the coriander (cilantro).

KASHMIRI CHICKEN
SERVES 4 OR MORE AS PART OF A MULTI-COURSE MEAL

To be honest, I never knew how popular Kashmiri chicken was until I wrote a recipe for it that was in *The Curry Guy Light*. In that recipe, it was cooked from scratch without any base sauce, but here I give you the authentic curry-house version. Some people like to throw a few raisins into the mixture when adding the banana, and you could too. If it sounds good, why not?

PREP TIME: 10 MINS, PLUS
   MAKING THE BASE SAUCE
   AND COOKING THE CHICKEN
COOKING TIME: 10 MINS

3 tbsp melted ghee or rapeseed
   (canola) oil
2.5cm (1in) piece of cinnamon stick
Seeds from 3 green cardamom pods
2 cloves
1 small onion, very finely chopped
1 tbsp garlic and ginger paste (see
   page 172)
2 tbsp ground almonds
½ green (bell) pepper, thinly sliced
1½ tsp mixed powder (see page 169)
   or curry powder (see page 171)
½ tsp Kashmiri chilli powder
70ml (¼ cup) tomato purée (see page
   172)
500ml (2 cups) base curry sauce (see
   page 164 or 166), heated
1 tsp tamarind concentrate
700g (1lb 9oz) tandoori chicken tikka
   (see page 259)
½ banana, sliced into coins
2 tbsp raisins (optional)
2 tsp smooth mango chutney (see
   page 331)
3 tbsp plain yoghurt
Salt, to taste
Coriander (cilantro), to garnish

Heat the oil in a large frying pan over a medium–high heat. Add the cinnamon, cardamom seeds and cloves and let them infuse into the oil for about 30 seconds. Add the onion and fry for about 5 minutes until soft and translucent. Stir in the garlic and ginger paste and the ground almonds and stir it all up to simmer for about 30 seconds. Toss in the green (bell) pepper and cook for a further minute.

Add the mixed powder and chilli powder and give it a good stir. Add the tomato purée and about half the base curry sauce and bring to a simmer, only stirring if it is sticking to the pan. Stir in the tamarind concentrate and simmer over a medium–high heat, adding more base sauce as it simmers down. Be sure to scrape any sauce that caramelizes to the sides of the pan into the sauce for even more flavour. Stir in the chicken tikka and cook until the chicken is heated through – this should take no more than about 2 minutes. Stir in the banana, raisins (if using) and smooth mango chutney and continue to simmer until you are happy with the consistency. If too saucy, let it cook down; if too dry, add a bit more sauce or stock. To finish, whisk in the yoghurt, 1 tablespoon at a time. Season with salt and garnish with the coriander (cilantro).

CHICKEN TIKKA MASALA

SERVES 4 OR MORE AS PART OF A MULTI-COURSE MEAL

When people order a chicken tikka masala, they know what they want, and if it isn't just like they expect it to be, you can see the disappointment in their faces. The thing is, there are hundreds of recipes for this world-famous curry. Some chefs add loads of coconut flour or block coconut, whereas others leave the coconut out. And many people like this curry super-sweet, whereas others prefer it to be more savoury. This BIR combo is my favourite version and should get you the result you're looking for. If you use this as a guide, you can then adjust the sweetness and coconut flavour to taste. Be sure to use tandoori chicken tikka (see page 259) for this one.

For the photograph, I made two curries from the same batch but used red food colouring powder for the dish on the left. This is how the famous bright red colour of this curry is achieved. The two dishes tasted identical.

PREP TIME: 10 MINS, PLUS
MAKING THE BASE CURRY
SAUCE AND COOKING THE
CHICKEN
COOKING TIME: 10 MINS

4 tbsp ghee, rapeseed (canola) oil or seasoned oil (see page 8)
2 tbsp garlic and ginger paste (see page 172)
1 tbsp sugar, or to taste
2 tbsp ground almonds
2 tbsp coconut flour (optional)
6 tbsp tomato purée (see page 172)
2 tbsp mixed powder (see page 169)
2 tbsp tandoori masala (see page 168)
1 tbsp sweet paprika
700ml (3 cups) base curry sauce (see page 164 or 166), heated
About 125ml (½ cup) cooking stock (see page 176) or spice stock (see page 167), (optional)
800g (1lb 12oz) grilled chicken tikka (see page 259)
200ml (generous ¾ cup) single (light) cream, plus a little more to finish
1 tbsp red food colouring powder (optional)
Salt, to taste
Juice of 1 lemon
Small bunch of coriander (cilantro), chopped
1 tbsp dried fenugreek leaves (kasoori methi)
1 tsp garam masala (see page 167)

Heat the ghee or oil in a large pan over a medium–high heat. When small bubbles begin to appear, stir in the garlic and ginger paste; it will sizzle. Add the sugar, ground almonds and coconut flour (if using) followed by the tomato purée. This will cool the pan slightly.

Swirl this all together into one big happy tomato party, then stir in the mixed powder, tandoori masala and paprika, followed by 250ml (1 cup) of the base curry sauce. When the sauce begins to bubble, add the rest of the base curry sauce and let it simmer nicely for a few minutes. As it simmers, the sauce will begin to brown on the side of the pan. Stir this in from time to time.

If you have some cooking stock from pre-cooked stewed chicken or spice stock, you can add it for extra flavour. Add the grilled chicken to the simmering sauce to heat through.

When the sauce has cooked down to your desired thickness, add the cream and food colouring (if using) and simmer for a further 2 minutes. If the sauce becomes too thick, you can add a little more base sauce, cooking stock or spice stock.

To finish, taste and season with salt. If you like your CTMs sweet, add a little more sugar. Squeeze in the lemon juice and sprinkle with the chopped coriander (cilantro), dried fenugreek leaves (kasoori methi) and the garam masala. A swirl of cream on top adds a nice finishing touch.

Chicken tikka masala, two ways – with the addition of red food colouring powder (left) and without (right)

CHICKEN KORMA

SERVES 4 OR MORE AS PART OF A MULTI-COURSE MEAL

There are hundreds of recipes for authentic Indian korma. Korma, which means 'braising' in Hindi, is actually a style of cooking where meat and vegetables are braised in a sealed pot with a little liquid. The sauce can be creamy, nutty and mild like our British kormas but they can also be quite spicy and cooked in stock or water. What we know as a korma may share the same name but it isn't really a korma at all.

I prefer to use a combination of block coconut and coconut flour to give my kormas a nice coconut flavour, but you could substitute thick coconut milk, adding it with the first batch of base curry sauce and letting it cook down to your preferred consistency (you might want to reduce the amount of base curry sauce). Never use desiccated coconut or your sauce will become grainy. My recipe will achieve a nice yellow colour, as expected. If you desire the more intense yellow colour found at many restaurants, you will need to add yellow food colouring powder to your dish. Chicken korma is best served with white rice and a good mild dhal.

PREP TIME: 10 MINS, PLUS
   MAKING THE BASE CURRY
   SAUCE
COOKING TIME: 10 MINS

4 tbsp ghee, rapeseed (canola) oil or
   seasoned oil (see page 8)
2.5cm (1in) piece of cinnamon stick
   or cassia bark
4 green cardamom pods, lightly
   bruised
1 tsp garlic and ginger paste (see page
   172)
3 tbsp sugar, or to taste
6 tbsp ground almonds
2 tbsp coconut flour
700ml (3 cups) base curry sauce (see
   page 164 or 166), heated
100g (3½ oz) block coconut
800g (1lb 12oz) raw chicken breast,
   cut on the diagonal into 5mm
   (¼in) slices, or pre-cooked stewed
   chicken (see page 176)
1 tbsp garam masala (see page 167)
125ml (½ cup) single (light) cream,
   plus a little extra to finish
1 tbsp rose water, or to taste
2 tbsp cold butter (optional)
Salt, to taste

Heat the ghee or oil in a large frying pan over a medium heat. When small bubbles begin to appear, toss in the cinnamon stick or cassia bark and cardamom pods. Let the whole spices flavour the oil for about 30 seconds, then stir in the garlic and ginger paste. Fry for about 20 seconds before adding the sugar, ground almonds and coconut flour. Mix into the oil and pour in about 250ml (1 cup) of the base curry sauce; it will bubble up nicely. Break up the block coconut and add it to the simmering sauce. It will dissolve and give your korma a nice light yellow tone.

Pour in the rest of the base curry sauce, then add the chicken. If using raw chicken, press it right into the sauce so that it cooks quickly and evenly. You can add a little more base curry sauce if you need to, as it will boil down anyway. Swirl in the garam masala.

When your chicken is cooked/heated through (about 10 minutes for raw or 2 minutes for pre-cooked), remove the cardamom pods and cinnamon, and stir in the cream. Add the rose water and finish with the butter, if you want. Season with salt and check the sweetness, adding more sugar if needed.

CHICKEN CEYLON

SERVES 4 OR MORE AS PART OF A MULTI-COURSE MEAL

Based on the bright flavours of Sri Lanka, chicken Ceylon is a good all-rounder. I prefer it really spicy hot and add a lot more fresh chillies and chilli powder than suggested in this recipe, so feel free to do that too. I've also taken the liberty of adding a few ingredients that are rarely included in curry-house Ceylon curries but are very Sri Lankan all the same.

PREP TIME: 10 MINS, PLUS
MAKING THE BASE CURRY
SAUCE AND COOKING THE
CHICKEN
COOKING TIME: 10 MINS

4 tbsp rapeseed (canola) oil or
  seasoned oil (see page 8)
2 star anise
7.5cm (3in) piece of cinnamon stick
  or cassia bark
4 green cardamom pods, bashed
20 fresh or frozen curry leaves
2 tbsp garlic and ginger paste (see
  page 172)
2 green bird's eye chillies, finely
  chopped
2 tbsp coconut flour
3 tbsp finely chopped coriander
  (cilantro) stalks
1 tsp Kashmiri chilli powder
2 tbsp mixed powder (see page 169)
1 tbsp tandoori masala (see page 168)
½ tbsp freshly ground black pepper
125ml (½ cup) tomato purée (see
  page 172)
625ml (2½ cups) base curry sauce
  (see page 164 or 166), heated
800g (1lb 12oz) tandoori chicken
  tikka (see page 259)
125ml (½ cup) spice stock (see page
  167) or pre-cooked stewed chicken
  stock (see page 176)
100g (3½oz) block coconut, cut into
  small pieces
1 tsp dried fenugreek leaves (kasoori
  methi)
2 tbsp smooth mango chutney (see
  page 331)
1–2 tbsp raw cashew paste (see page
  173) (optional)
Salt, to taste
Sugar, to taste
Juice of 1 lime
1 tsp garam masala (see page 167)
3 tbsp chopped coriander (cilantro),
  to finish

Heat the oil in a large pan over a medium–high heat until it is visibly hot. Add the star anise, cinnamon stick or cassia bark and cardamom pods, and stir around for about 30 seconds until fragrant; be careful not to burn them. Add the curry leaves and fry for 30 seconds until their scent fills the room.

Add the garlic and ginger paste and the chopped chillies. Both will sizzle in the pan as they release their moisture and flavour into the oil. When they quieten down, after about 30 seconds, add the coconut flour and mix it all together for a few seconds before adding the coriander (cilantro) stalks, chilli powder, mixed powder, tandoori masala, black pepper and tomato purée.

Now stir in about 250ml (1 cup) of the base curry sauce and let it reduce for about 1 minute, stirring the caramelized bits into the sauce. Add the pre-cooked chicken, the rest of the base curry sauce, the stock and block coconut pieces. Let the sauce simmer for about 5 minutes until you are happy with the consistency, only stirring if it looks like it is catching on the pan.

Stir in the dried fenugreek leaves (kasoori methi), mango chutney and cashew paste (if using). Fish out the whole spices if you want and add salt and sugar to taste. Squeeze the lime juice over the top and sprinkle with the garam masala and chopped coriander (cilantro) to serve.

CHICKEN KEEMA SHIMLA MIRCH

SERVES 4 OR MORE AS PART OF A MULTI-COURSE MEAL

Shimla mirch means bell pepper or capsicum and you get a lot of that in this one. You could try making this curry with tandoori chicken tikka but I prefer it with chicken keema. Both are really good. At restaurants, this popular keema curry is usually prepared with minced lamb. You could use your minced meat of choice. Turkey is nice too. The curry is often topped with julienned ginger, spring onions (scallions), coriander (cilantro) and freshly chopped green chillies, and that is exactly what you'll be doing here. The toppings take a good curry and make it great!

PREP TIME: 15 MINS, PLUS
    MAKING THE BASE CURRY
    SAUCE
COOKING TIME: 15 MINS

3 tbsp rapeseed (canola) oil
1 onion, roughly chopped
2 large green (bell) peppers, roughly
    chopped
1–2 green chillies, finely chopped,
    plus extra sliced chillies to serve
2 tbsp garlic and ginger paste (see
    page 172)
1–2 tbsp curry powder (see page 171)
1 tsp ground cumin
1 tsp ground coriander
1 tsp red chilli powder
½ tsp ground turmeric
3 tbsp plain passata (sieved tomatoes)
    or tomato purée (see page 172)
600ml (2½ cups) base curry sauce
    (see pages 164 or 166), heated
600g (1lb 5oz) minced (ground)
    chicken
200ml (generous ¾ cup) thick
    coconut milk
5 small tomatoes, quartered
Salt, to taste

TOPPINGS TO SERVE
5cm (2in) piece of ginger, peeled and
    julienned
4 spring onions (scallions), roughly
    chopped
5 tbsp finely chopped coriander
    (cilantro)

Heat the oil over a medium–high heat. When it's visibly hot, add the chopped onion, green (bell) peppers and green chillies and fry for 3–4 minutes until the onion is translucent but still quite crisp. Add the garlic and ginger paste and stir it all in for about 1 minute.

Now add the ground spices and stir them into the vegetables. Pour in the passata (sieved tomatoes) and 250ml (1 cup) of the curry sauce. Bring this to a simmer, stirring only if the sauce is sticking to the pan.

Add the chicken and stir it into the sauce. Let this simmer for about 10 minutes until the chicken is cooked through. (In restaurants, pre-cooked keema would be used as a time saver so if you're working ahead, feel free to do the same, following my recipe on page 178.) Once cooked through, add the rest of the base sauce and the coconut milk and stir it all to combine.

Add the quartered tomatoes. Season with salt and add more of the ground spices, if you want. Serve at the table with the ginger, spring onions (scallions), coriander (cilantro) and sliced chillies on the side or as a garnish. I have provided quantities for the toppings to start, but you might just find you like them so much you want to add more.

CHICKEN DOPIAZA
SERVES 4 OR MORE AS PART OF A MULTI-COURSE MEAL

Dopiaza curries are big on flavour and can be mild or quite spicy, depending on the restaurant. Broken down, the word 'do' means two and 'piaza' means onions. So the authentic Indian version of this dish is a curry with onions cooked in two different ways. If you count the base curry sauce, and fried onion petals, this recipe is actually made with onions cooked in four different ways so the name doesn't quite fit. That's just being technical, though.

PREP TIME: 10 MINS, PLUS MAKING THE BASE CURRY SAUCE AND COOKING THE CHICKEN
COOKING TIME: 10 MINS

4 tbsp rapeseed (canola) oil or seasoned oil (see page 8)
1 small onion, quartered and divided into petals
6 green cardamom pods, bashed
1 tsp cumin seeds
1 tsp coriander seeds, roughly chopped
3 tbsp garlic and ginger paste (see page 172)
2 tbsp mixed powder (see page 169)
1 tsp ground cumin
1–2 tsp mild or hot chilli powder, to taste
125ml (½ cup) tomato purée (see page 172)
500ml (2 cups) base curry sauce (see page 164 or 166), heated
600g (1lb 5oz) pre-cooked stewed chicken (see page 176), plus 250ml (1 cup) of its cooking stock, or more base curry sauce
7 tbsp onion paste made with yoghurt (see page 173)
1 tsp dried fenugreek leaves (kasoori methi)
Salt, to taste
Small bunch of coriander (cilantro), chopped
2 handfuls of fried onions (see page 173)
1 tsp garam masala (see page 167)

Heat 1 tablespoon of the oil in a large pan over a high heat. When good and hot, toss in the onion petals and sear them until they are nicely charred but still quite crisp. Remove with a slotted spoon to a plate.

Reduce the heat to medium–high and pour in the rest of the oil. When bubbles start to appear, add the whole spices. Stir the spices around in the oil for about 30 seconds and enjoy the aroma of that awesome meal you're making.

Stir in the garlic and ginger paste and let it sizzle until fragrant, then add the mixed powder, ground cumin, chilli powder and tomato purée. Give this all a good stir and then add 250ml (1 cup) of the base curry sauce. The curry sauce will begin to bubble rapidly and, when it does, add the rest of the sauce and the stock or extra sauce. Turn up the heat and simmer; some of the sauce may begin to caramelize on the side of the pan, so just stir this in from time to time for more flavour.

Add the chicken pieces and continue to simmer, without stirring, for about 2 minutes until the chicken is warmed through. The sauce will cook down and become thicker, but if it becomes too thick for your liking, add a little more chicken or spice stock or base curry sauce. Stir in the onion paste 1 tablespoon at a time, then the dried fenugreek leaves (kasoori methi) and charred onion petals. Season with salt, then sprinkle with the coriander (cilantro), fried onions and garam masala to serve.

CHICKEN CHASNI

SERVES 4 OR MORE AS PART OF A MULTI-COURSE MEAL

Some say that chicken chasni is the new chicken tikka masala. It's sweet, not spicy, and delicious over rice or naans. For me, tandoori chicken tikka is the only way to go with this one. The flavours work so well together.

A friend of mine, Alex Wilke, worked for several years in a Glasgow Indian takeaway. He told me how customers expected their chasni curries to be bright red. If they weren't the correct red, they'd be handed right back. At the takeaway, this curry was so popular they had a glowing red chasni sauce ready to speed things up and to ensure that the chasnis were always uniform. If that's the colour you prefer, you'll need some bright red food colouring powder. Just stir it in until you're happy with the colour. Personally, I have nothing against using a bit of bright red food colouring but it adds no flavour to the dish. I didn't add any to mine this time.

PREP TIME: 10 MINS, PLUS MAKING THE BASE CURRY SAUCE AND COOKING THE CHICKEN
COOKING TIME: 10 MINS

3 tbsp ghee or rapeseed (canola) oil or seasoned oil (see page 8)
2 tbsp garlic and ginger paste (see page 172)
½ tsp ground turmeric
500ml (2 cups) base curry sauce (see page 164 or 166), heated
800g (1lb 12oz) pre-cooked stewed chicken (see page 176), plus 125ml (½ cup) of its cooking stock, or more base curry sauce
3 tbsp smooth mango chutney (see page 331)
2 tbsp mint sauce
3 tbsp tomato ketchup
1 tbsp ground cumin
200ml (generous (¾ cup) double (heavy) cream
Salt, to taste
Juice of 1–2 lemons, to taste
Bright red food colouring powder (optional)
½ tsp garam masala (see page 167)
3 tbsp very finely chopped coriander (cilantro)

Heat the ghee or oil in a large pan over a medium–high heat. When the oil is visibly hot, add the garlic and ginger paste; it will sizzle as it releases its moisture into the hot oil. Add the turmeric and fry for about 40 seconds, stirring continuously, then pour in 250ml (1 cup) of the base curry sauce. Let this come to a rapid simmer and scrape any caramelized sauce from the sides of the pan into the sauce.

Add the rest of the base sauce with the pre-cooked chicken and the stock or extra sauce. Let this cook for about 5 minutes, only stirring if the sauce is obviously catching on the pan, and stirring in any caramelized sauce from the side of the pan.

Stir in the mango chutney, mint sauce and ketchup followed by the cumin. Pour in the cream and simmer until good and hot. Season with salt and squeeze in the lemon juice to taste. Add red food colouring powder if you want and sprinkle with the garam masala and chopped coriander (cilantro) to serve.

CHICKEN PATHIA

SERVES 4 OR MORE AS PART OF A MULTI-COURSE MEAL

Pathia curries were probably first made by Bangladeshi chefs here in Britain in an attempt to come up with an Indian dish that could compete with the sweet-and-sour chicken that was becoming popular at Chinese takeaways. It seems to have caught on because you rarely find a curry house or takeaway that doesn't have pathia on the menu.

You need to make the sauce so that it is both sweet and sour. I've seen mint sauce used as a souring agent and pineapple juice, sugar and ketchup used for sweetening. With this, my favourite combo, you get the sour flavour from the lemon and the sweetness from the sugar and mango chutney. Go ahead and adjust these ingredients to your own preferences, or even try some of the other alternative ingredients mentioned. Sometimes the best curries are discovered through a bit of experimentation.

Like chicken tikka masala and chasni curries, pathia curries are often coloured red with food colouring. I did this in this recipe, but remember that there is no flavour in food colouring so it is not an essential ingredient.

PREP TIME: 10 MINS, PLUS
MAKING THE BASE CURRY
SAUCE AND COOKING THE
CHICKEN
COOKING TIME: 10 MINS

4 tbsp rapeseed (canola) oil or
seasoned oil (see page 8)
1 small onion, very finely chopped
2 tbsp garlic and ginger paste (see
page 172)
Salt, to taste
2 tbsp mixed powder (see page 169)
1 tsp chilli powder
2 tbsp sugar, or to taste
125ml (½ cup) tomato purée (see
page 172)
500ml (2 cups) base curry sauce (see
page 164 or 166), heated
800g (1lb 12oz) pre-cooked stewed
chicken (see page 176), plus 125ml
(½ cup) of its cooking stock, or
more base curry sauce
1 tbsp smooth mango chutney (see
page 331), or to taste
½ tsp tamarind concentrate
1 tsp dried fenugreek leaves (kasoori
methi)
Juice of 1–2 lemons, to taste
Red food colouring powder (optional)
3 tbsp chopped coriander (cilantro)

Heat the oil in a large pan over a medium–high heat until bubbling hot. Stir in the chopped onion and fry for about 5 minutes until translucent and soft, then add the garlic and ginger paste and let it sizzle for about 1 minute. Then, when your kitchen smells all garlicky and gingery, sprinkle a little salt over the mixture as this will help release moisture. Cook for about another minute, then add the mixed powder, chilli powder and sugar. Stir briskly.

Stir in the tomato purée and 250ml (1 cup) of the base curry sauce. Let this come to a rolling simmer and scrape back in any caramelized sauce from the sides of the pan. Add the rest of the base sauce and the stock, followed by the pre-cooked chicken. Let this bubble and spit until reduced down to your preferred consistency. Add a little more base sauce or stock if you want more sauce.

To finish, stir in the mango chutney, tamarind, dried fenugreek leaves (kasoori methi) and lemon juice to taste. Taste the curry, and if you want it to be sweeter, add some more sugar or mango chutney, or more lemon juice if you want it to have more of a tang. If using food colouring, you can stir it in now. Start with ½ teaspoon and add more if you want a redder hue.

Season with salt and garnish with coriander (cilantro) to serve.

TIP
Prawns (shrimp) are an excellent and popular alternative to chicken.

CHICKEN METHI CURRY
SERVES 4 OR MORE AS PART OF A MULTI-COURSE MEAL

Fresh fenugreek leaves are, surprisingly, still difficult to come by at most supermarkets. You will almost definitely find them at Asian grocers. Last year I tried to grow some of my own and the plants actually thrived! I kill everything I plant, but for some reason my fenugreek just took off. So if you enjoy growing your own herbs, give it a try.

PREP TIME: 10 MINS, PLUS
  SOAKING, MAKING THE BASE
  CURRY SAUCE AND COOKING
  THE CHICKEN
COOKING TIME: 10 MINS

½ tsp salt
Large handful of fresh fenugreek
  leaves*, roughly chopped
3 tbsp rapeseed (canola) oil
2 star anise
1 Indian bay leaf (cassia leaf)
1 tsp coriander seeds
1 tsp fennel seeds
1 onion, finely chopped
2 tbsp garlic and ginger paste (see
  page 172)
2 green chillies, finely chopped
Stalks from a large bunch of
  coriander (cilantro)
1 tbsp mixed powder (see page 169) or
  curry powder (see page 171)
1 tsp bassar curry masala or chilli
  powder
75ml (5 tbsp) plain passata (sieved
  tomatoes) or blended chopped
  tomatoes
500ml (2 cups) base curry sauce (see
  page 164 or 166), heated
700g (1lb 9oz) pre-cooked chicken
  (see page 176), plus 120ml (½ cup)
  of the cooking stock
4 tbsp plain yoghurt
Salt, to taste
3 tbsp chopped coriander (cilantro)
  leaves
½ tsp garam masala (see page 167)
1 tsp dried fenugreek leaves (kasoori
  methi)

Fresh fenugreek has a tendency to be very bitter. To reduce the bitterness, pour the ½ teaspoon salt over the leaves and mix thoroughly by hand. Set aside for 10 minutes. After 10 minutes, squeeze the leaves to get rid of any excess water, which will also get rid of the bitterness. Finely chop the leaves.

Now heat the rapeseed (canola) oil in a large pan over a medium–high heat. When visibly hot, stir in the star anise, bay leaf, coriander seeds and fennel seeds and temper them in the oil for about 40 seconds. Add the finely chopped onion and fry for about 2 minutes, followed by the garlic and ginger paste. Stir this all up well, then add the green chillies, coriander (cilantro) stalks, fenugreek leaves, mixed powder or curry powder and bassar curry masala or chilli powder.

Fry for a further 30 seconds, then add the passata (sieved tomatoes), 250ml (1 cup) of the base curry sauce and the cooked chicken. Move the pieces of chicken around in the sauce to coat them but only stir the sauce if it is obviously sticking to the pan. Add the remaining base sauce and the cooking stock and bring to a rapid simmer. Cook until the sauce is your preferred consistency, then whisk in the plain yoghurt, 1 tablespoon at a time. Season with salt and garnish with the coriander (cilantro), garam masala and dried fenugreek leaves (kasoori methi).

FENUGREEK SUBSTITUTES
*Fresh fenugreek and dried fenugreek leaves (kasoori methi) are available at most Asian grocers. Dried is easier to come by than fresh. When asking for them in an Asian shop, don't ask for fenugreek leaves, as you will probably get a blank stare in return.

If all you can find is dried fenugreek leaves, this can be substituted for fresh. I suggest stirring in the dried leaves to taste at the end of cooking. A good alternative to using dried or fresh fenugreek is chopped celery leaves. They have a similar, but not as bitter, flavour. Another option would be to use a handful or two of chopped spinach with some ground fenugreek. This will give the look and flavour of using fresh fenugreek leaves. Remember, though, fenugreek is bitter and can quickly become overpowering. Add dried fenugreek in small ½ teaspoon amounts to taste.

CHICKEN PASANDA

SERVES 4 OR MORE AS PART OF A MULTI-COURSE MEAL

Authentic Indian pasandas can be spicy or mild, sweet and/or savoury. What makes them 'pasanda' has nothing to do with the sauces, which can vary greatly, but relates to the use of flattened meat, tenderized with a meat mallet before being added to the pan. Here in the UK, our pasandas are quite similar to our kormas but usually not quite as sweet. I have yet to try one with flattened meat in a curry house, although I do use thinly sliced raw chicken rather than the standard pre-cooked chicken tikka. Either could be used. My friends at Eastern Eye in Brick Lane, London, recommend adding a splash of red wine to the sauce. Great advice! I think it really gives the sauce a unique and delicious flavour. This curry is perfect for kids and those who aren't fans of spicy dishes.

PREP TIME: 10 MINS,
PLUS MAKING THE
BASE CURRY SAUCE
COOKING TIME: 10 MINS

4 tbsp almond flakes
4 tbsp rapeseed (canola) oil or seasoned oil (see page 8)
3 tbsp coconut flour
3 tbsp ground almonds
2 tbsp sugar
About 20 sultanas
500ml (2 cups) base curry sauce (see page 164 or 166), heated
100g (3½ oz) block coconut, cut into small pieces
800g (1lb 12oz) skinless, boneless chicken breast, cut into thin slices on the diagonal
Splash of red wine (125ml/½ cup) (optional)
Salt, to taste
100ml (scant ½ cup) single (light) cream
1 tsp garam masala (see page 167)

Toast the almond flakes in a dry pan over a medium–high heat until nicely browned. Transfer to a plate and set aside.

Add the oil to the pan. When nice and bubbly, add the coconut flour, ground almonds and sugar. Stir this around for about 30 seconds, then add the sultanas, base curry sauce and block coconut pieces. When the sauce begins to simmer, stir in the chicken.

Let this simmer for about 5 minutes until the chicken is cooked through and the sauce has cooked to your preferred consistency. If the sauce caramelizes to the sides, stir it back into the sauce. At this time, you could add a splash of red wine to simmer in the sauce until the alcohol cooks out.

To serve, check for seasoning, adding salt, more coconut and sugar if desired, to taste. Stir in the cream and sprinkle with the garam masala and the toasted almond flakes.

CHICKEN DHANSAK

SERVES 4 OR MORE AS PART OF A MULTI-COURSE MEAL

Chicken dhansak is one of the most popular curries served at curry houses around the UK. British dhansak is a play on a curry served by the Parsi community around Mumbai. There, it's usually made with goat's meat or mutton and it is a real party piece. It's traditionally served with brown rice and usually has other nice vegetables thrown in like pumpkin, aubergine (eggplant) and potato. Four different lentils are used to make the sauce, along with a long list of spices. Our British version is a lot less complicated, although it is a sweet-and-sour curry like the original. Cooked red split lentils (try my tarka dhal on page 321) are added to the sauce, and it is usually sweetened with pineapple juice and chunks or rings of pineapple, with lemon juice used as a souring agent.

PREP TIME: 10 MINS, PLUS
MAKING THE BASE CURRY
SAUCE AND COOKING THE
CHICKEN AND LENTILS
COOKING TIME: 10 MINS

4 tbsp rapeseed (canola) oil or seasoned oil (see page 8)
2 tbsp garlic and ginger paste (see page 172)
1 tsp ground turmeric
2 tbsp mixed powder (see page 169)
1 tbsp chilli powder, or to taste
125ml (½ cup) tomato purée (see page 172)
500ml (2 cups) base curry sauce (see page 164 or 166), heated
180g (1 cup) red split lentils, rinsed and cooked in water until soft
800g (1lb 12oz) pre-cooked stewed chicken (see page 176), plus a little of its cooking stock or some spice stock (page 167)
115ml (scant ½ cup) pineapple juice
3–4 tinned (canned) pineapple rings, cut into pieces
Salt, to taste
Juice of 1–2 lemons, to taste
3 tbsp chopped coriander (cilantro)

Heat the oil in a pan over a medium–high heat. Spoon in the garlic and ginger paste along with the turmeric, and let sizzle for about 30 seconds. The turmeric will become darker as you do this. Now add the mixed powder, chilli powder and tomato purée and stir briskly.

Pour in half of the base curry sauce and let it simmer for about 1 minute. Add the cooked lentils and stir it all up. Watch closely as lentils have a tendency to scorch on the bottom of the pan, so reduce the heat if necessary. Now add the rest of the sauce and the pre-cooked stewed chicken along with a splash of cooking stock or spice stock for additional flavour. Pour in the pineapple juice and add the pineapple pieces. Simmer for a further 3–5 minutes, adding more base curry sauce or stock if the mixture becomes too thick.

Season with salt, stir in the lemon juice and top with the coriander (cilantro) to serve.

CHICKEN JALFREZI

SERVES 4 OR MORE AS PART OF A MULTI-COURSE MEAL

I visited **The Balti House, Rishton,** after hearing great things about the chef and owner, Hussain Rashid. He invited me to come and watch him cook in person and I wasn't going to pass that offer up. I liked how he was promoting only using the freshest ingredients, so I knew I was going to be offered a good meal for my long drive, if nothing else. He asked me what I'd like to see him prepare, and as I could see a basket full of fresh tomatoes, green bird's eye chillies, peppers and onions, I chose a jalfrezi. We sat down to one heck of a good curry and rice meal. This is my interpretation of the recipe.

Jalfrezi curries are quick stir-fries that are usually served quite dry with lots of crunchy vegetables. Of course, if you like more sauce, you're in control of that one.

PREP TIME: 10 MINS, PLUS
MAKING THE BASE CURRY
SAUCE AND COOKING THE
CHICKEN
COOKING TIME: 10 MINS

4 tbsp rapeseed (canola) oil or
    seasoned oil (see page 8)
1 onion, thinly sliced
1 red (bell) pepper, deseeded and
    thinly sliced
3 green bird's eye chillies, roughly
    chopped
2 tbsp finely chopped coriander
    (cilantro) stalks
2 tbsp garlic and ginger paste (see
    page 172)
6 tbsp tomato purée (see page 172)
2 tbsp mixed powder (see page 169)
1 tsp chilli powder (optional)
500ml (2 cups) base curry sauce (see
    page 164 or 166), heated
700g (1lb 9oz) pre-cooked stewed
    chicken (see page 176), plus 100ml
    (scant ½ cup) of its cooking stock
2 tomatoes, quartered
1 tsp dried fenugreek leaves (kasoori
    methi)
Salt, to taste
1 tsp garam masala (see page 167)
Coriander (cilantro) leaves, chopped
Green finger chillies, cut in half
    lengthways

Heat the oil in a large frying pan over a medium–high heat, then add the sliced onion, red (bell) pepper, green chillies and coriander (cilantro) stalks. Mix this all up in the pan and sauté until the vegetables are beginning to cook through but are still crisp.

Stir in the garlic and ginger paste and fry for about 1 minute. Add the tomato purée, mixed powder, chilli powder and about 250ml (1 cup) of the base curry sauce. This will come to an instant bubble. Add the chicken, stock and the rest of the base curry sauce.

Let this simmer over a medium heat for about 5 minutes, without stirring unless it is obviously catching on the pan. If the sauce begins to caramelize around the edges of the pan, stir this back into the curry. Add more base sauce or cooking stock if the sauce becomes too thick.

About 2 minutes before serving, add the quartered tomatoes and dried fenugreek leaves (kasoori methi).

When the tomatoes are cooked through but still crisp and you are happy with the consistency, season with salt and sprinkle with the garam masala. Finish by garnishing with the chopped coriander (cilantro) leaves and sliced chillies.

CHICKEN CHILLI GARLIC
SERVES 4 OR MORE AS PART OF A MULTI-COURSE MEAL

Garlicky and spicy, chicken chilli garlic curries are one of my curry-house favourites – I do love my garlic. I have experimented with this recipe many times and I think it's a winner.

It's spicy but not numbingly so. You can always add a few more chillies at the end if you want to turn the zing into a zap. By the way, if you are eating this for lunch, you probably don't want to go back to work that day. You won't be very popular.

PREP TIME: 10 MINS, PLUS
   MAKING THE BASE CURRY
   SAUCE AND COOKING THE
   CHICKEN

COOKING TIME: 10 MINS

4 tbsp rapeseed (canola) oil or
   seasoned oil (see page 8)
15 garlic cloves, cut into thin slivers
1 onion, finely chopped
½ tsp salt
2 tbsp garlic and ginger paste (see
   page 172)
3 (or more) fresh green chillies, sliced
   into thin rings, plus extra to serve
   (optional)
1 tsp chilli powder
2 tbsp mixed powder (see page 169)
2 tbsp tandoori masala (see page 168)
125ml (½ cup) tomato purée (see
   page 172)
500ml (2 cups) base curry sauce (see
   page 164 or 166), heated
800g (1lb 12oz) tandoori chicken
   tikka (see page 259), plus 125ml (½
   cup) pre-cooked stewed chicken
   stock (see page 176) or spice stock
   (see page 167)
1 tsp dried fenugreek leaves (kasoori
   methi)
Salt, to taste
Small bunch of coriander (cilantro),
   finely chopped
Dried garlic flakes, to serve (optional)

Heat the oil in a pan over a medium heat and add the garlic slivers. It is very important not to burn the garlic, so watch the pan and move the slivers around in the pan until they become soft and are just beginning to brown.

Now add the onion and fry for a further 3 minutes until soft and translucent, sprinkling a little salt over the onions to help release moisture. Stir in the garlic and ginger paste and chillies, and fry for about 20 seconds.

Increase the heat to medium–high, add the ground spices and tomato purée and sizzle for a further 30 seconds, stirring continuously. Add half the base curry sauce and bring to a rolling simmer. (You don't need to stir the sauce unless it is obviously catching on the pan.) Be sure to scrape any sauce that caramelizes on the sides of the pan back into the sauce.

Pour in the rest of the base sauce, the chicken and the cooking stock or spice stock, and let this bubble without disturbing until the chicken is heated through (about 2 minutes) and your sauce consistency is how you like it.

Stir in the dried fenugreek leaves (kasoori methi) and season with salt. Sprinkle with the coriander (cilantro), dried garlic flakes and a few more chilli rings, if you like.

CHICKEN REZALA

SERVES 4 OR MORE AS PART OF A MULTI-COURSE MEAL

One thing I really love about doing what I do is meeting and learning from so many great curry-house chefs around the UK. On one visit to London, I took my wife to Sheba Brick Lane and told her she had to try their rezala curry. She loved it. Chicken rezala is a lot like chicken tikka masala but it is a bit spicier and there are a lot fewer ingredients. I learned Sheba's famous biryani recipe when I was writing my first cookbook, so I asked the floor manager, Mohith Khan, if I could see how they make their rezala. A couple of days later, I was back in the Sheba kitchen cooking with Chef Faruk Miah. You are going to love this one. Chicken rezala is delicious served with white or pilau rice. Naans are also very nice!

PREP TIME: 10 MINS, PLUS MAKING THE BASE CURRY SAUCE AND COOKING THE CHICKEN
COOKING TIME: 10 MINS

3 tbsp rapeseed (canola) oil
2 tbsp garlic and ginger paste (see page 172)
1 onion, finely chopped
Pinch of salt, plus more to taste
3 green chillies, finely chopped
2 tbsp mixed powder (see page 169)
1 tsp Kashmiri chilli powder
70ml (¼ cup) tomato purée (see page 172)
500ml (2 cups) base curry sauce (see page 164 or 166), heated
800g (1lb 12oz) pre-cooked chicken (see page 176), plus 70ml (¼ cup) of its cooking stock, or more base curry sauce
125ml (½ cup) single (light) cream
½ tsp garam masala (see page 167)
2 tbsp finely chopped coriander (cilantro)
1–2 tbsp butter

Heat the oil in a frying pan over a medium–high heat. Add the garlic and ginger paste and let it sizzle, stirring continuously, for about 30 seconds. Add the onion and salt (the salt will help release the moisture from the onion into the pan). Fry for about 3 minutes until the onion is just becoming translucent, then add the green chillies and fry for a further 30 seconds. Stir in the mixed powder and chilli powder. Add the tomato purée and about 70ml (¼ cup) of the base sauce – the sauce should evaporate quite quickly. When almost dry, add another 125ml (½ cup) of the base sauce and the chicken with the cooking liquid, if you have some, or more base curry sauce.

Bring this to a rolling simmer, stirring only if the sauce is obviously sticking to the pan. Be sure to scrape any sauce that caramelizes on the side of the pan back in as this adds fantastic flavour. Add the remaining base sauce and simmer until the sauce has thickened to your liking.

To finish, swirl in the cream, garam masala, coriander (cilantro) and butter. When the butter has melted into the sauce, season with salt.

MANGO CHICKEN CURRY
SERVES 4 OR MORE AS PART OF A MULTI-COURSE MEAL

My friend Richard Sayce (AKA Misty Ricardo) records popular YouTube videos demonstrating his take on BIR cooking, and he sent me this recipe to try. This is my interpretation of it. It's spicy and sweet. Kids love it too, but you might want to omit or reduce the amount of fresh chillies and chilli powder. Richard adds large chunks of fresh mango to this curry, but I opted for small chunks. It's a personal thing, so do what you think will taste best.

PREP TIME: 10 MINS, PLUS MAKING THE BASE CURRY SAUCE AND COOKING THE CHICKEN
COOKING TIME: 15 MINS

2 tbsp rapeseed (canola) oil
2 tbsp garlic and ginger paste (see page 172)
1 tbsp mixed powder (see page 169) or curry powder (see page 171)
1 tsp chilli powder (or to taste)
3 tbsp finely chopped coriander (cilantro) stalks
2 fresh green chillies (bird's eye or bullet), thinly sliced
600ml (2½ cups) base curry sauce (see page 164 or 166), heated, plus extra if needed
6 tbsp coconut flour
4 tbsp smooth mango chutney (see page 331)
700g (1lb 9oz) pre-cooked chicken (see page 176)
1 small mango, cut into bite-size chunks (tinned/canned mango can be used)
Salt, to taste
1 tsp garam masala (see page 167)
1 tsp dried fenugreek leaves (kasoori methi)
3 tbsp finely chopped coriander (cilantro) leaves, to serve

Heat the oil in a frying pan over a medium–high heat. When visibly hot, stir in the garlic and ginger paste and let it fry for about 30 seconds. Stir in the mixed powder and chilli powder, along with the finely chopped coriander (cilantro) stalks and fresh chillies. Stir these ingredients really well into the hot oil, then add about 250ml (1 cup) of the base curry sauce.

Let this come to a rolling simmer, stirring only if it is sticking to the pan. Add the coconut flour and mango chutney, followed by another 125ml (½ cup) of base curry sauce. Stir in the chicken and heat it through for about 1 minute in the bubbling sauce. Now add the mango chunks and the rest of the base curry sauce. Let the curry cook for another 4 minutes or so until it has reduced down to your preferred consistency. You can always add more base sauce or a little water if it becomes too dry.

To finish, season with salt and sprinkle the garam masala and dried fenugreek leaves (kasoori methi) over the top. Give it a good stir and garnish with the coriander (cilantro) to serve.

LAMB BHUNA

SERVES 4 OR MORE AS PART OF A MULTI-COURSE MEAL

Authentic Indian bhunas are quite a lot more difficult to make than this British restaurant-style version. Bhuna is a style of cooking where hot oil or ghee is used to release the flavours of whole spices before raw meat is added, often as small pieces still on the bone. Once the meat is added, stock or water is drizzled into the pan in small amounts, cooking the meat as it reduces down. This process is repeated for 1 hour or more until the meat becomes fall-off-the-bone tender. It is then served in the thick sauce it was cooked in. This time-consuming style of cooking wouldn't be possible in most restaurants.

This bhuna is still a dry curry, but it is made in a fraction of the time, using cooked boneless meat instead of braised raw meat. It is delicious served with chapattis or naans to soak up all that amazing sauce.

You can try my authentic chicken bhuna recipe on page 85. Chicken takes a lot less time to cook in authentic bhuna style, but you could use the same method to cook an authentic lamb bhuna. You will just need to add more water during cooking.

PREP TIME: 10 MINS, PLUS
MAKING THE BASE CURRY
SAUCE AND COOKING THE
LAMB
COOKING TIME: 10 MINS

3 tbsp ghee, rapeseed (canola) oil or seasoned oil (see page 8)
1 small onion, finely chopped
¼ red (bell) pepper, deseeded and roughly chopped
2 tbsp garlic and ginger paste (see page 172)
2 tbsp finely chopped coriander (cilantro) stalks (from the bunch below)
125ml (½ cup) tomato purée (see page 172)
2 tbsp mixed powder (see page 169)
2 tbsp tandoori masala (see page 168)
500ml (2 cups) base curry sauce (see page 164 or 166), heated
800g (1lb 12oz) pre-cooked stewed lamb (see page 177), plus 250ml (1 cup) of its cooking stock, or more base curry sauce
2 tbsp Greek yoghurt
Salt and freshly ground black pepper, to taste
Small bunch of coriander (cilantro), leaves finely chopped
Juice of 1–2 limes, to serve (optional)
Sliced red chilli, to serve (optional)

Heat the ghee or oil in a large pan over a medium–high heat. When it is bubbling, add the onion and red (bell) pepper and sizzle them in the oil for about 5 minutes until the onion is translucent and soft. Stir in the garlic and ginger paste, and coriander (cilantro) stalks, and stir these around in the oil for about 30 seconds.

Add the tomato purée and, when it starts to bubble, stir in the mixed powder and tandoori masala, followed by 250ml (1 cup) of the base curry sauce. Let this simmer for about 2 minutes, without stirring unless it is obviously catching on the pan. Scrape any caramelized sauce at the edges of the pan back in.

Increase the heat to high and add the pre-cooked lamb and the rest of the sauce along with the cooking stock. Let this bubble undisturbed until it reduces down to a thick sauce.

To finish, reduce the heat to medium and whisk in the yoghurt 1 tablespoon at a time. Season with salt and black pepper. Top with the coriander (cilantro) and serve with a good squeeze of lime juice and/or some sliced red chilli, if you like.

LAMB SAAG

SERVES 4 OR MORE AS PART OF A MULTI-COURSE MEAL

Good British lamb saag (saag gosht) is very close to the authentic Punjabi version. In the subcontinent, the meat is slowly cooked on the bone in a large karahi until the lamb almost falls off the bone into the rich spinach sauce. Some British Pakistani and Punjabi restaurants still prepare the curry in this way and promote it as one of their house special dishes. At most curry houses, however, it's made in under 10 minutes using prepared ingredients and plenty of cooking stock from pre-cooked lamb. This recipe might be quick but when done correctly it will taste like it's been gently simmering for hours. If you like buttery ghee, this is a good one to use it in. Lamb saag is delicious served with plain or pilau rice.

PREP TIME: 10 MINS, PLUS
    MAKING THE BASE CURRY
    SAUCE AND COOKING THE
    LAMB
COOKING TIME: 10 MINS

225g (8oz) baby spinach leaves
A little water or spice stock (see page 167)
3–6 fresh green bullet chillies, to taste
Bunch of coriander (cilantro), leaves only (reserve stalks, see below)
4 tbsp ghee, rapeseed (canola) oil or seasoned oil (see page 8)
1 onion, finely chopped
2 tbsp garlic paste and 1 tbsp ginger paste*, or 3 tbsp garlic and ginger paste (see page 172)
3 tbsp finely chopped coriander (cilantro) stalks
1 tbsp ground cumin
1 tbsp ground coriander
1 tbsp mixed powder (see page 169)
1 tsp chilli powder
180ml (¾ cup) tomato purée (see page 172)
375ml (generous 1½ cups) base curry sauce (see page 164 or 166), heated
600g (1lb 5oz) pre-cooked stewed lamb (see page 177), plus 250ml (1 cup) of its cooking stock
Salt and freshly ground black pepper, to taste
2 tbsp plain yoghurt
Juice of 1 lemon
1 tbsp garam masala (see page 167)

* I prefer to use more garlic than ginger in this recipe, but you could use garlic and ginger paste if you prefer. To make the garlic paste, blend 2–4 cloves of garlic with just enough water to make a paste. For the ginger paste, blend a 5cm (2in) piece of ginger with just enough water to make a smooth paste.

Put the spinach, chillies and coriander (cilantro) leaves in a food processor and blend to a smooth paste with a little water or spice stock. Set aside.

Heat the ghee or oil in a frying pan over a medium–high heat. When hot, add the onion and fry for about 5 minutes until translucent and soft but not overly browned. Add the garlic and ginger pastes, and allow to sizzle for about 30 seconds. Add the coriander (cilantro) stalks, ground cumin and coriander, mixed powder and chilli powder, and stir to combine.

Swirl in the tomato purée and about 250ml (1 cup) of the base curry sauce and let it come to a happy simmer. Add the stock and the rest of the base sauce. You can let it simmer for a few minutes and you don't need to stir unless it is obviously catching on the pan. Be sure to stir in any caramelized sauce from the sides of the pan from time to time.

Add the pre-cooked lamb pieces and simmer in the sauce until heated through. When the sauce is about the consistency you prefer, pour in the spinach purée and stir it all up. The bright green spinach will become darker as it cooks. Simmer for a further 2 minutes. If the sauce becomes too dry for your liking, just add a little more base sauce and/or lamb stock. To finish, season with salt and black pepper. Stir in the yoghurt 1 tablespoon at a time, then top with a squeeze of lemon juice and the garam masala.

OTHER IDEAS

To make this curry even more interesting, you could add more texture with ingredients such as chickpeas (garbanzo beans) or pre-cooked potatoes (see page 179).

LAMB ROGAN JOSH

SERVES 4 OR MORE AS PART OF A MULTI-COURSE MEAL

Just like many of the British versions of Indian curries, our lamb rogan josh is quite a lot different to those made in India. Mutton or lamb rogan josh originates from the Kashmir region of India, where it is made with tempered whole spices such as cloves, cinnamon, bay leaves, cardamom and deseeded Kashmiri dried chillies. Meat on the bone is braised in a sauce that is deep red, from both the Kashmiri chillies and rattanjot, which is a natural red food colouring and difficult to come by in the West, where the red colouring is achieved with paprika and tomato. You might also want to try my authentic Kashmiri lamb rogan josh recipe on page 107.

PREP TIME: 10 MINS, PLUS
    MAKING THE BASE CURRY
    SAUCE AND COOKING THE
    LAMB
COOKING TIME: 10 MINS

4 tbsp rapeseed (canola) oil or seasoned oil (see page 8)
2 tbsp garlic and ginger paste (see page 172)
2 tbsp paprika
1 tsp chilli powder, or more to taste
125ml (½ cup) tomato purée (see page 172)
500ml (2 cups) base curry sauce (see page 164 or 166), heated
1 tbsp ground cumin
1½ tbsp mixed powder (see page 169)
700g (1lb 9oz) pre-cooked stewed lamb (see page 177), plus 200ml (generous ¾ cup) of its cooking stock
2 tomatoes, quartered
2–3 tbsp raw cashew paste (see page 173)
3 tbsp plain yoghurt, plus extra to garnish
1 tsp dried fenugreek leaves (kasoori methi)
1 tsp garam masala (see page 167)
Salt, to taste
3 tbsp chopped coriander (cilantro) leaves
Chopped red onion, to garnish

Heat the oil in a large frying pan over a medium–high heat until hot. Add the garlic and ginger paste and let it sizzle for about 30 seconds, stirring continuously. Add the paprika and chilli powder and fry for about 30 seconds. The mixture should turn a darker red as it cooks. Pour in the tomato purée, which should start to bubble as soon as it hits the pan. Cook it down by about half, then stir in 250ml (1 cup) of the base curry sauce, the cumin and mixed powder.

Allow the sauce to simmer for about 2 minutes, without stirring unless it is obviously catching on the pan. Some of the sauce should caramelize to the sides of the pan; you want to scrape it off from time to time as it adds a nice smoky flavour. Add the pre-cooked lamb and the rest of the base sauce with the stock.

Let the sauce come to a boil until it reduces to your preferred consistency, only stirring if it is catching. Add the tomato wedges to the sauce.

To serve, swirl in the cashew paste, then add the yoghurt 1 tablespoon at a time, stirring continuously. Sprinkle with the dried fenugreek leaves (kasoori methi) and garam masala and season with salt. Top with coriander (cilantro) and garnish with chopped red onion and a little plain yoghurt.

ALOO GOSHT
SERVES 4 OR MORE AS PART OF A MULTI-COURSE MEAL

Aloo gosht, or potatoes with meat, makes an excellent meal on its own. I do usually serve it with rice, chapattis and/or naans, but there are plenty of carbs in the potatoes, so you could simply serve it on its own as you would a stew. The bassar curry masala mentioned in this recipe is used mainly in Pakistani cuisine. It is spicy like chilli powder but has other ingredients thrown in, including mustard oil powder. It should be cooked before it is eaten and adds a really nice flavour.

PREP TIME: 10 MINS, PLUS
MAKING THE BASE CURRY
SAUCE, COOKING THE
POTATOES AND MEAT
COOKING TIME: 15 MINS

5 tbsp rapeseed (canola) oil, vegetable oil or ghee
1 tsp cumin seeds
1 onion, finely chopped
2 tbsp garlic and ginger paste (see page 172)
1 tsp red chilli (hot pepper) flakes
1 tsp bassar curry masala or chilli powder, or to taste
1 tsp paprika
½ tsp ground turmeric
2 tsp ground cumin
1 tsp ground coriander
500ml (2 cups) base curry sauce (see page 164 or 166), heated
125ml (½ cup) plain passata (sieved tomatoes) or blended chopped tomatoes
750g (1lb 10oz) pre-cooked lamb (see page 177) or the meat from the lamb masala curry on page 96, plus 150ml (generous ½ cup) stock from the lamb masala curry, or more base curry sauce
450g (1lb) cooked potatoes, peeled and diced
Salt, to taste
1 tsp garam masala (see page 167)
3 tbsp finely chopped coriander (cilantro) leaves

Heat the oil in a large saucepan over a medium–high heat. When visibly hot, add the cumin seeds and temper in the oil for about 30 seconds. Add the chopped onion and fry until soft and translucent – about 5 minutes should do the job. (This is a curry that benefits from cooking the chopped onion longer until browned though, so you can do that if you have time.)

Stir in the garlic and ginger paste and allow it to sizzle for about 30 seconds, then add the chilli (hot pepper) flakes, bassar curry masala or chilli powder, paprika, turmeric, cumin and ground coriander. Stir this into the onion mixture. It will become quite fragrant after 30 seconds. When this happens, stir in half of the base curry sauce and the passata (sieved tomatoes). Bring to a rolling simmer, only stirring if the sauce is sticking to the pan.

Stir in the lamb pieces and potato chunks with the cooking stock and the rest of the base curry sauce. Heat everything through and reduce the sauce down to your preferred consistency. Season with salt. To serve, sprinkle with the garam masala and chopped coriander (cilantro).

LAMB MADRAS
SERVES 4 OR MORE AS PART OF A MULTI-COURSE MEAL

Dining out with friends at a curry house right after I moved to the UK, I was told how to order from the menu by spice level. A simple lamb curry would be mild. A madras would be the same but with more chilli powder. The vindaloo would have substantially more chilli powder and the phal would be dangerously hot. That advice did me well back then, but nowadays the better chefs ensure each of these curries have a flavour all their own. It's not just down to the spiciness anymore.

I love this sweet-and-sour madras. The addition of smooth mango chutney and a twist or two of lime juice makes this the perfect blend that can take centre stage at any curry feast. Spicy curries like this are delicious served with rice and kachumber salad (see page 326).

PREP TIME: 10 MINS, PLUS MAKING THE BASE CURRY SAUCE AND COOKING THE LAMB
COOKING TIME: 10 MINS

3 tbsp rapeseed (canola) oil or seasoned oil (see page 8)
2–4 Kashmiri dried red chillies, to taste
A few green cardamom pods, lightly bruised
3 tbsp garlic and ginger paste (see page 172)
2 fresh green chillies, or to taste, finely chopped
125ml (½ cup) tomato purée (see page 172)
2 tbsp ground cumin
1 tsp ground coriander
¼ tsp ground turmeric
1–2 tbsp chilli powder, to taste
2 tbsp mixed powder (see page 169)
500ml (2 cups) base curry sauce (see page 164 or 166), heated
800g (1lb 12oz) pre-cooked stewed lamb (see page 177), plus 250ml (1 cup) of its cooking stock, or more base curry sauce
1–2 tbsp smooth mango chutney (see page 331), to taste
Juice of 1 lime
Salt, to taste
Pinch of garam masala (see page 167)
Coriander (cilantro), to garnish

Heat the oil in a pan over a medium–high heat until hot. Add the dried chillies and cardamom pods, and allow to sizzle for about 30 seconds. Be sure to count the cardamom pods in and count them back out again at the end of cooking if you don't like biting into whole spices. Scoop in the garlic and ginger paste along with the chopped chillies. Allow them to sizzle for about 20 seconds, then stir in the tomato purée followed by the ground cumin, coriander and turmeric, the chilli powder and mixed powder.

Now add 250ml (1 cup) of the base curry sauce along with the lamb. Simmer for about 2 minutes, without stirring unless it is obviously catching on the pan, scraping back in any caramelized sauce from the sides of the pan. Pour in the rest of the base curry sauce and the stock, and let it simmer over a high heat until it has reduced down to your preferred consistency.

To serve, stir in the mango chutney and lime juice. Season with salt, sprinkle with the garam masala and garnish with the coriander (cilantro).

TIP
If you are looking for a more savoury flavour, spicy lime pickle can be substituted for the mango chutney.

LAMB ACHARI

SERVES 4 OR MORE AS PART OF A MULTI-COURSE MEAL

In Hindi, 'achar' means pickle. Achari is a very popular Punjabi curry made with the spices often used to make pickles, such as the panch poran and dried chillies used in this recipe. The sweet flavour of the mango chutney and sourness in the lime pickle give this curry the well-rounded flavour loved by so many.

PREP TIME: 10 MINS, PLUS
  MAKING THE BASE CURRY
  SAUCE AND COOKING THE
  LAMB
COOKING TIME: 10 MINS

4 tbsp rapeseed (canola) oil or
  vegetable oil
1 tbsp panch poran (see page 171)
2 Kashmiri dried red chillies, split
  lengthways and deseeded
1 onion, thinly sliced into rings
2 tbsp garlic and ginger paste (see
  page 172)
2 bird's eye chillies, finely chopped
125ml (½ cup) tomato purée (see
  page 172), plain passata (sieved
  tomatoes) or blended tinned
  (canned) tomatoes
2 tbsp mixed powder (see page 169)
  or curry powder (see page 171)
1 tsp ground coriander
1 tsp Kashmiri chilli powder
600ml (2½ cups) base curry sauce
  (see page 164 or 166), heated
750g (1lb 10oz) pre-cooked lamb (see
  page 177), plus 200ml (generous ¾
  cup) of the cooking stock
2 tbsp lime pickle (see page 328), or
  1 tbsp each of lime pickle and
  smooth mango chutney (page 331)
4 tbsp plain yoghurt
1 tsp dried fenugreek leaves (kasoori
  methi)
1 tsp garam masala (see page 167)
Salt, to taste
Juice of 1 lemon
3 tbsp finely chopped coriander
  (cilantro) leaves, to garnish

Heat the oil in a frying pan over a medium–high heat. When the oil is visibly hot, add the panch poran and Kashmiri chillies. The panch poran will begin to crackle as the spices release their flavour into the oil. Toss in the sliced onion and fry until soft and translucent – about 5 minutes. A sprinkle of salt will help release moisture from the onion and cool down the pan.

Add the garlic and ginger paste and bird's eye chillies and fry for a further 30 seconds while stirring continuously. Pour in the tomato purée followed by the mixed powder, ground coriander, chilli powder and 250ml (1 cup) of the base curry sauce. It will sizzle and bubble, but don't be tempted to stir unless it is obviously burning onto the pan. Be sure to scrape any caramelized sauce from the side of the pan into the sauce for additional flavour.

Add the meat and its stock and the rest of the curry sauce and simmer until it has reduced down to your preferred consistency. Stir in the lime pickle and mango chutney (if using), then add the yoghurt 1 tablespoon at a time. You need to stir continuously so that the yoghurt doesn't curdle.

Swirl in the dried fenugreek leaves (kasoori methi) and garam masala and season with salt. Squeeze the lemon juice over the top and garnish with the coriander (cilantro) to serve.

LAMB KEEMA
SERVES 4 OR MORE AS PART OF A MULTI-COURSE MEAL

Now you get to put that pre-cooked keema (see page 178) to work. I've specified lamb keema here but any meat keema will do. Whenever I make this curry, I usually also prepare a selection of different samosas the same day using the pre-cooked keema. I just take out what I need for the samosas and use the rest in the curry. I would like to stress how much magnificent additional flavour you get by pre-cooking the keema meat. You could throw it in raw for this recipe, but you would be missing one of the flavour boosts that makes BIR dishes so amazing.

To make this dish even more exciting, try adding a few more complementary ingredients. Chickpeas, blended spinach, pre-cooked potatoes (see page 179) and/or tandoori prawns (page 291), for example, could be all that's needed to take this popular curry and make it into a personal masterpiece. Thick curries like this are always nice scooped up with hot chapattis.

PREP TIME: 10 MINS, PLUS MAKING THE BASE CURRY SAUCE AND COOKING THE LAMB
COOKING TIME: 10 MINS

3 tbsp rapeseed (canola) oil or seasoned oil (see page 8)
½ onion, very finely chopped
¼ red (bell) pepper, deseeded and finely chopped
2 tbsp garlic and ginger paste (see page 172)
2 fresh green bullet chillies, finely chopped
2 tbsp finely chopped coriander (cilantro) stalks
2 tbsp mixed powder (see page 169)
1 tsp ground cumin
1 tsp chilli powder or to taste
125ml (½ cup) tomato purée (see page 172)
500ml (2 cups) base curry sauce (see page 164 or 166), heated, plus extra sauce or meat stock (see page 177) if desired
1 quantity pre-cooked keema (see page 178)
150g (1 cup) frozen peas
1 tomato, cut into 8 wedges
1 tsp dried fenugreek leaves (kasoori methi)
Salt, to taste
1 tsp garam masala (see page 167)
3 tbsp chopped coriander (cilantro) leaves
5cm (2in) piece of ginger, peeled and julienned

Heat the oil in a pan over a medium–high heat until sizzling hot. Add the onion and red (bell) pepper and fry for about 5 minutes until the onion is soft and just beginning to brown. Add the garlic and ginger paste, chillies and coriander (cilantro) stalks, and move it all around in the pan so that everything is nicely coated in the oil.

Stir in the mixed powder, cumin and chilli powder, give it all a good stir and then add the tomato purée. Let this sizzle for about 30 seconds and then pour in about 250ml (1 cup) of the base curry sauce and let it bubble for about 30 seconds. There's no need to stir unless it is obviously catching on the pan. Stir in the pre-cooked keema and the rest of the base curry sauce. This is usually a dry curry, but if you prefer more sauce, go ahead and add it, or a little meat stock.

Add the peas, tomato and dried fenugreek leaves (kasoori methi) and cook for a further 2–3 minutes until the peas are heated through. Be careful not to overcook them; they need to be plump and still have a bit of a bite to them. Simmer them too long and they will turn wrinkly and rather unappetizing.

Season with salt and sprinkle with the garam masala, coriander (cilantro) and ginger to serve.

LAMB NAGA PHALL

SERVES 1–2

How hot you make your phall curries is really down to you. You could, for instance, use ghost chillies, which are the spiciest you can get. I don't do that though. I do like a good spicy phall from time to time, but I also like to taste all the ingredients that are in it. If you make it too spicy, the spice overtakes the curry. Still, this phall will be too hot for most people, which is why I have only given a one- to two-person serving. I'm not allowed to cook this in the house anymore because it's nearly impossible to breathe without coughing. This is one I have to cook outdoors. Mr Naga pickle is available from most Indian grocers and online. It's spicy but also has a great flavour, so I recommend picking some up. As this is so hot, so you might want to serve with rice, naans, a few papadams and a couple of ice-cold lagers to help cool things down.

PREP TIME: 10 MINS, PLUS
MAKING THE BASE SAUCE
AND COOKING THE LAMB
COOKING TIME: 10 MINS

4 habanero chillies, finely chopped
2 tbsp rapeseed (canola) oil or mustard oil
½ small onion, finely chopped
½ red (bell) pepper, diced
1 tbsp garlic and ginger paste (see page 172)
1 tbsp Mr Naga chilli pickle (optional but delicious)
1 tbsp mixed powder (see page 169) or curry powder (see page 171)
2 tsp Kashmiri chilli powder
70ml (¼ cup) tomato purée (see page 172)
300ml (1¼ cups) base curry sauce (see page 164 or 166), heated
200g (7oz) lamb tikka (see page 286) or pre-cooked lamb in sauce (see page 177)
Salt, to taste
1 tsp dried fenugreek leaves (kasoori methi)
½ tsp garam masala (see page 167)
2 tbsp finely chopped coriander (cilantro)

Blend the habanero chillies with just enough water to make a paste, then set aside.

Heat the oil in a large frying pan over a medium–high heat. When it is visibly hot, add the onion and fry for 5 minutes, or until soft and translucent. Stir in the red (bell) pepper and cook for a further minute or so. Add the garlic and ginger paste, the blended habaneros and Mr Naga chilli pickle (if using) and cook for a further 30 seconds, stirring regularly.

Add the mixed powder and Kashmiri chilli powder followed by the tomato purée, and stir to combine, then add about 125ml (½ cup) of the base sauce. Allow this to come to a simmer, then add the lamb tikka or the pre-cooked lamb with a drop of the cooking liquid. Cook for about 5 minutes to heat the meat through, adding more base sauce as needed. Only stir the sauce if it is sticking to the pan and be sure to scrape any caramelized sauce around the edges into the curry for extra flavour. Cook the curry until you are happy with the consistency and season with salt. Sprinkle the dried fenugreek leaves (kasoori methi) over the top by rubbing the leaves between your fingers.

Garnish with the garam masala and coriander (cilantro) to serve.

LAMB VINDALOO

SERVES 4 OR MORE AS PART OF A MULTI-COURSE MEAL

Many restaurants include potato in their vindaloo curries. 'Aloo' means potato in Hindi, so a lot of the original self-taught Bangladeshi and Pakistani chefs in the UK mistakenly added potatoes to this fiery curry, and it stuck. Vindaloo, however, owes its origins to Portuguese-controlled Goa in the 15th century, where the dish was usually served with pork. The name vindaloo was most likely a mispronunciation of the similar Portuguese dish *carne de vinho e alho* (meat with wine and garlic). So our vindaloo is completely different to the authentic Goan version other than it is quite spicy and often packs a vinegary punch. I don't add potatoes, but if you would like to, I've included instructions. If you would like to try a recipe for the original Goan pork vindaloo, you'll find it on page 110.

PREP TIME: 10 MINS, PLUS MAKING THE BASE CURRY SAUCE AND COOKING THE LAMB AND POTATOES

COOKING TIME: 10 MINS

3 tbsp rapeseed (canola) oil or seasoned oil (see page 8)
6 green cardamom pods, bashed
2 star anise
1 Indian bay leaf (cassia leaf)
2 tbsp garlic and ginger paste (see page 172)
2 fresh green bullet chillies, finely chopped
2 Scotch bonnet chillies, finely chopped
1 tsp ground turmeric
2 tbsp hot chilli powder (be careful – if unsure, add less)
2 tbsp mixed powder (see page 169)
125ml (½ cup) tomato purée (see page 172)
2 tsp jaggery or sugar
600ml (2½ cups) base curry sauce (see page 164 or 166), heated
800g (1lb 12oz) pre-cooked stewed lamb (see page 177), plus some (generous ¾ cup) of its cooking stock
2 tbsp white wine vinegar
1 tsp dried fenugreek leaves (kasoori methi)
2 pre-cooked stewed potatoes (see page 179) (about 8 pieces) (optional)
3 tbsp chopped coriander (cilantro)
Salt and freshly ground black pepper, to taste

Heat the oil in a pan over a medium–high heat. When it begins to bubble, add the whole spices and bay leaf. If you don't like biting into whole spices, be sure to count them in and count them back out again before serving.

Scoop in the garlic and ginger paste and fry in the hot oil for about 1 minute. Add the chopped chillies, turmeric, chilli powder and mixed powder, followed by the tomato purée and jaggery or sugar. The tomato purée will bubble as it heat ups.

Pour in about 250ml (1 cup) of the base curry sauce and let it come to a rolling simmer. Don't stir the sauce unless it looks like it is beginning to catch. Scrape back in any sauce that caramelizes around the sides of the pan.

The pan should be going crazy over the heat. Swirl in the remaining base curry sauce and add the pre-cooked meat with a little of the cooking stock. Let the sauce simmer over the high heat until it cooks down to your desired consistency.

To finish, add the vinegar, dried fenugreek leaves (kasoori methi), potatoes (if using) and the coriander (cilantro). Season with salt and black pepper.

VEGETABLE BHAJI
SERVES 4 OR MORE AS PART OF A MULTI-COURSE MEAL

Any seasonal vegetables can be used for this recipe. I've recommended a few, but feel free to add whatever you like. Vegetable bhaji is essentially a stir-fry with a little base curry sauce and spices mixed in. Be careful not to overcook the vegetables in the sauce. They need to have a bit of bite to them.

Consider this a slightly fancier version of the pre-cooked onions and vegetables on page 175. Vegetable bhaji can be served as a curry on its own, or you could mix a few spoonfuls into the curry of your choice.

PREP TIME: 10 MINS, PLUS
    MAKING THE BASE CURRY
    SAUCE
COOKING TIME: 10 MINS

2 tbsp rapeseed (canola) oil or
   seasoned oil (see page 8)
1 tsp mustard seeds
10 fresh or frozen curry leaves
2 onions, thinly sliced
1 yellow and 1 red (bell) pepper, thinly
   sliced
2 tbsp garlic and ginger paste (see
   page 172)
2 green bird's eye chillies, finely
   chopped
½ tsp ground turmeric
2 tbsp mixed powder (see page 169)
125ml (½ cup) tomato purée (see
   page 172)
1 small carrot, peeled and thinly sliced
10 button mushrooms
20 green beans, cut into 2.5cm (1in)
   pieces
Handful of shredded cabbage
400ml (scant 1¾ cups) base curry
   sauce (see page 164 or 166), heated
1 tomato, quartered
1 tbsp dried fenugreek leaves (kasoori
   methi)
Salt and freshly ground black pepper,
   to taste
1 tbsp garam masala (see page 167)

Heat the oil in a large wok or frying pan over a high heat. When hot, throw in the mustard seeds. When they begin to crackle (after about 30 seconds), reduce the heat to medium–high, then add the curry leaves and stir to combine.

Now add the sliced onions and yellow and red (bell) peppers and fry for about 5 minutes until the onions are translucent and soft. Add the garlic and ginger paste, chillies, turmeric and mixed powder, followed by the tomato purée. Let these sizzle for 1 minute, then stir in the rest of the vegetables to fry for about 2 minutes, stirring continuously.

Pour in the base curry sauce and simmer undisturbed, stirring only if it is catching on the pan.

When the vegetables are cooked to your liking, add the tomato wedges and dried fenugreek leaves (kasoori methi). Season with salt and black pepper and sprinkle with the garam masala to serve.

TIP
A couple of pre-cooked potatoes (see page 179) and a little of the cooking sauce is a nice addition.

PRAWN MASALA CURRY

SERVES 4 OR MORE AS PART OF A MULTI-COURSE MEAL

If you like prawn (shrimp) curries, this is a straightforward one that my youngest daughter, Jennifer, makes all the time. One of her tips for getting extra flavour into the curry (that isn't in the recipe method below) is to purchase your prawns unpeeled. Peel and clean them and then sauté the shells in the oil. The shells will turn pink as they cook. Press the shells down to extract every last bit of flavour and then remove and discard them, leaving as much oil in the pan as possible. Then, start the recipe as described below. This extra step really adds depth and flavour to the sauce.

PREP TIME: 10 MINS, PLUS
MAKING THE BASE CURRY
SAUCE
COOKING TIME: 10 MINS

3 tbsp rapeseed (canola) oil or ghee
1 tsp mustard seeds
2.5cm (1in) piece of cinnamon stick
10 curry leaves (optional)
2 tbsp garlic and ginger paste (see page 172)
2 green chillies, finely chopped
2 tbsp mixed powder (see page 169) or curry powder (see page 171)
50ml (3½ tbsp) tomato purée (see page 172)
400ml (scant 1¾ cups) base curry sauce (see page 164 or 166), heated
600g (1lb 5oz) raw bite-size prawns (shrimp), peeled and cleaned
200ml (scant 1 cup) thick coconut milk
2 tbsp light soy sauce or coconut amino*
Small bunch of coriander (cilantro), finely chopped
Salt and freshly ground black pepper, to serve
Juice of 1–2 limes
1 tsp garam masala (see page 167)

Heat the oil in a large frying pan. When visibly hot, toss in the mustard seeds and cinnamon stick. The mustard seeds will begin to pop after about 30 seconds. When they do, add the curry leaves and fry for about 15 seconds until they become fragrant.

Stir in the garlic and ginger paste and bring to a good sizzle before adding the chopped chillies. Stir it all up well, then add the mixed powder, tomato purée and about 125ml (½ cup) of the base curry sauce. Allow this to come to a simmer, only stirring if the sauce is catching on the pan. If the sauce caramelizes on the sides of the pan, stir it in as it adds nice flavour.

Tip in the raw prawns (shrimp) and the rest of the base curry sauce and simmer until the prawns are cooked through and you are happy with the consistency of the sauce. Now add the coconut milk and the soy sauce or coconut amino. Stir in the coriander (cilantro) and season with salt and black pepper.

To serve, squeeze the lime juice over the top and sprinkle with the garam masala.

NOTE

*Most soy sauces are not gluten-free. If this is important to you, use coconut amino instead.

RESTAURANT-STYLE QUICK BIRYANI

SERVES 2 OR MORE AS PART OF A MULTI-COURSE MEAL

The kacchi lamb biryani on page 98 is a very authentic recipe. You could use that same process to cook a chicken biryani too, just as it's done all over India. The cooking process is quite lengthy, so it wouldn't be possible for curry houses to cook their biryanis in this way unless it was for a special event. The chefs never know how many people will order the different biryani options – chicken or lamb, prawns (shrimp) or vegetarian – so a recipe like this quick restaurant-style biryani is how they make it. It is essentially a fried pilau rice with the preferred main ingredient added and then served with a sauce or raita. This is a great way to use up leftover rice as the rice needs to be cooked cold from the fridge.

PREP TIME: 10 MINS, PLUS
THE TIME TO COOK AND
COOL THE RICE AND COOK
THE MAIN INGREDIENT OF
YOUR CHOICE
COOKING TIME: 15 MINS

3 tbsp rapeseed (canola) oil or ghee
2.5cm (1in) piece of cinnamon stick
2 green cardamom pods, smashed
3 cloves
½ tsp cumin seeds
1 onion, finely chopped
1 tbsp garlic and ginger paste (see page 172)
250g (8oz) pre-cooked meat, chicken, prawns (shrimp) or vegetables
3 tbsp tomato purée (see page 172)
1 tbsp mixed powder (see page 169) or curry powder (see page 171)
¼ tsp ground turmeric
2 tbsp plain yoghurt
500g (2 cups) cooked and cooled basmati rice*
Pinch of saffron infused in 2 tbsp hot milk (optional)
3 tbsp finely chopped coriander (cilantro), plus extra to serve if desired
70g (¼ cup) fresh or frozen peas
Salt, to taste
½ onion, fried until crisp (see page 173) or the equivalent shop-bought fried onions
2 tbsp ghee, for pouring over the top (optional)

*It is important to cool leftover rice quickly (within an hour) after cooking. When reheating, take care to fully heat it all the way through before using.

Heat the oil in a large frying pan over a medium–high heat and toss in the cinnamon stick, cardamom pods, cloves and cumin seeds. Stir these whole spices around in the oil for about 30 seconds and the add the onion. Fry for about 5 minutes, or until the onion is soft and translucent, then stir in the garlic and ginger paste. Fry for a further 30 seconds or so.

Add your pre-cooked main ingredient of choice and the tomato purée and stir it all up to combine with the onion mixture. Now stir in the ground spices. Add the yoghurt 1 tablespoon at a time and mix it all in. This is your base masala ready for the rice.

Reduce the heat to medium and add the cold, cooked rice. Carefully and delicately stir the rice into the sauce. It is important not to stir the rice too roughly or it will split and become mushy.

Once the rice is heated through and coated with the oily sauce mixture, add the saffron-infused milk (if using). Then add the coriander (cilantro) and peas and continue cooking over a medium heat until the peas are cooked. This should take about 3 minutes. Season with salt.

To finish, transfer the biryani to a heated serving plate. Garnish with the fried onions and a little more chopped coriander (cilantro), if liked. Now this is totally optional, but drizzling a bit of hot melted ghee over the top tastes amazing!

BALTI, KARAHI AND HANDI DISHES

I receive so many requests for balti, karahi and handi recipes, mainly due to people having a favourite dish at their local Indian restaurant that includes one of these titles. The thing is, the reference to balti, karahi and handi is not about the ingredients used but rather the style of pan in which the ingredients are supposedly cooked, as well as how they are cooked. I say supposedly because this isn't always the case.

I think it is a good idea here to explain what the differences are between the pans, followed by a number of recipes that are best cooked in them.

KARAHI PAN

An authentic karahi is a deep-sided, cast-iron pan used for slow-cooking and stir-frying in Pakistan and other parts of the subcontinent. It looks a lot like a wok with handles. They are now also made of steel, aluminium and non-stick materials, but personally I think these don't compare to the original – and still most popular – heavy cast-iron pans. Karahis are available in sizes from small one-serving pans right up to pans large enough to prepare a curry for more than fifty people.

HANDI PAN

Handi pans can be used in the same way as a karahi. They have a rounded, heavy base like a wok so that meat and vegetables can be cooked for long periods of time without catching on the base, just like a karahi. Handis are different in shape to karahis in that they are narrow in the centre and have a wide mouth at the top.

Some handis have lids, making them perfect for steaming rice as well as for slow-cooking amazing curries. They are manufactured in many different metals and also clay. Handis, like karahis, are available as both large and more decorative small pans, used in many curry houses for presentation.

BALTI PAN

Balti was invented in Birmingham. I know there are those who say that balti cooking comes from Baltistan or that balti pans are really only small karahis, but that simply isn't the case.

I spent a few days visiting Birmingham's Balti Triangle with my friend and respected balti historian Andy Munro. Andy grew up there in the 1950s, 60s and 70s, long before it was called the Balti Triangle – in fact, he claims he coined the now-famous phrase for the area. Few people know balti like Andy.

There are many well-known Balti Triangle restaurateurs who were influential in the balti craze of the 1980s. Through Munro's meticulous research, however, he believes that one man is responsible for the balti-style pan and how baltis were – and in a few restaurants still are – served in the authentic style.

Mohammed Arif was the owner of the long-established Adil's. He had substantial experience from several of Birmingham's Indian restaurants and knew how much Brummies loved a good curry. In the late 1970s, Pakistani restaurants were attracting only the local Pakistani community, and Arif wanted to get the larger population of Birmingham curry fans to Adil's.

One-pot cooking was popular in Pakistan as it made it possible to serve large groups of people. Slow-cooked curries would be prepared, usually with meat on the bone, and simmered in stock and spices until the meat was falling off the bone into the succulent sauce. Arif wanted to bring this style of cooking to the greater population, but understood that most Western curry fans wouldn't be prepared to wait an hour or longer to be served. He needed single-serving pans capable of heating up faster than cast-iron karahis.

Arif got a local company to design a one-serving pan that looked like a karahi but was made out of thin, pressed steel, with a flat bottom rather than the rounded base of a karahi. This had the added benefit of heating up faster than cast iron. These balti pans had a matt steel finish, which quickly turned their trademark black colour over the fierce heat of the flame.

The balti caught on fast in the early 1980s. It was new and fun. There was something about going out for a balti with friends and family, having the baltis served in the intensely hot pans they were cooked in and then mopping it up with a huge naan that was shared around the table.

So why is it called balti? There is a lot of speculation, but in Munro's opinion, after speaking with Arif and many other Balti Triangle restaurateurs, the answer is quite simple and believable. Pakistani restaurateurs at the time understood that chicken tikka masala and chicken biryani were the most common curries in British curry houses and the extent of most people's Indian cuisine vocabulary. They felt that describing the dish as a karahi was deceptive as it was not karahi-style cooking so much as the pan looked like a karahi. They also believed that the word karahi wasn't the catchiest or easiest word to pronounce. Balti in Hindi means bucket, and the word was already being used by many Pakistanis to describe a container that held food for weddings. Balti just seemed to slip off the tongue. It was catchy and, as we all now know, it caught on in a big way.

BALTI DHAL FRY
SERVES 2

This recipe is a balti so I only cook it to serve one or two people. Authentic British baltis are cooked in a stainless steel balti pan over a high heat and then served in the same pan they were cooked in. That's how I hope you serve this too. There's just something about dipping fresh naans into a flaming hot balti pan laden with delicious sizzling curry. If you don't have a balti pan, do make this anyway!

The recipe calls for a cup of cooked chana dhal. I always make a good-size batch for ease, following the cooking instructions on the bag and freezing any leftovers; however if you just want to make enough for this recipe you will need to soak and cook 100g (½ cup) chana dhal as the lentils double in weight and size when cooked.

PREP TIME: 10 MINS, PLUS
DHAL COOKING TIME IF
USING HOME-COOKED
COOKING TIME: 10 MINS

2 tbsp coconut oil
2 cloves
2.5cm (1in) piece of cinnamon stick
½ onion, very finely chopped
2 green chillies, finely chopped
1 large tomato, diced
2 tsp finely chopped coriander
   (cilantro) stalks
3–4 garlic cloves, finely chopped
1 tsp chilli powder
½ tsp ground turmeric
½ tsp ground cumin
½ tsp ground coriander
200g (1 cup) cooked chana dhal
Salt and freshly ground black pepper,
   to taste
Coriander (cilantro), to garnish
   (optional)

FOR THE TARKA
2 tbsp ghee, vegetable ghee or
   rapeseed (canola) oil
3 Kashmiri dried red chillies
1 tsp cumin seeds
Pinch of asafoetida*

Melt the coconut oil in a saucepan over a high heat. When it is good and hot, stir in the cloves and cinnamon stick. Let the spices temper into the oil for about 30 seconds and then add the chopped onion. Fry for about 2 minutes, then add the green chillies. Stir well and add the tomato and coriander (cilantro) stalks followed by the garlic and ground spices. Stir in the cooked dhal and simmer over a low heat while you make the tarka.

Melt the ghee or oil in another pan. When visibly hot, add the Kashmiri chillies, cumin seeds and asafoetida. Allow to sizzle for about 30 seconds, then pour it all over the dhal.

Season to taste with salt and black pepper, and garnish with coriander (if using).

NOTE

*If you are gluten-free, please check the asafoetida packaging as some brands contain wheat flour.

AUBERGINE BALTI

SERVES 2

If you like a good balti, try this one with my balti dhal fry (see page 238). The two curries go so well together and they are a lot of fun to serve in the flaming hot balti pans. In barbecue season, I omit the oil for the skin and prick the aubergine (eggplant) before cooking it right on the hot coals. I turn it a few times until it's cooked through. The smoky flavour you get is out of this world and perfect for this dish. Baltis are meant to be served with naans or chapattis to soak up that last bit of sauce.

PREP TIME: 10 MINS
COOKING TIME: 30 MINS

1 aubergine (eggplant), about 300g
    (10½ oz)
2 tbsp rapeseed (canola) oil
1 tsp cumin seeds
1 onion, finely chopped
1 green chilli, finely chopped
2 tbsp garlic and ginger paste (see
    page 172)
2 tomatoes, diced
½ tsp ground turmeric
1 tsp ground cumin
½ tsp ground coriander
½ tsp chilli powder
Salt, to taste
3 tbsp finely chopped coriander
    (cilantro), to garnish

Preheat the oven to its highest setting. Rub the skin of the aubergine (eggplant) with about ½ teaspoon of the oil and place it on a roasting tray in the oven for about 20 minutes, or until the skin blackens and blisters. Transfer the aubergine to a chopping board and slice it in half lengthways. Scoop out all the flesh. Discard the skin and cut the flesh into small cubes. Set aside.

Now heat the remaining oil in a frying pan over a medium–high heat. When visibly hot, toss in the cumin seeds. Temper the cumin in the oil for about 20 seconds. Add the chopped onion and fry for about 5 minutes until it is soft, translucent and lightly browned. Stir in the chilli and garlic and ginger paste. Fry for a further minute or so, then stir in the diced tomatoes.

Add the dry spices while stirring, then add the diced aubergine. Let the aubergine cook until it is soft and most of the liquid has dried up, about 3–5 minutes. Season with salt and garnish with the coriander (cilantro).

SPECIAL BALTI

SERVES 1–2

Go out for an authentic balti meal and chances are the special balti is going to catch your eye. There are lots of different recipes for it because it is the chef's own special mix of ingredients. This one is mine. Use this recipe as a guide and try coming up with a special balti recipe that is all your own.

Curries like this are best made when you're having a curry house-style curry feast for friends and/or family as you will have a good selection of pre-cooked meats, seafood and vegetables on hand to add to it. Add whatever main ingredients sound good and you really can't go wrong. Baltis are traditionally eaten with hot naans, but you could also serve this with rice.

PREP TIME: 10 MINS, PLUS
  PREPPING THE PRE-COOKED
  INGREDIENTS
COOKING TIME: 10 MINS

3 tbsp rapeseed (canola) oil
½ onion, finely chopped
1 large tomato, diced
2 green chillies, finely chopped
200g (7oz) pre-cooked lamb keema
  (see page 178)
2 tbsp tomato purée (see page 172)
1 tsp paprika
½ tsp ground turmeric
1 tsp mixed powder (see page 169) or
  curry powder (see page 171)
1 tsp chilli powder (optional)
150ml (generous ½ cup) base curry
  sauce (see page 164 or 166), heated
3 pieces of tandoori chicken tikka (see
  page 259)
3 pieces of tandoori lamb tikka (see
  page 286)
100ml (3½ fl oz) thick coconut milk
2 handfuls of chopped spinach
3 prawns (shrimp), shelled and
  cleaned
Salt, to taste
½ tsp dried fenugreek leaves (kasoori
  methi)
Handful of tinned (canned) chickpeas
  (garbanzo beans) (optional)
Juice of ½ lemon

Heat a balti pan or similar pan over a medium–high heat and add the oil. When hot, add the onion and fry for about 3 minutes, then stir in the tomato and chillies. Stir well to combine, then add the pre-cooked keema and tomato purée, followed by all the ground spices. Spoon in about half the base sauce and then the chicken and lamb tikka. Bring to a simmer and add more base sauce when it's looking thirsty.

Now add the coconut milk and spinach. It will look like there is a lot in the pan right now, but the spinach cooks down quickly. When it does, add the prawns (shrimp) and cook for about 2 minutes until they are pink and cooked through. Be sure to top up the curry with some base sauce as needed. Season with salt.

To finish, add the dried fenugreek leaves (kasoori methi) by rubbing the leaves between your fingers into the pan. Add the chickpeas (if using) and squeeze the lemon juice over the top.

AUTHENTIC CHICKEN HANDI

SERVES 4 OR MORE AS PART OF A MULTI-COURSE MEAL

I am asked for chicken handi recipes all the time, but that's a difficult one. Simply asking for a chicken handi recipe may or may not get you the curry you want to recreate. Just like balti and karahi curries, handis are called handis because of the handi pot they are cooked and/or served in. These days, more often than not, the handi will be cooked in a frying pan at restaurants and then served in an ornamental metal handi pan. The first handis were cooked in earthenware handi pots and the recipes varied from chef to chef. There is a lot of ghee in this one, which might be one of the reasons it's so good.

PREP TIME: 15 MINS
COOKING TIME: 40 MINS

125ml (½ cup) ghee
2 medium red onions, thinly sliced
2 tbsp garlic and ginger paste (see page 172)
1 tsp cumin seeds
2 tomatoes, diced
4 green chillies, sliced
1 tsp ground turmeric
1 tsp red chilli powder
1 tsp ground coriander
800g (1lb 12oz) skinless chicken thighs on or off the bone, cut into small pieces
125ml (½ cup) water, unsalted chicken stock or spice stock (see page 167)
250g (1 cup) plain yoghurt, whisked until creamy smooth
70ml (¼ cup) single (light) cream (optional)
1 tsp dried fenugreek leaves (kasoori methi)
1 tsp garam masala (see page 167)
Salt, to taste
Bunch of coriander (cilantro), chopped
5cm (2in) piece of ginger, peeled and julienned

Heat the ghee in a handi pan or large saucepan over a medium–high heat. When visibly hot, add the onions and fry for about 10 minutes, or until golden brown and crispy-looking but not burnt. Stir in the garlic and ginger paste and cumin seeds and fry for about 30 seconds, then add the tomatoes and green chillies and stir it all up to combine.

Stir in the ground spices and mix it all up. This is the base of your curry. Toss in the chicken thighs and stir continuously for 3–4 minutes to brown the meat in the sauce mixture. Add the water/stock, cover the pan and simmer for about 15 minutes over a medium heat until the chicken is cooked through and the stock is thick.

Stir in the yoghurt 1 tablespoon at a time and continue to simmer until you are happy with the consistency of the sauce. If using cream, add it now, then sprinkle in the dried fenugreek leaves (kasoori methi) by rubbing the leaves between your fingers, followed by the garam masala. Season with salt and garnish with the coriander (cilantro) and ginger.

CHICKEN BALTI
SERVES 1

Almost any curry can be cooked as a balti. At Shababs, in Birmingham, they seem to have hundreds of combinations that can be ordered. The restaurant was packed when I visited with my friend and balti historian Andy Munro. He commented that making baltis correctly was probably best left to the professionals, and after watching chef-owner Zafar Hussain cook a few, I could understand why. Don't let that stop you making this one, though!

Authentic baltis are cooked over a high gas flame that is much hotter than is possible on most conventional hobs. As they are cooked, the whole pan turns into a big ball of fire as the oil catches light. You might think that this would burn the other ingredients but it doesn't. Only the oil is burned off, making the balti healthier and adding a delicious smoking flavour. When they place those sizzling hot curries in front of you, you know you're in for something special. Cook it in a large one-serving balti pan just like at Shababs! A good frying pan can be substituted.

PREP TIME: 10 MINS, PLUS
MAKING THE BASE CURRY
SAUCE
COOKING TIME: 10 MINS

3 tbsp rapeseed (canola) oil or
seasoned oil (see page 8)
1 small onion, roughly chopped
1 green (bell) pepper, deseeded and
roughly chopped
1 tomato, diced
1 tbsp garlic and ginger paste (see
page 172)
1 tbsp green chilli paste (see page 172)
1 tsp ground cumin
1 tsp ground turmeric
1 tsp paprika
250ml (1 cup) base curry sauce (see
page 164 or 166), heated
200g (7oz) skinless chicken breast or
thigh meat, cut into small pieces
(tikka)
1 tbsp garam masala (see page 167)
1 tsp dried fenugreek leaves (kasoori
methi)
Salt, to taste
Chopped coriander (cilantro), to serve

Heat the oil in a frying pan (or wok, karahi or balti pan) over a high heat until almost smoking. Add the onion, green (bell) pepper and tomato, and fry for about 1 minute. Stir in the garlic and ginger paste and chilli paste. The oil will sizzle as they release their moisture.

If you're feeling brave and have a gas hob, tilt the pan towards the flame and see if you can get the oil to catch fire. Don't panic if it lights, and never throw water on the flame or you will probably have to call the fire service and may need a new kitchen.

Add the ground spices and 5 tablespoons of the base curry sauce. Let this come to a boil then add the chicken pieces and another 5 tablespoons of the base sauce. Stir occasionally so that the sauce doesn't catch, and scrape the caramelized sauce from the sides of the pan.

Pour in the remaining base sauce and let the curry simmer until the chicken is cooked through and the sauce is quite thick. Baltis are usually served with fresh naans or chapattis, which are used to soak up the sauce and meat instead of cutlery, and your sauce needs to be thick enough to do this.

To finish, stir in the garam masala and dried fenugreek leaves (kasoori methi) and check for seasoning. If there is any oil on the surface, skim it off for a healthier curry. Top with chopped coriander (cilantro) to serve.

LAMB KARAHI

SERVES 4 OR MORE AS PART OF A MULTI-COURSE MEAL

I got to watch this curry being prepared at Imran's in Birmingham by head chef Talib Hussain. It was drop-dead gorgeous and I've made it many times since. At Imran's, the meat is cut into small pieces still on the bone. Boneless lamb can be substituted, but personally I like it their way. It may be messier to eat, but dipping your naan into this delicious sauce and trying to gnaw every last bit of meat off the bone is part of the experience. This curry is fun to serve and can be quite impressive when presented in a sizzling hot karahi at the table.

PREP TIME: 10 MINS, PLUS
    MARINATING TIME
COOKING TIME: 1 HOUR

800g (1lb 12oz) lamb leg and
    shoulder, cut into pieces, ideally
    still with bone in
4 tbsp rapeseed (canola) oil
2 tbsp garlic and ginger paste (see
    page 172)
1 quantity fried onions (see page 173)
1 tbsp pungent dried red chilli flakes
2 large tomatoes, diced
1½ tbsp ground cumin
1½ tbsp ground coriander
1 tbsp Kashmiri chilli powder
Salt, to taste
7.5cm (3in) piece of ginger, peeled
    and julienned
2 fresh green bullet chillies, roughly
    chopped
1 tsp garam masala (see page 167)
Coriander (cilantro), to serve

FOR THE MARINADE
1 tbsp rapeseed (canola) oil
100g (scant ½ cup) Greek yoghurt
2 tbsp garlic and ginger paste (see
    page 172)
1 tsp salt
1 tbsp freshly ground black pepper

Mix the meat pieces with the marinade ingredients in a large bowl and cover with cling film (plastic wrap). Leave to marinate in the fridge for at least 2 hours or ideally overnight – the longer the better.

When ready to cook, heat the oil in a pan over a medium–high heat and add the garlic and ginger paste. Stir this around for about 30 seconds, then add the meat and all the marinade. Using a large spoon, stir to coat the meat with the garlicky oil. Add the fried onions, chilli flakes and tomatoes and again stir it all up to combine.

Now sprinkle in the ground cumin, coriander and chilli powder. Pour in just enough water to cover and let it all simmer for a good 40 minutes to 1 hour. You may need to top up the water from time to time.

Check for seasoning and add more salt or spices to taste. This is a quite dry curry so that it can easily be soaked up with fresh naans. When the meat is really tender, add the ginger, fresh chillies and garam masala and serve topped with coriander (cilantro).

That's it! This may be simple, but believe me no one will know. Serve it to friends and they'll think you've been secretly working as the head chef of Imran's!

LAMB KEEMA SAAG BALTI
SERVES 4

In order to make a traditional Birmingham balti, it must be made and served in an authentic balti pan. In balti kitchens, the curries are cooked over intensely high heat. Often the curry catches fire but it doesn't burn. The fire is just the oil being burned and it gives a nice smoky, charred flavour to the curry. For the home chef, go ahead and use a pan you're comfortable using and turn the heat right up. A good wok will do the job just fine. It won't be the 'real deal' but it will still taste amazing! If you're really into baltis, you might be happy to know that authentic balti pans like those produced in the 1970s are once again being made in the UK. (See suppliers on page 343 for more information.) These are great not only for cooking in but also for serving right from the pan, just as baltis are meant to be eaten. They are wonderful served with hot naans – perfect for mopping up the curry.

PREP TIME: 10 MINS, PLUS
    MAKING THE BASE SAUCE, IF
    USING
COOKING TIME: 15 MINS

3 tbsp rapeseed (canola) oil or ghee
1 tsp panch poran (see page 171)
2 onions, finely chopped or thinly
    sliced
2 tbsp garlic and ginger paste (see
    page 172)
2 red or green chillies, finely chopped
2 tbsp curry powder (see page 171)
500g (1lb 2oz) minced (ground) lamb
150ml (generous $\frac{1}{2}$ cup) plain passata
    (sieved tomatoes) or blended
    chopped tomatoes
150g (5$\frac{1}{2}$oz) baby spinach leaves,
    washed and shredded
Up to 250ml (1 cup) base curry sauce
    (see page 164 or 166), heated
    (optional)
Salt, to taste
1 tsp garam masala (see page 167), to
    serve

Heat the oil over a medium heat. When visibly hot, toss in the panch poran and temper the spices for about 30 seconds, then add the onions. Sauté for about 5 minutes until soft and translucent.

Add the garlic and ginger paste and the chopped chillies. Fry for a further minute, then stir in the curry powder followed by the lamb. Brown the meat for about 2 minutes, then stir in the passata (sieved tomatoes) and shredded spinach. The spinach will wilt and cook into the sauce.

To finish, stir in the base curry sauce if you prefer a saucier curry. Let it simmer until it cooks down to your preferred consistency. Season with salt and sprinkle with garam masala to serve.

CHARSI KARAHI

SERVES 4 OR MORE AS PART OF A MULTI-COURSE MEAL

The first time I tried charsi karahi I was blown away by how something so simple could taste so amazing. I guess one reason is all that tasty lamb fat, so if you're on a low-calorie diet, just skip this one or better yet... take a break from your diet. This recipe is all about the delicious chunks of lamb cooked in meat fat. There aren't even any spices used, which is pretty unique to say the least. Give this one a try. I promise, you'll thank me for it. It is so good soaked up and devoured with fresh naans.

PREP TIME: 5 MINS
COOKING TIME: 50 MINS

2 tbsp garlic paste*
2 tbsp rapeseed (canola) oil
900g (2lb) small chunks of lamb or
    mutton on the bone
250g (9oz) lamb fat, cut into 2.5cm
    (1in) chunks
5 medium tomatoes, quartered
10 green bullet chillies or similar, cut
    lengthways
Salt, to taste
1 tsp dried fenugreek leaves (kasoori
    methi)

*To make this, blend 2–4 cloves of
garlic with just enough water to make
a smooth paste.

In a jug, whisk the garlic paste into 1 litre (4½ cups) of water and set aside. Heat the oil in a large karahi or wok over a medium–high heat. Add the lamb meat and fat chunks and brown for about 5 minutes. Pour in about 250ml (1 cup) of the garlic water. Bring to a rolling simmer, stirring from time to time. As the water reduces down, pour in a little more and continue doing this, stirring regularly, for about 30 minutes. Be sure to keep about 400ml (scant 1¾ cups) of the garlic water back for later use. As the water reduces, it will cook the lamb, making it mouthwateringly tender.

After about 30 minutes, place the tomatoes on top and cover the pan. Add more water at this point if the curry is looking dry. Simmer for about 10 minutes, then smash the tomatoes into the meat using a wooden spoon or spatula. If needed, add a little more of the garlic water and also the green chillies.

Continue simmering the meat until all the water has been used. Taste a piece: if it is fall-apart tender, your job is almost done; if not, add a little water and continue simmering until the meat is tender to your liking. As the meat simmers, the oil will rise to the top – this is a good clue that the curry is ready. You can skim the fat off at this point or enjoy the curry with all the fat in. The curry should be quite moist, but there shouldn't be a lot of sauce.

To serve, season with salt and add the dried fenugreek leaves (kasoori methi) by rubbing the leaves between your fingers into the sauce.

LAMB KORMA HANDI

SERVES 4 OR MORE AS PART OF A MULTI-COURSE MEAL

This korma is a lot different to the sweet, creamy and mild kormas you might be familiar with from UK curry houses. Our British-style kormas are actually kormas only in name. Korma or quorma is actually a style of cooking where meat or vegetables are braised and cooked in one big pot. Handis are used traditionally because of their large belly and smaller mouth, which is perfect for korma-style cooking. The meat is usually cooked on the bone for flavour, but you could use lamb off the bone for easier eating. Do you really need all that ghee? Yep, if you want to make it authentic, but use less if you must. Served with chapattis and homemade lime pickle (see page 328), this is a must-try!

PREP TIME: 15 MINS
COOKING TIME: 1 HOUR

6 garlic cloves, roughly chopped
5cm (2in) piece of ginger, peeled and roughly chopped
3 green chillies, roughly chopped
1 tsp Kashmiri chilli powder
3 generous tbsp ground coriander
1 tsp ground turmeric
1 tbsp ground cumin
Onion paste made with 2 medium onions (see page 173) or the equivalent made with shop-bought fried onions
250g (1 cup) plain yoghurt
800g (1lb 12oz) lamb, cut into small pieces on or off the bone
8 generous tbsp (¾ cup) ghee
10 black peppercorns
5 cloves
2.5cm (1in) piece of cinnamon stick
10 green cardamom pods, smashed
Salt, to taste
1 tsp rose water

Place the garlic, ginger and green chillies in a spice grinder or blend with just enough water to make a paste. Add the ground spices and onion paste and blend further: this is your korma paste. Add the yoghurt by running it through a fine-mesh strainer. This is done to prevent the yoghurt from curdling. Place the meat in a mixing bowl and pour over the marinade, mixing well. Leave to marinate for at least 30 minutes or overnight.

When ready to cook, heat the ghee over a medium–high heat in a handi or high-sided saucepan. When bubbling hot, add the whole spices and stir them around for about 30 seconds. Tip in the marinated meat with all its marinade. Reduce the heat to medium and simmer for about 15 minutes, stirring regularly. The yoghurt will become thin and the ghee will rise to the top. Add 1 litre (4½ cups) of water and bring to a rolling simmer. Cover and reduce the heat to low and cook for a further 15 minutes without lifting the lid. Give it all a good stir, cover again and continue cooking for another 15 minutes – do not lift the lid during this time. Check the meat. It should still be a bit tough but beginning to become tender. Cover again and continue cooking, covered, for a further 20–30 minutes, or until the meat is deliciously tender.

Season with salt and stir in the rose water just before serving.

GRILLING, BARBECUE AND ROASTING

This chapter shows how to make some of my favourite tandoori dishes. Given the word tandoori, it would be fair to assume everything is cooked in a tandoor oven, but this isn't always the case. Most Indian restaurants have a tandoor oven, but many only use it for naans and parathas.

Some of the best 'tandoori' dishes I've had were cooked on skewers or on a grill over an open flame. I have a home tandoor oven, but also often only use it for naans, especially when having friends round. Cooking the meat, seafood, paneer and vegetables over the barbecue and the naans in the tandoor means all the food can be served hot, at the same time.

Don't get me wrong. I do cook meat in the tandoor and do recommend getting one. Small home tandoor ovens cost about the same as a good gas barbecue and achieve superior results. They reach temperatures near to 400°C (750°F), which is how meat and seafood get so nicely charred.

These recipes use both indirect and direct grilling methods, and I have explained both. I've also given instructions for conventional ovens as well as tandoor cooking, just in case you're tempted.

PREPARING THE BARBECUE FOR DIRECT HEAT GRILLING

Cooking over open flames is the simplest of the three methods used. When food is exposed to intense direct heat, it gets a wonderful, smoky char on the exterior, while the interior remains deliciously juicy.

When preparing the charcoal, it is a good idea to build a two-level fire. For ease, use a barbecue chimney starter to light the coals. When the coals are white-hot, pour the charcoal into the basin of the barbecue, then spread the charcoal so that two-thirds of the coals are stacked about twice as high as the remaining one-third. This way, you can easily move whatever it is you are cooking from the hot side of the grill to the cooler side if it begins to burn before it's cooked through.

I use a lot of charcoal – about two full shoe boxes* – as it is important to achieve that intense heat. Light the charcoal and let it heat up until the coals are white-hot. To check if the coals are ready, hold your hand about 5cm (2in) above the cooking grate. If your hand becomes uncomfortably hot in 2 seconds, you're ready to start cooking.

I like to cook using flat skewers when cooking this way. Skewering meat, seafood, paneer and vegetables gives the finished dish that authentic tandoori restaurant look. You could also use a grill.

PREPARING THE BARBECUE FOR INDIRECT COOKING

This method is used for roasting and you will need a barbecue that has a tight-fitting lid. Fill the barbecue on one side only with about two shoe boxes full of charcoal*, leaving the other half empty. Light a few firelighters and pile in the charcoal. Let it heat until white-hot, then place the grill on top and whatever it is you are cooking over the side with no coals. Cover and cook. If you are barbecuing for a long period of time, you will need to throw a few handfuls of charcoal on the fire every 30 minutes or so.

PREPARING THE HOME TANDOOR FOR COOKING

Open the bottom vent completely and place a few firelighters in the tandoor opposite the vent. Pour in about two shoe boxes full of charcoal* and light, ensuring that you strategically stack as many pieces of charcoal as you can over the flames. It is important that your charcoal is as far away from the vent as possible so that air can flow freely.

Once the fire is burning nicely, place the lid on, leaving a crack open so that air can flow from the vent to the top. Close the bottom vent so that it is only one-third open. You can now relax with a beer or two for about an hour while it heats up.

To work properly, the clay walls of the oven need to be extremely hot and the tandoor needs to be at least 300°C (570°F). I usually cook my naans between 300°C (570°F) and 325°C (615°F) and meat, fish, poultry and vegetables at a higher temperature of around 400°C (750°F).

If you are cooking with a tandoor for the first time, be sure to read the manual first, and cure the clay walls before cooking anything. Tandoor cooking really does take some practice, so if you purchase a tandoor keep working on it until you get it right.

OVEN COOKING

Ovens vary, but I usually crank mine up to 200°C (400°F/Gas 6) and cook the meat on a wire rack near the top. To get that charred appearance and flavour, place the roasted meat under a hot grill (broiler) for about 2 minutes after cooking, just before serving.

*The amount of charcoal you use depends on the size of your barbecue. Refer to your owner's manual for the manufacturer's recommendations. The Thüros Kebab Grill (see page 343) shown in many of the photos in this section requires a lot less than larger kettle barbecues.

TANDOORI WHOLE CHICKEN
SERVES 4

Over the years, this tandoori whole roast chicken has been one of my family's favourite Sunday night dinners. It is so easy to make and tastes amazing. The recipe calls for tandoori masala, which is commercially available, but I hope you try my homemade tandoori masala on page 168.

This is my recipe for cooking in the oven. If you prefer a smokier flavour, cook it on the barbecue using the indirect cooking method (see page 255). Cooking times may vary. Just aim to get your barbecue to about 250°C (480°F). You could also use smoked instead of regular paprika.

PREP TIME: 10 MINS, PLUS
MARINATING TIME
COOKING TIME: 1 HOUR

2.5kg (5lb 8oz) whole free-range
    skinless chicken
Melted butter, for basting
Juice of 1–2 limes
Salt, to taste

FOR THE MARINADE
4 tbsp Greek yoghurt
2 tbsp garlic and ginger paste (see
    page 172)
2 tsp paprika
1 heaped tbsp tandoori masala (see
    page 168) (more or less to taste)

Make the marinade by mixing together all of the marinade ingredients. Rub about a quarter of the marinade inside the chicken. Make shallow incisions into the chicken breasts, legs and thighs and truss it tightly. (If you aren't familiar with how to truss a chicken, no worries. Just tie the legs together tightly with a piece of string. It won't win you any awards for presentation but it will help the chicken cook evenly.) Rub the remaining marinade all over the chicken, ensuring that all of the incisions are covered in marinade. Allow to marinate in the fridge for 3–48 hours.

Remove the chicken from the fridge a good half an hour before cooking. When ready to cook, preheat the oven to its highest setting. Once the oven is hot, place the chicken in a roasting pan and roast for 40 minutes to 1 hour, basting regularly with the melted butter and cooking juices. Your chicken is ready when the juices run clear when you prick the thigh with a knife. If using a meat thermometer, aim for 75°C (165°F).

Squeeze over the lime juice and season with salt.

TANDOORI CHICKEN TIKKA

SERVES 4 OR MORE AS PART OF A MULTI-COURSE MEAL

Red food colouring powder is often added to chicken tikka to give it the appearance of being spicy hot. I often add red food colouring to my chicken tikka but it doesn't add any flavour and can be left out. Beetroot powder is often used as a substitute but it doesn't achieve that bright red curry-house look.

This recipe is amazing on its own but you could also use it in curries such as chicken tikka masala (see page 186) and chicken chilli garlic (page 208). I usually cook these chicken pieces (tikka) on skewers over a hot charcoal fire, but you could also cook them on a rack in the oven at about 200°C (400°F/Gas 6).

PREP TIME: 15 MINS, PLUS
    MARINATING TIME
COOKING TIME: 15 MINS

1kg (2lb 3oz) skinless, boneless
    chicken breasts, cut into bite-size
    pieces (tikka)
Juice of 2 lemons
Salt, to taste
3 tbsp garlic and ginger paste (see
    page 172)
Red food colouring powder (optional)

FOR THE MARINADE
200g (¾ cup) Greek yoghurt,
    whisked
1 tbsp ground cumin
1 tbsp ground coriander
1 tbsp garam masala (see page 167)
1 tbsp tandoori masala (see page 168)
1 tsp amchoor (dried mango powder)
1 tsp ground turmeric
1 tsp paprika or chilli powder
2 fresh green chillies, finely chopped
    or green chilli paste (see page 172)
3 tbsp finely grated Parmesan cheese
20g coriander (cilantro) leaves, finely
    chopped
1 tsp salt
1 tbsp freshly ground black pepper

Place the chicken pieces (tikka) in a large bowl, squeeze the lemon juice over them and sprinkle with a little salt. Stir in the garlic and ginger paste and some red food colouring if you want the authentic chicken tikka colour. Mix it all up really well and set aside while you make the marinade.

Place the marinade ingredients in a bowl and mix with your hands until good and smooth. Cover the chicken pieces with the marinade, ensuring they are completely coated. Cover and marinate in the fridge for 6–48 hours – the longer the better.

When ready to cook, prepare the barbecue for direct cooking (see page 255). When the coals are white-hot, thread the chicken tikka onto skewers and place over the coals, turning occasionally until the chicken is cooked through and the edges are blackened. You can also do this on a grill.

Season with salt and serve hot, or use in your curries.

TIPS
- When grilling skewered chicken, the raw pieces will move around a lot when turned. I suggest leaving to cook through on one side before turning. The meat will expand as it cooks and you will not experience as much annoying movement on the skewers.
- Try to leave a little space between each piece of chicken on the skewer so that it cooks evenly. For better presentation, you could move the meat chunks closer together, once cooked through, if serving on the skewers.

From top: Tandoori chicken tikka (above); chicken soola kebabs (page 261); and tandoori murgh malai tikka (page 260)

TANDOORI MURGH MALAI TIKKA

SERVES 4 OR MORE AS PART OF A MULTI-COURSE MEAL

I've learned so much from my friend Chef Palash Mitra over the past few years. This recipe is one I simply had to share with you. The tender chunks of chicken are awesome served on their own with a tasty raita. It is equally as good added to a curry, such as the butter chicken (see page 79).

Before I watched Palash prepare this marinade, I used to simply throw my marinades together in a couple of minutes. Palash took his time and blended the ingredients together by hand into a smooth emulsion. It is obvious he loves what he does, and his meticulous style and attention to detail really do make a big difference. These kebabs are featured in the photograph on page 258.

PREP TIME: 15 MINS, PLUS MARINATING TIME
COOKING TIME: 15 MINS

1kg (2lb 3oz) skinless chicken thighs, boned and diced

FOR THE FIRST MARINADE
5 tbsp rapeseed (canola) oil
2 tbsp garlic and ginger paste (see page 172)
1½ tsp salt
1½ tsp ground turmeric
2–4 green bird's eye chillies, finely chopped
2 tsp lemon juice
Pinch of saffron threads

FOR THE SECOND MARINADE
2 tbsp ghee
2 tsp royal (black) cumin seeds
125ml (½ cup) double (heavy) cream
3 tbsp cream cheese
4 tbsp finely chopped coriander (cilantro)
100g (scant ½ cup) Greek yoghurt

To make the first marinade, pour the oil into a deep tray and add the garlic and ginger paste, salt, turmeric, chopped chillies, lemon juice and saffron. Add the chicken pieces and stir well to combine. Set aside for up to 20 minutes while you make the second marinade.

For the second marinade, heat the ghee in a small pan over a low heat, add the royal (black) cumin seeds and let them splutter. Cool the ghee to room temperature, pour it over the chicken and mix well.

Push the chicken with its marinade to one side of the tray and spoon in the cream, cream cheese, chopped coriander (cilantro) and yoghurt to the other side of the tray.

Work these ingredients together with your hands until they are completely emulsified. This takes about 5 minutes. Mix into the chicken, cover and marinate in the fridge for 24 hours.

To cook the chicken, thread the pieces onto skewers and grill, using the direct heat method (see page 255), until lightly charred on the underside. Flip over the chicken skewers and grill the other side until cooked through. Alternately, bake in the oven at 200°C (400°F/Gas 6) for 6–8 minutes, or until cooked through.

NOTE
Palash adds 1 teaspoon of sandalwood powder to his marinade. It isn't easy to find but if you come across some, give it a go!

CHICKEN SOOLA KEBABS
SERVES 4 OR MORE AS PART OF A MULTI-COURSE MEAL

The soola marinade in this recipe is popular not just for chicken but red meat and vegetables too. Red meat such as venison, beef and lamb can be marinated for three days and the end result is so good. With chicken, duck and other poultry and feathered game, I usually marinate the meat for 24–48 hours. Seafood only needs about 20 minutes. These kebabs are pictured on page 258. I like to serve them with a simple green salad and coriander, garlic and chilli raita (page 339).

For me, mustard oil is a must with this recipe. You could substitute rapeseed (canola) oil but you will get a different flavour.

PREP TIME: 15 MINS, PLUS
MARINATING TIME
COOKING TIME: 15 MINS

8 skinless, boneless chicken breasts, cut into bite-size pieces (tikka)
Juice of 2 limes
1 tsp chaat masala (see page 168)
Salt and freshly ground black pepper, to taste

FOR THE MARINADE
1 tbsp cloves
Seeds from 6 black cardamom pods
2 tbsp black peppercorns
1 tbsp fennel seeds
1 tbsp cumin seeds
1 tbsp coriander seeds
3 tbsp ghee
2 tbsp mustard oil
1 large onion, finely chopped
8 garlic cloves, finely chopped
2 large bunches of coriander (cilantro), leaves only
100g (scant ½ cup) plain yoghurt

To make the marinade, heat a frying pan over a medium heat. Throw in the cloves, cardamom seeds, peppercorns and the fennel, cumin and coriander seeds, and move them around in the pan so that they roast evenly. When they become warm and fragrant, tip onto a plate, allow to cool a little, then grind them into a powder using a spice grinder or pestle and mortar.

Heat the ghee and mustard oil together in the frying pan. Add the onion and fry until translucent and soft, but not browned. Add the garlic and fry for a further minute, then remove from the heat and allow to cool.

Transfer to a food processor with the ground spices, coriander (cilantro) leaves and 1 teaspoon of salt, and blend until smooth. Transfer to a bowl, add the yoghurt and whisk together. Add the chicken pieces and stir to coat, then cover and marinate in the fridge for 3–48 hours – the longer the better.

When ready to cook, light the barbecue using the direct cooking method (see page 255). Thread the chicken pieces onto skewers and cook, turning them until nicely charred on the exterior and cooked through. Transfer to a warm plate and squeeze the lime juice over the top. Sprinkle with the chaat masala and season with salt and black pepper.

TANDOORI BEER CAN CHICKEN

SERVES 4 OR MORE AS PART OF A MULTI-COURSE MEAL

This is one you are very unlikely to find at a curry house but it was too good to leave out of the book. I've been making beer can chicken for many years and this Indian-inspired version is one of my current favourites. You could also easily make this in a conventional oven – see my tip below.

PREP TIME: 10 MINS, PLUS
    MARINATING TIME
COOKING TIME: 1–1½ HOURS

100ml (scant ½ cup) rapeseed
    (canola) oil
1 x 440ml (15fl oz) can of your
    favourite beer or lager
900g (2lb) whole chicken

FOR THE MARINADE
2 tbsp garlic and ginger paste (see
    page 172)
1 tbsp paprika
1 tsp ground cumin
1 tsp dried oregano
½ tsp red chilli powder
1 tsp ground turmeric
Small bunch of coriander (cilantro),
    blended with a little water
Salt and freshly ground black pepper,
    to taste

Blend all the marinade ingredients into a paste or pound them using a pestle and mortar.

Slowly drizzle the rapeseed (canola) oil into the paste, whisking continuously until you have a smooth emulsion. Cover the chicken inside and out with the marinade and allow to marinate for 8 hours or overnight. I carefully rub about half of the marinade under the skin but don't worry if you can't be bothered.

When ready to cook, set up the barbecue for indirect cooking (see page 255). Drink half the can of beer or lager and add 1 teaspoon of marinade from the chicken dish to the can. The beer might foam up when you add the marinade but that isn't a problem.

When your barbecue is good and hot you're ready to cook. If you have a thermometer, aim for a cooking temperature of 190–200°C (375–390°F). Place the chicken on the beer can and stand it directly on the barbecue on the side with no coals. Cover and cook for about 1–1¼ hours until the chicken is cooked through and the juices run clear when stuck with a knife in the thigh. You can't be too careful with chicken so if you have a meat thermometer, check that your chicken is 82°C (180°F).

When cooked through, transfer to a serving plate and cover with foil to sit for about 10 minutes before serving.

TIP
You can also cook the chicken in the oven. Preheat the oven to 230°C (450°F/Gas 8). Place the chicken on a half-full beer can in a roasting tray and roast for 20 minutes. Reduce the heat to 200°C (400°F/Gas 6) and continue to roast until cooked through and the juices run clear, about another 30 minutes. Season with salt and black pepper. Let the chicken rest for about 10 minutes before carving.

SHAWARMA KEBABS

SERVES 4–6

You've got to love a good shawarma kebab! Perfectly marinated pieces of meat that are nice and crisp on the exterior and juicy and tender in the centre. I'm getting hungry just writing about it. At UK takeaways, beef, chicken and lamb are marinated and then placed on a rotating spit. The meat is shaved off with a large electric knife and then served in fresh naans topped with salad, hot sauce and/or yoghurt dressing.

I don't have a large spit, nor the need to cook as much meat as takeaways do, so I decided to downsize this recipe a bit. You will need metal skewers and a good barbecue for best results. I like to add vegetables like red onions and (bell) peppers to the skewers – they are delicious served with the marinated, grilled meat.

PREP TIME: 15 MINS, PLUS
   FREEZING AND MARINATING
COOKING TIME: 15 MINS

6 large chicken breasts
Red and green chillies
Red onion and green and/or yellow
   (bell) peppers, chopped
Naans, buns or tortillas, to serve
Sauces of your choice, to serve

FOR THE MARINADE
5 tbsp olive oil
2 tbsp garlic and ginger paste (see
   page 172)
1 tbsp ground cumin
1 tbsp ground coriander
1 tsp ground allspice
½ tsp ground turmeric
½ tsp ground cinnamon
1 tbsp paprika
Salt and freshly ground black pepper,
   to taste

Place the chicken breasts in the freezer for 30 minutes – this will help you slice them. Remove from the freezer and slice into thin discs.

Place all the marinade ingredients in a bowl and mix well. Add your chicken discs to the marinade and ensure it is all nicely coated. Marinate for 30 minutes–24 hours.

When ready to cook, light your charcoal using the direct cooking method (see page 255) and wait until white-hot.

In the meantime, skewer the marinated chicken discs on the metal skewers so that they are pressed tightly together. I like to include some chillies, red onions and peppers for colour.

Place the skewers over the heat and rotate often until charred on the outside and cooked through – about 15 minutes. Remove the meat and vegetables and chop the meat into small pieces. Serve the meat and vegetables on their own or wrapped in fresh naans, buns or tortillas with your sauces of choice.

From left: Shawarma kebab (above); mean and green chicken tikka kebab (page 267); shawarma kebab; and tandoori lamb tikka (see page 286)

TANDOORI METHI CHICKEN TIKKA
SERVES 4 OR MORE AS PART OF A MULTI-COURSE MEAL

Like most of the recipes in this book, this methi chicken tikka is a mix of about ten different recipes I've seen prepared. I took the best ingredients and ideas from each and came up with this version that's a big favourite at our family barbecues.

PREP TIME: 15 MINS, PLUS
MARINATING TIME
COOKING TIME: 10 MINS

Juice of 2 lemons
800g (1lb 12oz) skinless chicken
thighs or breasts, cut into 7.5cm
(3in) pieces
1 tbsp garlic and ginger paste (see
page 172)
50g (3½ tbsp) unsalted butter, melted
Salt, to taste
Raita and naan breads, to serve

FOR THE MARINADE
2 large bunches (about 100g/3½ oz)
of fresh fenugreek leaves*
3 tbsp rapeseed (canola) oil or
mustard oil
1 tbsp cumin seeds
250g (1 cup) Greek yoghurt
2 tbsp garlic and ginger paste (see
page 172)
5 tbsp finely chopped coriander
(cilantro) leaves
1 tbsp green chilli paste (see page 172)
1 tbsp red chilli powder
1 tbsp garam masala (see page 167)
1 tbsp gram (chickpea) flour
3 tbsp cream cheese
1 tbsp rapeseed (canola) oil

*Fresh fenugreek is best, but see page
200 if you would like to use dried or
alternative ingredients.

Squeeze the lemon juice over the chicken and rub in 1 tablespoon of the garlic and ginger paste. Set aside while you make the marinade.

Chop up your fresh fenugreek leaves and thin stalks finely. Blanch in a pot of boiling water for about 30 seconds. Drain and squeeze out the excess moisture and set aside to cool slightly. Using a food processor or blender, blend the fenugreek leaves until you have a smooth purée. You may need to add a little fresh water to help it blend. Set aside.

Now heat the oil in a large frying pan over a medium–high heat until visibly hot. If using mustard oil, it will give off a strong, nutty aroma. Throw in the cumin seeds. When they begin to pop, add the fenugreek purée you prepared. Stir it into the oil and fry for about 30 seconds, then set aside to cool.

Put the yoghurt in a large bowl and whisk it until smooth. Add the rest of the garlic and ginger paste, the coriander (cilantro), chilli paste, red chilli powder, garam masala, gram (chickpea) flour, cream cheese and rapeseed (canola) oil. Work this together with your hands until all of the ingredients become a smooth emulsion. Add the cooled fenugreek mixture to this and continue to work it into a smooth marinade.

Cover the chicken and marinate for 3–24 hours. When ready to cook, light about two shoe boxes full of charcoal on the barbecue. When the charcoal is white-hot, you're ready to cook.

Skewer your chicken, leaving a small space between each piece, and grill on one side until nicely charred. Flip the skewers over and continue grilling until cooked through – it will take about 10 minutes.

Just before the meat is cooked, baste it with the melted butter. Remove to a warm plate and let rest for about 5 minutes before serving. Check the seasoning and serve with your favourite raita and naans.

NOTE
You can also roast the chicken in the oven at 200°C (400°F/Gas 6) until cooked through. Once cooked, placing the meat under a grill (broiler) will give a nice charred finish.

MEAN AND GREEN CHICKEN TIKKA KEBABS

SERVES 4 OR MORE AS PART OF A MULTI-COURSE MEAL

I love the deep green colour of these kebabs and the flavour is out of this world. Just look at the photograph on page 264! Be sure to keep some of the marinade aside to brush over the chicken pieces just before they're cooked through. You can also cook these on a grill (broiler) if the barbecue isn't set up, or even in the oven if you wish. See the note below.

PREP TIME: 15 MINS, PLUS
    MARINATING TIME
COOKING TIME: 20 MINS

800g (1lb 12oz) skinless chicken
    breast, cut into bite-size pieces

FOR THE MARINADE
4 tbsp rapeseed (canola) oil
1 onion, finely chopped
8 green chillies, finely chopped (use
    less if you don't like it very hot)
1 tbsp ground cumin
½ tsp ground turmeric
3 large handfuls of baby spinach
    leaves
3 tbsp garlic and ginger paste (see
    page 172)
Juice of 2 lemons
10 cashew nuts
100g (3½ oz) butter
15 mint leaves
Large bunch of coriander (cilantro)
3 tbsp thick Greek yoghurt
1 tbsp garam masala (see page 167)
    (or more or less to taste)
Salt and freshly ground black pepper,
    to taste

To make the marinade, heat the oil in a large pan over a medium–high heat. Tip in the onion and green chillies and sizzle until the onion is translucent and soft, about 5 minutes. Add the cumin and turmeric and stir it all up. Stir the spinach and the garlic and ginger paste into the onion. As you cook, the spinach will wilt. Remove from the heat and allow to cool for a few minutes.

In a blender or food processor, blend the spinach and onion mixture with the lemon juice, cashew nuts, butter, mint and coriander (cilantro) – you might need to add a drop of water. Whisk the mixture in a bowl with the yoghurt until smooth and creamy, add the garam masala and season with salt and black pepper.

Remove about 250ml (1 cup) of the marinade and set aside for later. Pour the remaining marinade over the chicken pieces and allow to marinate for 3–48 hours.

When ready to cook, light your charcoal using the direct cooking method (see page 255). Skewer the chicken pieces (tikka), leaving a small space between each piece, and place over the hot coals. Allow the meat to cook and get a good char on the underside before turning. Flip the skewers over and cook through. You can rotate the skewers from time to time for more even cooking.

Just before serving, baste with the marinade you set aside earlier.

NOTE

You can also roast the chicken in the oven at 200°C (400°F/Gas 6) until cooked through. Once cooked, placing the meat under a grill (broiler) will give a nice charred finish.

PIRI PIRI CHICKEN

SERVES 4 OR MORE AS PART OF A MULTI-COURSE MEAL

Piri piri dishes are now popular all over the world. Originally a Portuguese recipe that is believed to have been first made in the former Portuguese colony of Mozambique, piri piri was introduced to the native population of Goa during the Portuguese occupation. The sauce was made from red sweet (bell) peppers, paprika and red piri piri chillies, but many other varieties are used now.

It is believed that the red piri piri sauce was the inspiration behind chicken cafreal, which is made with similar ingredients but with additional green chillies, coriander (cilantro) and mint to make a green sauce. So it's little wonder that this spicy Portuguese dish that was loved by the Goan population is now finding its way on to many Indian restaurant menus. Double the sauce recipe if you like a lot of sauce.

PREP TIME: 15 MINS, PLUS
    MARINATING AND CHILLING
    TIME
COOKING TIME: 1–1¼ HOURS

1.5kg (3lb 5oz) chicken thighs, bone-
    in and skin left on
Salt and freshly ground black pepper,
    to taste
1 tbsp smoked or regular paprika
Lime slices, to serve

FOR THE PIRI PIRI SAUCE
5 tbsp rapeseed (canola) oil
½ onion, finely chopped
1 red (bell) pepper, roughly chopped
8 garlic cloves, peeled
4 green or red chillies, roughly
    chopped
1 tbsp smoked or regular paprika
1 tbsp cayenne pepper (more or less to
    taste)
1 tsp freshly ground black pepper
1 tbsp dried chilli (hot pepper) flakes
Salt, to taste
3 tbsp lemon juice
70ml (¼ cup) white wine vinegar

To make the sauce, heat the oil in a saucepan over a medium–high heat and add the onion and red (bell) pepper. Fry until the onion is translucent and soft (about 5 minutes), then add the garlic and chillies. Fry for a further minute or so, then add the paprika, the cayenne chilli powder, black pepper and chilli (hot pepper) flakes and season with salt.

Add the lemon juice and vinegar and simmer for about 5 minutes. Allow to cool slightly, then blend until very smooth and place this marinade in the fridge for about 30 minutes.

When ready to prepare your chicken, season the thighs generously with salt and pepper and the paprika and pour over half of the piri piri sauce. Stir it all up so that the chicken is nicely coated and marinate in the fridge for no more than 3 hours.

When ready to cook, heat the oven to its highest temperature. Remove as much of the marinade as you can and stir it into the marinade you set aside. Place the chicken in a roasting tray and cook for 40 minutes–1 hour until the chicken is crisp and cooked through.

Transfer the chicken to a warm serving plate, then whisk the retained marinade into the cooking juices in the tray. Bring to a rolling simmer. You can either pour this over the chicken or serve it like a gravy at the table.

Serve the chicken drizzled with the sauce and topped with slices of lime. I love this dish cooked using the indirect cooking method (see page 255) on the barbecue.

SPICY GOURMET CHICKEN KEBABS

SERVES 4 OR MORE AS PART OF A MULTI-COURSE MEAL

This one is a real showpiece. I wouldn't exactly call it easy cooking, but it's well worth the effort. You want to freeze the chicken breasts for about 30 minutes before slicing as this will make slicing much easier. I usually cook this in my tandoor oven, which always makes the chicken taste amazing. To do this, I skewer a small raw onion or shallot between each kebab and at both ends of the skewer to help keep the stuffing in.

PREP TIME: 30 MINS, PLUS
    OPTIONAL MARINATING TIME
COOKING TIME: 20 MINS

2 large boneless, skinless chicken
    breasts, placed in the freezer for
    30 minutes
3 tbsp melted ghee or butter, for
    basting

FOR THE FIRST MARINADE

3 tbsp garlic and ginger paste (see
    page 172)
Juice of 1 lemon
½ tsp salt

FOR THE SECOND MARINADE

200g (¾ cup) Greek yoghurt
1 tbsp gram (chickpea) flour
1 tbsp Kashmiri chilli powder (more
    or less to taste)
1 tsp ground turmeric
1 tsp chaat masala (see page 168)
2 tsp garam masala (see page 167) or
    tandoori masala (see page 168)
1½ tsp amchoor (dried mango
    powder)
2 tbsp mustard oil or rapeseed
    (canola) oil
Salt, to taste

FOR THE STUFFING

1 tbsp rapeseed (canola) oil
2 shallots, finely chopped
2 tbsp garlic and ginger paste (see
    page 172)
3 green bird's eye chillies, finely
    chopped or blended to a paste
1 tsp ground cumin
1 tsp ground turmeric
120g (4oz) minced (ground) chicken
2 tbsp Parmesan cheese (finely
    grated)
2 tbsp finely chopped coriander
    (cilantro)
1 tbsp cider or white wine vinegar
Salt and freshly ground black pepper,
    to taste

Place one of the chicken breasts on a clean surface and place one hand over the top – this will make slicing easier. Using a sharp knife, slice horizontally into four very thin chicken steaks. If you are lacking in knife skills, no worries: aim for three steaks per breast. Using a meat mallet or something that will work as one (like a heavy cup), pound the steaks until they are about 2mm thick. They should be really thin but not falling apart.

Place the pounded chicken steaks in a mixing bowl and mix well with all of the first marinade ingredients. Set aside for about 10 minutes while you make the second marinade.

Whisk all the second marinade ingredients together in a bowl until creamy smooth. Set aside.

To make the stuffing, heat the oil in a large frying pan over a medium heat and fry the shallots for about 5 minutes, or until soft and translucent. Add the garlic and ginger paste, green chillies, cumin and turmeric and stir it all up to combine. Continue cooking for about 45 seconds, then add the minced chicken. Cook for about 5 minutes, or until completely cooked through, then stir in the Parmesan, coriander (cilantro) and vinegar. Season with salt and black pepper. Transfer the stuffing to a bowl to cool.

Lay one of the chicken breast steaks lengthways in front of you. Place 2–3 tablespoons of the stuffing on one end and roll it up tightly lengthways. Secure with a toothpick or two and repeat with the remaining steaks. Place these rolled bundles of deliciousness into the second marinade so that they are completely covered in sauce. You could cook these now or let them sit for a few hours or overnight for best results.

When ready to cook, heat the barbecue for direct cooking (see page 255). Pick up the chicken rolls and remove as much marinade as possible. Retain the excess marinade. Skewer the chicken pieces though the centre of the mince filling. It is important that each of the chicken bundles is pressed together on the skewer to help keep the stuffing in. I usually put 3 or 4 on one skewer.

Cook over the coals for about 5 minutes until the underside is cooked through and lightly charred. Then turn the skewers over to cook the other side for about 5 more minutes. The kebabs are ready when the exterior is nicely charred and the stuffing is sizzling hot. Baste with a little melted ghee or butter before serving.

Place the retained marinade into a saucepan and bring to a simmer over a medium heat. If you don't have a lot left, you could stir in some more yoghurt. Once the sauce has come to a simmer, let it cook for a couple of minutes to cook off the raw chicken juices and then try it. This sauce is delicious served with the chicken, so adjust the flavours to your liking by adding more spices, salt and/or yoghurt.

HONEY ROAST WHOLE QUAILS
SERVES 4 OR MORE AS PART OF A MULTI-COURSE MEAL

Free-range quails have stronger skin than barn-reared birds, so source those if you can. This is my version of a unique Indian recipe that I learned on a trip to Mumbai. I was told it stems back to the days of the British Raj when wild quails or similar would be used on hunting days, though the recipe was presumably less spicy. It's rare to cook poultry with the skin on in Indian cooking, but I'm sure you'll agree, it's worth every calorie. The quails are spicy, sweet, sour and savoury – all of my favourite taste sensations in one dish! I like to serve this with rice and mixed vegetable pickle (see page 329) or kachumber salad (see page 326) and a good chutney or hot sauce.

PREP TIME: 30 MINS
COOKING TIME: 40 MINS

4 free-range quails, skin on

FOR THE FIRST MARINADE
Juice of 2 lemons
2 tsp garlic and ginger paste (see page 172)
1 tbsp Kashmiri chilli powder
70ml (¼ cup) rapeseed (canola) oil

FOR THE SECOND MARINADE
1 quantity of fried onion paste using yoghurt (see page 173)
Seeds of 8 green cardamom pods
2 tbsp garlic and ginger paste (see page 172)
3 green bird's eye chillies, minced to a paste
1 tsp ground cumin
1 tsp ground coriander
1 tsp garam masala (see page 167)
1 tsp freshly ground black pepper
1 tsp salt
250g (1 cup) Greek yoghurt

FOR BASTING
125ml (½ cup) clear honey
4 tbsp melted ghee
Flaky salt, to taste

Carefully move a finger between the skin and meat of the quails to separate (but not remove) the skin from the meat. Using a small knife, try to make slits in the meat under the skin in a few places.

Mix all the first marinade ingredients together in a bowl and divide equally under the skin of the birds. If there is any remaining, you can rub it onto the skin of the quails. Marinate for about 20 minutes while you make the second marinade.

Whisk all the second marinade ingredients together in a bowl and rub under the skin too, and also inside the carcasses. Again, if there is any left over, rub it over the skin.

Set up the barbecue for indirect cooking (see page 255). When very hot (around 220°C/430°F), place the quails on the grill away from the burning coals and cook for 10 minutes. Swiftly transfer to a plate and cover the barbecue.

Spread the honey lightly all over the skin of the quails and leave for about 10 minutes to dry onto the skin (you don't have to use all the honey, just a thin coating will do). Brush the quails with the ghee and return to the barbecue to cook for about 20 minutes, or until the quails are cooked through and the skin is nicely browned and crispy. Season with flaky salt.

LAMB AND BEEF GOLA KEBABS
SERVES 4 OR MORE AS PART OF A MULTI-COURSE MEAL

Gola kebabs are usually pan-fried on wooden skewers so that they have a hole in the middle to look like a minced kebab should. Although the pan-frying method is very good, I like to cook them on the barbecue. What makes these kebabs really unique is the flavour of the allspice berries and mace. Unlike seekh kebabs, the meat is formed into small oblong balls, which makes them easier to thread onto the skewers. The finished kebabs can be eaten as they are with naans or rice and all the sauces and vegetables of your choice, or they could also be used as kofta in any of the curry house-style curries (see page 182–235). I have served them here with rice and kachumber salad (see page 326).

PREP TIME: 15 MINS
COOKING TIME: 15 MINS

12 dried allspice berries
2 x 2.5cm (1in) mace
1 tbsp cumin seeds
1 tbsp coriander seeds
10 black peppercorns
500g (1lb 2oz) lamb/beef mix
  (20% fat)
2 tbsp garlic and ginger paste (see
  page 172)
1 tsp salt, or to taste
3 green bird's eye chillies, finely
  chopped
3 tbsp finely chopped coriander
  (cilantro)
6 tbsp golden brown fried onions (see
  page 173 for homemade or use
  shop-bought)
3 tbsp melted ghee
Flaky sea salt, to taste

Heat a dry frying pan over a medium–high heat and add the allspice berries, mace, cumin seeds, coriander seeds and peppercorns. Roast until warm to the touch and fragrant but not yet smoking. Be sure to move the spices around in the pan so that they roast evenly. Transfer to a plate to cool slightly, then place in a spice grinder or pestle and mortar and grind to a fine powder.

Place the meat in a food processor with the prepared spice powder and the remaining ingredients except for the melted ghee, and blend until very finely minced. Prepare the barbecue for direct heat cooking.

Divide the meat into about 12 small oblong balls the size of limes. Oiling your hands lightly will help in doing this. Lightly oil four skewers and slide the balls onto them, leaving a little space between each. Be sure to squeeze the kebabs onto the skewers so that they remain firmly in place.

When the coals are white-hot and it is unbearably hot to hold your hand at cooking level for more than 2 seconds, you're ready to cook. Cook the kebabs on one side for about 5 minutes until they are beginning to brown on the underside. Then flip them over and cook the other side for another 5 minutes, or until nicely charred and cooked through. Baste the kebabs with the melted ghee as they cook and sprinkle with a little flaky salt. Remove the kebabs from the skewers and serve.

LAMB SEEKH KEBABS
SERVES 4 OR MORE AS PART OF A MULTI-COURSE MEAL

How can you not love a good grilled lamb seekh kebab? They're great on their own, simply dipped into a spicy raita or chutney or two, and even more delicious wrapped into a hot homemade naan with lots of crispy cold salad. They are especially good with the mint, coriander and mango chutney on page 335.

I've tried more complicated recipes but this is my go-to recipe. Use the best-quality minced meat you can find and the rest of the ingredients will bring out its natural flavour to perfection. Texture is important! If you have a good butcher, ask him or her to run the meat through their grinder three or four times. You can also achieve this texture at home with the method I describe below. It's what my friend Hasan Chaudhry calls 'lacing' and it really makes these kebabs special.

PREP TIME: 25 MINS
COOKING TIME: 15 MINS

1kg (2lb 3oz) lean minced (ground) lamb
1 egg
2 tbsp green chilli paste (see page 172)
2 onions, finely chopped
1 tbsp freshly roasted ground coriander (see page 163)
1 tbsp garam masala (see page 167)
Large bunch of coriander (cilantro), finely chopped
1 tsp salt

Place the minced lamb in a large bowl. Mix in the remaining ingredients and begin kneading the mixture with your hands. When all the ingredients are nicely mixed, begin pressing down on the meat, scraping it against the bottom of the bowl. The meat should streak against the bottom of the bowl, giving a 'lace' texture (see above), which will take about 5 minutes of kneading.

Form the mixture into meatballs the size of tennis balls. Slide a meatball onto a large, flat skewer and squeeze with a wet hand into a sausage shape around the skewer. Turn the skewer over and do the same, squeezing again with your hand to make it longer. Continue this process until you have a long kebab with visible finger marks that is securely on the skewer. Repeat with the rest of the meat mixture.

Heat the barbecue using the direct heat method (see page 255), then place the kebabs over the heat. Char well on one side, then flip them over and do the same on the other side until nicely blackened and cooked through. You could also pan-fry the kebabs, but I tend not to. It just isn't the same.

ALTERNATIVE MEAT MIXTURE
To make an eggless version of these kebabs, mix 800g (1lb 12oz) minced lamb with 200g (7oz) minced chicken. The chicken is stickier than the lamb and helps keep the meat on the skewer, just as the egg does.

GRILLED LAMB CHOPS
SERVES 4 OR MORE AS PART OF A MULTI-COURSE MEAL

Sometimes simplicity is best, and that is certainly the case with the famous lamb chops served at Lahore Kebab House in Shoreditch. After trying their lamb chops on a visit there, I arranged to meet Emran Siddique, one of the owners, to find out how they were prepared. I guess you could say I needed that recipe! These delicious marinated lamb chops are cooked over a flame grill, which produces a tasty char. Lahore uses only top-quality ingredients and marinates the lamb for three days. This makes all the difference. These lamb chops are out-of-this-world gorgeous! I recommend serving them with cucumber raita (see page 339) and lime wedges.

PREP TIME: 15 MINS, PLUS
   MARINATING TIME
COOKING TIME: 15 MINS

8–10 lamb chops on the bone, with most surface fat removed
Salt and freshly ground black pepper, to taste
Coriander (cilantro), to serve

FOR THE MARINADE
1 tbsp rapeseed (canola) oil
1 tbsp green chilli paste (see page 172)
2 tbsp garlic and ginger paste (see page 172)
1 tbsp garam masala (see page 167)
½ tsp ground turmeric
1 tsp chilli powder
Juice of 1 lemon
100g (scant ½ cup) Greek yoghurt

Mix all of the marinade ingredients up to and including the lemon juice together in a large glass or ceramic bowl. Add the lamb chops and massage the marinade into the meat. Let this stand for about 20 minutes.

Whisk the yoghurt until nice and creamy, then pour it over the meat, massaging it right into the flesh, ensuring every piece is coated. As you massage the yoghurt into the meat, it will take on the colours of the spices in the marinade. Marinate the meat for 24–72 hours. (You could marinate for a shorter time, but the longer the better.)

When ready to cook, set up the barbecue for direct heat cooking (see page 255), until the coals are extremely hot. Grill each lamb chop until nicely charred underneath, then flip over and do the same on the other side. When nicely blackened, remove from the heat to rest for about 5 minutes. Season with salt and black pepper and serve garnished with coriander (cilantro).

NOTE
The chargrilled exterior of these lamb chops is one of the things that makes them so delicious. I don't recommend pan-frying.

LAMB CHOPS WITH LEMON ANCHOVY BUTTER

SERVES 4 OR MORE AS PART OF A MULTI-COURSE MEAL

The flavour and aroma of smoky lamb chops covered in lemon and anchovy butter is to die for. I make this recipe all the time during barbecue season and I think you might do the same once you've tried these chops. The salty flavour of the anchovies and tart lemon goes so well with the lamb.

PREP TIME: 15 MINS, PLUS
MARINATING TIME
COOKING TIME: 8 MINS

FOR THE LEMON ANCHOVY
BUTTER
40g (3 tbsp) unsalted butter
8–10 anchovy fillets, crushed to a
paste
Juice of 1 lemon

FOR THE LAMB CHOPS
2 tbsp garlic and ginger paste (see
page 172)
1 tsp salt
8 lamb chops on the bone
1 tsp amchoor (dried mango powder)
2 tbsp mustard oil
2 tbsp crème fraîche
2 tsp white wine vinegar
2 green chillies, deseeded and finely
chopped
Large handful of coriander (cilantro)
stalks, finely chopped
Small handful of mint leaves, finely
chopped
1 tsp garam masala (see page 167)
1 tsp sugar
1 tsp chilli powder
A few drops of rose water
A few drops of Himalayan screwpine
water (optional; available online
and in Asian food shops)

Place the butter in a bowl and leave in a warm place for about 10 minutes. Then whisk it until smooth. Add the anchovies and lemon juice and fold it all together. Keep chilled.

Rub the garlic and ginger paste and salt into the lamb chops and leave for 10 minutes.

Mix all the remaining ingredients together in a non-metallic bowl. Add the lamb chops to the bowl and rub the marinade into the meat well. Leave for 30 minutes–48 hours.

When ready to cook, fire up the barbecue using the direct grilling method (see page 255) and place the lamb chops on the grill. Grill for about 8 minutes, turning only once, or until the exterior is crispy and blackened and medium rare in the centre. (Alternatively, you could sear them in a hot frying pan with a little oil. About 2 minutes per side should get them nicely charred. Then turn regularly until cooked to your preferred doneness.)

Let rest on a warmed plate for a few minutes, then place the chargrilled lamb chops on warm plates, top with the lemon anchovy butter and serve.

FALL-APART HABANERO GRILLED RAAN

SERVES 6 OR MORE AS PART OF A MULTI-COURSE MEAL

I have experimented a lot with lamb raan recipes over the years, but this is my go-to recipe now, especially when cooking outdoors. Lamb raan simply doesn't get any better. You could do the initial cooking in your oven if you wish, but I like to cook the whole recipe first over indirect heat on the barbecue and then flame-grill over intense direct heat to finish. This is great served with a green salad and naans or chapattis. In the picture here I have served it with lemon wedges and grilled cauliflower.

PREP TIME: 20 MINS, PLUS
MARINATING TIME
COOKING TIME: 2 HOURS

1 leg of lamb, surface fat removed
5 garlic cloves, cut into thin slivers
3 tbsp melted ghee, for basting
Flaky sea salt, to taste

FOR THE MARINADE
1 red habanero chilli, plus extra if
   desired
5 tbsp crispy fried onions, homemade
   (see page 173) or shop-bought
3 green bird's eye chillies, roughly
   chopped
1 tbsp ground cumin
1 tbsp ground coriander
1 tbsp garam masala (see page 167) or
   tandoori masala (see page 168)
1 tbsp Kashmiri chilli powder
1 tbsp freshly ground black pepper
1 tbsp salt, plus extra to taste
2 tbsp white wine vinegar
4 tbsp lemon juice
4 tbsp garlic and ginger paste (see
   page 172)
500g (2 cups) Greek yoghurt

Place all of the marinade ingredients up to and including the garlic and ginger paste in a food processor or blender with about 5 tablespoons of the yoghurt and blend to a thick paste that is smooth, not grainy. Whisk this paste into the remaining yoghurt until creamy smooth. Set aside.

Make about eight deep slashes on each side of the leg of lamb; it should look mutilated, like roadkill! Take a sharp knife and make holes all over the meat and fill them with the garlic slivers. With this done, roll out a few large pieces of cling film (plastic wrap) and layer them in a baking dish. Place the lamb on top and pour the marinade over it. Rub the marinade all over the meat and into the slits.

Wrap the leg tightly with the cling film and allow to marinate for at least 3 hours or overnight – the longer the better. Sometimes I leave it to marinate for three days!

When ready to cook, set up the barbecue for indirect cooking (see page 255). You are aiming for a cooking temperature of 180°C (350°F/ Gas 4) and this can all be done in an oven if you wish. Unwrap the lamb and scrape off all the marinade. Transfer the marinade to a bowl and place in the fridge to be used later for the sauce. Place the lamb leg on the cooking tray and cover tightly with foil. Set it on the cooking grate and cook for 2–2½ hours, or until fall-apart tender. If cooking on a barbecue you will need to top up the coals from time to time to retain the heat.

Once the lamb is tender, remove it from the barbecue and add more charcoal for direct heat cooking. I usually add the equivalent of a couple of shoe boxes of lumpwood charcoal. The charcoal and cooking grate need to be flaming hot. Your fire is ready when it is unbearably uncomfortable to hold your hand just 5cm (2in) above the cooking grate. Now slam that leg right down on the grate and cook for about 5 minutes per side until nicely charred. Be sure to slather it with the melted ghee! Transfer to a warm platter to rest and season with flaky sea salt.

To make the sauce, pour the retained marinade into a small saucepan and place it on the cooking grate. Stir constantly until the sauce is heated through and serve alongside the lamb.

NARGISI KOFTA
(INDIAN SCOTCH EGG)
SERVES 4 OR MORE AS PART OF A MULTI-COURSE MEAL

These are excellent served outside, straight off the barbecue. You can prepare them indoors up to the end of the frying stage, then take them outside and cook over indirect heat (see page 255) on the barbecue. Like all of the tandoori recipes in this book, you can also cook them in the oven, as I have here. They are delicious served just as they are with a green salad and perhaps a good hot sauce.

Cook the hard-boiled eggs to your liking. For soft yolks, boil the eggs for no more than 7 minutes, and for hard yolks, 10–12 minutes. The meat is prepared exactly as the lamb seekh kebab recipe on page 277.

This is a great recipe for parties as most of the work can be done ahead of time. Even the frying can be done a good hour before guests arrive, so all you need to do is heat them up in the oven or on the barbecue.

PREP TIME: 15 MINS, PLUS
MARINATING TIME
COOKING TIME: 15 MINS

150g (5½ oz) seekh kebab minced
(ground) lamb (see page 277) per
egg
Hard-boiled eggs, 1 per person (see
cooking times above), peeled
Gram (chickpea) flour, for dusting
1 egg, beaten
Toasted breadcrumbs, for coating
Rapeseed (canola) oil, for frying

For each egg, roll out 150g (5½oz) minced lamb mixture between two layers of cling film (plastic wrap), so that it is about 5mm (¼in) thick, and flat. Remove the top layer of cling film and place a hard-boiled egg in the middle. Using the bottom sheet of cling film, bring the meat up and form it around the egg.

Dust in the gram (chickpea) flour, then coat in the beaten egg and roll in the breadcrumbs until fully coated. (This work can all be done ahead of time for ease. Just place the coated koftas on a plate, cover with cling film and store in the fridge.)

When ready to cook, pour about 5cm (2in) of oil into a wok and heat over a high heat. When a few breadcrumbs sizzle immediately when thrown in, it is ready. Lower a nargisi kofta into the oil and fry all over for about 3 minutes until nicely browned. Remove with a slotted spoon to a plate lined with paper towel and repeat until all the koftas are fried.

To finish, preheat the oven to 200°C (400°F/Gas 6) or prepare your barbecue for indirect cooking (see page 255). If refrigerated, remove the koftas from the fridge to come to room temperature. If oven cooking, place the fried koftas on a baking tray and roast in the oven for about 7 minutes. If using the barbecue, place the fried kofta on the grate over the side that has no coals and cover, cooking for about 7 minutes. The meat should already be cooked from the frying, so the oven or barbecue roasting will just warm them through.

TANDOORI LAMB TIKKA

SERVES 4 OR MORE AS PART OF A MULTI-COURSE MEAL

The marinade used in this recipe is good on any meat, not just lamb. The first time I made this I took it camping with my family. The meat had already been marinating for about 48 hours, but when we got there and I finally got my disaster of a tent put up, I was in no mood to start cooking. So we cooked the following evening, and I have to say that extra 24 hours of marinating really worked a treat! There is a lot of talk these days that meat doesn't benefit from excessively long marinating times. All I know is that meal was amazing and one we all still talk about. You can see a tandoori lamb tikka skewer pictured on page 264.

PREP TIME: 15 MINS, PLUS
    MARINATING TIME
COOKING TIME: 20 MINS

4 tbsp garlic and ginger paste (see page 172)
2 tbsp green chilli paste (see page 172)
800g (1lb 12oz) lamb leg meat, trimmed of fat and cut into cubes
Salad, raita and naan breads, to serve

FOR THE MARINADE
½ tsp salt (or to taste)
Juice of 2 limes
1 tbsp garam masala (see page 167)
1 tsp red chilli power
1 tbsp ground cumin
1 tsp ground coriander
1 tsp dried fenugreek leaves (kasoori methi)
1 tsp mustard oil
1 tsp English mustard
3 tbsp plain yoghurt
1 tbsp mint sauce

Rub the garlic and ginger and green chilli pastes into the meat and set aside for about 20 minutes.

Blend the marinade ingredients together until very smooth. Cover the lamb cubes with the marinade and allow to marinate for 3–72 hours – the longer the better.

When ready to cook, remove the meat from the marinade. Skewer the meat, leaving a little space between each piece so that it cooks evenly and the outside crisps right up. Heat the coals until very hot and white.

Grill the meat, turning regularly, for about 10 minutes, or until it is crisp and nicely browned on the outside. Don't worry too much about this. I am a rare-meat fan but have overcooked the lamb on occasion and it still comes out beautifully even when well done.

Serve as it is with a nice green salad and raita, or wrap it up in a homemade naan. The meat can also be used in any lamb curry.

BEEF BOTI KEBABS
SERVES 6 OR MORE AS PART OF A MULTI-COURSE MEAL

Here's one of my favourites, which I hope you find the time to try. Although the meat is usually cooked well done, as it is in this recipe, I like to build a really hot fire so that the meat chars quickly. Doing this, you will still have some pink juicy meat in the centre if medium-cooked sirloin is more to your liking.

PREP TIME: 15 MINS, PLUS
    MARINATING TIME
COOKING TIME: 15 MINS

900g (2lb) beef sirloin cut into 5cm
    (2in) cubes
3 tbsp melted ghee, for basting
Salt, to taste
Hot naans, salad, hot sauce and
    raitas, to serve

FOR THE MARINADE
1 tsp salt
1 tbsp Kashmiri chilli powder
1 tsp dried red chilli flakes
1 tsp ground turmeric
1½ tsp ground coriander
1½ tsp ground cumin
1 tsp garam masala (see page 167)
1½ tbsp amchoor (dried mango
    powder)
3 tbsp rapeseed (canola) oil
4 tbsp lemon or lime juice
3 tbsp garlic and ginger paste (see
    page 172) blended with 3 tbsp
    finely chopped onion
2 tbsp green chilli paste (see page
    172)
1 tbsp mint sauce
3 tbsp finely chopped coriander
    (cilantro)
200g (¾ cup) Greek yoghurt

Place all the marinade ingredients in a large mixing bowl and whisk to combine. Add the meat and mix well with your hands so that it is thoroughly coated in the marinade. Cover and leave to marinate for at least 30 minutes or overnight – the longer the better.

When ready to cook, set up the barbecue for direct heat cooking (see page 255). Skewer the meat, preferably on flat skewers if you have them, and place over the hot coals. Grill for about 5 minutes on one side, then turn the skewers over and grill for another 5 minutes, or until the exterior is charred. Be sure to brush the meat from time to time with the melted ghee. Season with salt and serve with hot naans, a salad, your hot sauce of choice and perhaps a raita or two.

TANDOORI LOBSTER
SERVES 2

If you love lobster like I do, nothing more needs to be said. Just look at it! You will need a sharp pair of kitchen scissors for removing the shells.

PREP TIME: 30 MINS, PLUS
    SEDATING THE LOBSTERS
COOKING TIME: 45 MINS

2 x 750g (1lb 10oz) live lobsters
2 tbsp ghee
1 tsp brown mustard seeds
20 fresh or frozen curry leaves
½ onion, very finely chopped
1 tbsp garlic paste*
1 tsp ground cumin
1 tsp chilli powder
1 tsp English mustard
2 tbsp plain yoghurt
150ml (generous ½ cup) double
    (heavy) cream
Pinch of saffron threads (optional)
Salt, to taste
4 tbsp grated Parmesan cheese
3 tbsp finely chopped coriander
    (cilantro)
Lemon or lime wedges, to serve

FOR THE LOBSTER STOCK
2 tbsp butter
Retained cracked claw shells with
    remaining meat
½ onion, finely chopped
2 Indian bay leaves (cassia leaves)
250ml (1 cup) dry white wine

*To make this, blend 1–2 cloves of
garlic with just enough water to make
a smooth paste.

Sedate the lobsters for 1 hour in the freezer before cooking. Transfer the lobsters from the freezer to a cutting board and firmly insert the tip of a sharp chef's knife into the cross on the back of the head, with the blade facing forward, and bring it down, slicing the head in half.

Cook your lobsters in a large pot of salty boiling water for no more than 4 minutes. Remove to cool. Remove the top of the shells from the tail and body with your scissors. Twist off the claws. Transfer the tail meat to a clean bowl and remove and discard the black and green innards from the body. Place the hollowed shells on a baking tray, cover and place them and the tail meat in the fridge.

Now crack open the claw shells (a messy job) and remove the meat from inside to another clean bowl. The small amount of meat you can't get at easily will help flavour the stock.

To make the stock, melt the butter in a large saucepan over a medium heat and add the retained cracked lobster claw shells. Stir the shells around in the hot butter for about 10 minutes, then add the onion and bay leaves. Pour in the wine and just enough water to cover. Simmer for about 20 minutes, then strain through a sieve into a clean bowl.

Preheat the oven to its highest setting or prepare your barbecue for indirect cooking (see page 255).

Melt the ghee in a pan over a high heat until bubbly hot and add the mustard seeds. When they begin to pop (after about 30 seconds), reduce the heat to medium and add the curry leaves. Add the onion and fry for about 5 minutes until translucent and soft but not browned. Now add the garlic paste, cumin, chilli powder and mustard, and stir to combine.

Pour in 150ml (generous ½ cup) of the lobster stock and turn up the heat to bring the mixture to a boil. Reduce this sauce by half, then whisk in the yoghurt, cream and saffron (if using). Simmer for another 5–10 minutes to thicken. Season with salt and set aside to cool slightly.

Pour the warm sauce over each bowl of lobster meat and spoon the mixture back into the shells. I usually place the meat from the two claws in the body and the tail meat in the tails. You may not be able to use all the sauce. Sprinkle with the Parmesan and transfer to the oven or barbecue for 4–5 minutes until the meat is just cooked through and hot. Watch closely so you don't overcook!

Transfer each to a hot plate, garnish with coriander (cilantro) and serve with lemon or lime wedges.

TANDOORI-STYLE KING PRAWNS
SERVES 4 OR MORE AS PART OF A MULTI-COURSE MEAL

These prawns (shrimp) are addictive. They are superb served on their own, dipped into a tasty raita, or added to a curry. That said, I think they are much too good to be thrown in a curry. I like to serve them drizzled with my honey mustard raita (see page 339), which goes so well with most seafood.

One of the spice blends used in the recipe is mace and ground cardamom powder, which is so simple to make: just grind equal amounts of mace and green cardamom seeds together into a powder. This delicate spice blend adds a subtle flavour that takes the tandoori prawns to a whole new level. The lemons you see in the photograph were charred on the grill. This not only looks great but helps draw the juice out of them when squeezed at the table.

PREP TIME: 10 MINS, PLUS
    MARINATING TIME
COOKING TIME: 10 MINS

500g (1lb 2oz) raw king prawns
    (jumbo shrimp), peeled and
    deveined with head and tail intact

FOR THE FIRST MARINADE
1 tbsp rapeseed (canola) oil
2 tsp garlic and ginger paste (see page
    172)
¼tsp ground turmeric
1 tsp salt
½ tsp ground white pepper

FOR THE SECOND MARINADE
2 tbsp Greek yoghurt
1 tbsp cream cheese
1 tbsp single (light) cream
1cm (½ in) piece of ginger, peeled and
    finely chopped
1 fresh green chilli, finely chopped
1 tbsp finely chopped coriander
    (cilantro)
1 tsp mace and cardamom powder
    (see above)
1 tsp salt
1 tsp garlic powder
1 tsp ajwain (carom) seeds

Prepare the barbecue for direct heat cooking (see page 255).

Mix the prawns (shrimp) with the ingredients for the first marinade and set aside. Combine all the ingredients for the second marinade and work them together with your hands until you have a smooth emulsion. Cover the prawns with this marinade and leave for about 20 minutes.

Thread the prawns onto skewers and place over the hot fire. (You can also cook them directly on a barbecue grill.) Cook, turning frequently, until lightly charred and cooked through.

TANDOORI WHOLE FISH
SERVES 2 OR MORE AS PART OF A MULTI-COURSE MEAL

I must make this recipe once a week in the summer. You only need to throw it on the barbecue for a few minutes and, voilà, you've got yourself a dinner that not only tastes great but looks amazing. My fishmonger gets wild sea bass and bream for me, which is a lot better than the farmed stuff. It's a little more expensive, but when you're making a fancy meal like this it's worth every penny.

PREP TIME: 10 MINS, PLUS
    MARINATING TIME
COOKING TIME: 15 MINS

2 whole bream or sea bass, cleaned
1 lemon, quartered

FOR THE MARINADE
1 tbsp garlic and ginger paste (see
    page 172)
4 tbsp white wine vinegar
1 tsp rapeseed (canola) oil
1 tsp chilli powder
2 tbsp tandoori masala (see page 168)
1 tsp garam masala (see page 167)
1½ tbsp plain yoghurt
Salt, to taste

Make shallow slits on each side of the fish. Put all of the marinade ingredients up to and including the yoghurt in a bowl and whisk to combine. Season with salt, then rub the marinade all over the fish, inside and out, and leave to marinate for about 30 minutes.

Meanwhile, prepare the barbecue for direct grilling (see page 255). Remove the fish from the marinade and place in a metal grill fish basket, or thread a couple of skewers through to hold it in place. Cook, turning regularly, until the skin is nicely charred and the fish is cooked through. Serve with a squeeze of lemon.

GRILLED STUFFED PANEER

SERVES 2–3 OR MORE AS PART OF A MULTI-COURSE MEAL

This stuffed paneer recipe is delicious fried, but I also like to cook it outdoors on skewers over the hot coals.
I usually marinate the paneer for about 2 hours or overnight, but I do this more for convenience than flavour.
Still, you will get a more intense flavour if you marinate the paneer for a while. If marinating, prick each piece
of paneer a few times with a fork to allow the marinade to really get into the cheese.

PREP TIME: 15 MINS
COOKING TIME: 10 MINS

400g paneer cheese, cut into 5cm
(2in) squares and 1cm (3/4in) thick,
or similar
Flaky sea salt, to taste

FOR THE MARINADE
4 tbsp Greek yoghurt
Juice of 1 lime
1 tsp ground turmeric
1 tbsp Kashmiri chilli powder
1 tbsp ground cumin
1/2 tsp salt
1 1/2 tbsp garlic and ginger paste (see
page 172)
2 tsp garam masala (see page 167)

FOR THE FILLING
3 tbsp Greek yoghurt
Large handful (1 cup) of mint leaves,
large stems removed
Large handful (1 cup) of coriander
(cilantro)
Large handful (1 cup) of baby spinach
leaves
5cm (2in) piece of ginger, peeled and
finely chopped
3 garlic cloves, smashed
3 green bird's eye chillies
1/2 tsp chaat masala (see page 168)
Juice of 1 lime
Salt, to taste

Whisk all the marinade ingredients together in a bowl until creamy
smooth. Prick the paneer with a fork and coat it with the marinade to
use immediately or marinate for a while in the fridge.

Set up the barbecue for direct heat cooking (see page 255). While it's
heating up, make the filling. Blend all the ingredients in a food processor
into a thick paste. Set aside.

The coals are ready when it is unbearably hot to hold your hand over
them for 2 seconds at cooking height. Skewer the paneer onto two or
three metal skewers, leaving a bit of space between each piece, and cook
over the coals on the grill, turning regularly for about 10 minutes, or until
the paneer has charred a brown colour all over.

Remove the paneer from the skewers. Spread the filling paste over half
of them and top with the other half to make a paneer sandwich. Season
with flaky salt and serve hot.

TIP
While you're marinating the paneer, you could also marinate some nice
vegetables, such as red onion or red (bell) pepper. Then skewer them with
the paneer. The additional vegetables look great and taste delicious served
with the paneer.

TANDOORI PANEER CHUKANDARI

SERVES 4 OR MORE AS PART OF A MULTI-COURSE MEAL

I was invited to the Radisson Blu Edwardian at Heathrow a few years back to try their new restaurant Annayu and write a review on my blog. The head chef at the time, Madhup Sinha, really went to town trying to impress, and impress he did. He has since moved on to become head chef of Global Street Food Kitchen and has been such a valuable source of information, with both recipes and techniques.

The evening of my visit, Madhup prepared about 15 different dishes for me. I didn't eat for two days after that! They were all spectacular, but this one really caught my eye; it was beautiful. I didn't want to ruin it by cutting into it, but of course I did. The good news is, it isn't difficult to make but don't tell anyone. Your guests will think you are some kind of master chef when you place this one in front of them.

PREP TIME: 15 MINS, PLUS
   MARINATING TIME
COOKING TIME: 1 HOUR

2kg (4lb 6oz) raw beetroot (beet), peeled
1 tsp fine sea salt
1 tsp ajwain (carom) seeds
1 tsp royal (black) cumin seeds
2 tbsp ground white pepper
1½ tbsp garlic powder
5 tbsp garam masala (see page 167)
700g (1lb 9oz) paneer cheese, cut into 7.5cm (3in) cubes or sliced 1cm (½ in) thick
350ml (1½ cups) balsamic vinegar
1½ tsp dried fenugreek leaves (kasoori methi)
1 tbsp tamarind concentrate
Sea salt
Chaat masala (see page 168), to serve

Preheat the oven to 200°C (400°F/Gas 6). Sprinkle the beetroot (beet) with sea salt and wrap in foil. Roast in the oven for about 45 minutes, or until the beetroot is very soft, like potatoes cooked for mash. Weigh out 1.5kg (3lb 5oz) cooled beetroot (reserve the rest) and blend to a smooth paste in a food processor. In a bowl, stir the ajwain (carom) seeds and cumin seeds, white pepper, garlic powder and garam masala into the beetroot paste.

Now add the paneer pieces and check for seasoning, adding a little more salt if needed. Stir gently to coat the paneer, cover and marinate in the fridge for 4 hours or overnight.

Put the reserved roasted beetroot through a juicer if you have one. If not, blend it and pass it through a fine sieve a few times to obtain the juice. Add the balsamic vinegar to the beetroot juice, tip into a pan and reduce by half over a medium heat. Keep warm (or reheat gently when ready to serve).

When ready to cook, preheat the oven to 180°C (350°F/Gas 4) or set up the barbecue for indirect cooking (see page 255). Stir the dried fenugreek leaves (kasoori methi) and tamarind pulp into the marinade, then remove the paneer and spread out in a single layer in a roasting tin if roasting in the oven, or place on a rack to barbecue. Roast or barbecue until the paneer feels soft, 5–10 minutes.

Immediately drizzle the hot beetroot and vinegar reduction over the paneer, sprinkle with some chaat masala and serve.

Top: Paneer shashlik (page 298)
Bottom: Tandoori paneer chukandari (above)

PANEER SHASHLIK
SERVES 4 OR MORE AS PART OF A MULTI-COURSE MEAL

These spicy paneer kebabs (pictured on page 297) are a real treat, with a crispy, charred crust on the exterior and a deliciously soft centre. If you're working ahead of time, you can marinate these early in the day and then simply skewer them up and grill just before serving. They are great served on their own or wrapped into hot homemade naans with the raita of your choice.

PREP TIME: 10 MINS, PLUS
   MARINATING TIME
COOKING TIME: 10 MINS

2 tbsp Greek yoghurt
1 tbsp garlic and ginger paste (see
   page 172)
1 tsp chilli powder
1 tsp ground cumin
1 tsp ground coriander
1 tsp mixed powder (see page 169)
1 tsp chaat masala (see page 168)
½ tsp amchoor (dried mango powder)
1 tbsp vegetable oil
Juice of 1 lemon
1 large red (bell) pepper, deseeded
   and cut into pieces
1 medium red onion, cut into pieces
300g (10½ oz) paneer cheese, cubed

Put the yoghurt, garlic and ginger paste, spices, amchoor, oil and lemon juice in a bowl and mix together by hand. Add the red (bell) pepper, onion and paneer to the marinade, stir to coat and leave to marinate for about 2 hours or overnight in the fridge.

When ready to cook, light the barbecue using the direct grilling method (see page 255). Thread the vegetables and paneer onto skewers and grill over direct heat for 8–10 minutes, turning regularly until the middle of the paneer is hot and soft.

You can serve these as they are, on a plate, or wrap a naan around the skewer and pull the hot paneer and vegetables off into the naan. Top with your favourite raita or hot sauce.

TANDOORI CAULIFLOWER

SERVES 4 OR MORE AS PART OF A MULTI-COURSE MEAL

The flavour of marinated and chargrilled cauliflower is amazing. This mildly spiced marinade can be substantially spiced up by using more chilli powder and/or blended green chillies to taste. Although this recipe is fine as simple finger food, I like to wrap the cauliflower up into hot chapattis with a sloppy helping of mint and coriander sauce (see page 335). It is photographed on page 283, next to the lamb raan.

PREP TIME: 5 MINS, PLUS
    OPTIONAL MARINATING TIME
COOKING TIME: 15 MINS

1 tsp salt
24 cauliflower florets with short
    stems still attached
2 tbsp melted unsalted butter
Flaky sea salt and freshly ground
    black pepper, to taste

FOR THE MARINADE
250g (1 cup) Greek yoghurt
1 tbsp garlic and ginger paste (see
    page 172)
½ tsp chaat masala (see page 168)
½ tsp Kashmiri chilli powder
1 tsp sweet paprika
1 tbsp amchoor (dried mango
    powder)
1 tsp ground cumin
Juice of ½ lemon (about 1 tbsp)
2 tbsp mustard oil or rapeseed
    (canola) oil

Bring 2 litres (2 US quarts) of water to the boil and add the salt and cauliflower florets. Simmer for 3 minutes, or until fork-tender but not at all mushy. Strain and set aside to cool.

In a large mixing bowl, whisk all of the marinade ingredients together until smooth. Place the cauliflower in the marinade and mix well. For the best results, allow to marinate for about 30 minutes, but this isn't really necessary.

When ready to cook, set up the barbecue for direct heat cooking (see page 255). When your hand becomes very hot when held at skewer height above the coals, you're ready to cook. Skewer the cauliflower florets through the stem and out through the top and place over the heat. Cook, turning regularly, for about 5 minutes, or until black marks appear on the cauliflower.

To finish, baste lightly with the melted butter and season with flaky salt and black pepper.

NOTE
This recipe is great served with a good raita and it can also be used as a meat substitute in the curry of your choice. It will already be cooked, so add it to curries just before serving.

GRILLED SPICE AND LIME CORN ON THE COB
SERVES 4–6 AS PART OF A MULTI-COURSE MEAL

Once you've tried this corn on the cob, you'll want to make it again and again! In barbecue season, I like to light up a lumpwood or log fire and cook the corn directly on the hot coals. Don't worry about burning the corn. You want about a quarter of the kernels to blacken as it cooks through. Only cook on the coals if you are using untreated charcoal.

PREP TIME: 5 MINS
COOKING TIME: 10 MINS

75g (5 tbsp) unsalted butter
4 long corn on the cobs (ears of corn)
2 limes, halved or quartered

FOR THE SPICE MIX
1 tsp amchoor (dried mango powder)
1 tsp ground cumin
½ tsp chaat masala (see page 168)
1 tsp chilli powder
1 tsp salt

Set up the barbecue for direct cooking (see page 255). Place a tray near the fire with the butter on and let it melt.

Mix together all the spice mix ingredients on a serving plate and set aside.

When ready to cook, place your corn either on the grate or right in the coals. As you hear the corn begin to crackle, turn it slightly. Continue doing this until you have a mixture of yellow and blackened corn kernels.

To serve, roll the corn around in the melted butter. Serve hot and tell friends to dip their corn in the spice mixture and then rub it all over the corn with the lime wedges, squeezing the juice out as they do.

MAKE IT VEGAN
Although the butter could be omitted, this corn should taste buttery to be authentic. If you'd like, you could try a non-dairy butter or vegetable ghee.

GRILLED MUSHROOMS WITH FIG AND MOZZARELLA STUFFING AND CURRY-LEAF DRESSING

SERVES 2–4

I have to say that this is one of my all-time favourite mushroom recipes. I first tried it at a local curry house that's no longer around but I did get to watch the chef there make this. I later heard that a similar dish was being served at a tandoori restaurant in Camden called Namaaste Kitchen. Knowing the brilliant restaurant and its talented chef/owner, Sabbir Karim, my bet is that the dish originated there. I didn't get Sabbir's recipe in time for this cookbook but I think you are going to like this one. There really is so much amazing flavour in the grilled mushrooms and dressing that all you need is a little rice to go with it and you will be in food heaven. Sometimes I do add a nice raita or coriander (cilantro) chutney though.

PREP TIME: 15 MINS
COOKING TIME: 20 MINS

4 large flat mushrooms, stems cut off and chopped for the stuffing
150g (5½ oz) fresh buffalo mozzarella, roughly chopped
3 spring onions (scallions), roughly chopped
3 soft dried figs, finely chopped
1 green chilli, finely chopped
Salt, to taste

FOR THE MARINADE
1 tbsp olive oil
1½ tbsp garlic and ginger paste (see page 172)
Pinch of ground cumin
Pinch of garam masala (see page 167)

FOR THE DRESSING
Large bunch of fresh curry leaves (about 50)
1 garlic clove, smashed
1cm (½in) piece of ginger, peeled and grated
2 tbsp extra virgin olive oil
2 tbsp lime juice
Pinch of salt
Pinch of red chilli powder
½ tsp ground cumin
Salt and freshly ground black pepper, to taste

Set up the barbecue for indirect cooking (see page 255).

While it is heating up, mix all of the marinade ingredients in a bowl, then add the mushroom tops. Coat them evenly and allow the mushrooms to marinate while you make the filling.

Mix the mozzarella, spring onions (scallions), figs, chopped mushroom stems and green chilli together in a bowl and season with salt. Now remove the mushroom tops from the marinade and fill them equally with the stuffing.

When the barbecue is up to heat, place the stuffed mushrooms over the cooler side and bake for about 20 minutes until cooked through and browned on the top.

While the mushrooms are baking, make the dressing. This can also be done a day or so in advance. Place the curry leaves in a pestle and mortar and pound until the leaves are broken into small pieces, but not a paste. This helps release their flavour. Now add the garlic and ginger and pound some more to incorporate. Add the rest of the ingredients and whisk them all together until you have a nice thick, leafy dressing. Check for seasoning and set aside until ready to use.

Place each of the baked mushrooms on a plate and drizzle the curry-leaf dressing over them to serve.

NOTE

You can also make this recipe in the oven. Place a baking tray with a wire rack in the oven and preheat it to 200°C (400°F/Gas 6). When the oven is up to heat, place the stuffed mushrooms on the rack over the baking tray and bake for about 20 minutes until cooked through and toasty brown on top.

MAKE IT VEGAN

The mozzarella could simply be left out, or there is good dairy-free mozzarella available that melts well and makes a great alternative.

BREAD, RICE AND SIDES

A good side dish or two is all it takes to make a good curry feast great. In this section I have chosen recipes for sides that every curry fan enjoys.

Of course, all the most popular naan and rice dishes are here, but I have also included a few new recipes for you to try.

As you will see, most of the recipes can be made ahead of time, making serving the finished meal much easier.

CHAPATTIS
MAKES 8–10 SMALL CHAPATTIS

You know those chapattis available at the supermarket? Well, don't bother. Make your own and you will be much happier. These are so much fluffier and worth every minute you spend making them.

It's important to slap them around in your hands a few times before adding them to the pan. This helps get rid of any excess flour that will burn when dry-fried. You can make delicious chapattis in a pan, but if you have a gas burner, use it. You can throw them directly onto the flame, which gives them more character and makes them lighter. They are great served with curries or wrapped around kebabs. All you really need though is a little butter and you'll be in chapatti heaven.

PREP TIME: 5 MINS, PLUS
    RESTING TIME
COOKING TIME: 1 MIN PER
    CHAPATTI

250g (2 cups) chapatti flour, plus
    extra for dusting
Rapeseed (canola) oil, for oiling the
    pan

Put the flour into a bowl and add about 125ml (1/2 cup) water a little at a time. Knead until you have a soft, pliable dough, then continue kneading for about 3 minutes. Set aside, covered with a tea (dish) towel, and allow to rest for at least 30 minutes.

Dust the work surface with a little flour and divide the dough into 8–10 balls.

Working in batches, depending on space in your kitchen (keep the waiting balls covered with a damp tea/dish towel), flatten each ball between your hands and then flatten them more with a rolling pin until they are about 12cm (5in) in diameter and 1 mm thick. Dust off any excess flour from a disc of dough, then slap it from hand to hand to remove any stubborn flour.

Oil the pan with just enough oil to create a film (1/2 teaspoon should do) and dry-fry the chapatti for 30 seconds, then flip it over and fry for another 30 seconds. Brown spots should appear on both sides.

If you are cooking on an electric hob, turn the chapatti over again and apply pressure to the surface with a spatula or sheet of paper towel. It should puff up with air. If it doesn't it should still be fine. If you are cooking over a gas flame, lift the chapatti out of the pan and carefully place it directly on the flame. This will cause it to puff up into a nice light chapatti.

Transfer to a bowl lined with paper towel to keep warm while you make the remaining chapattis. For best results, serve immediately, but they can also be warmed up in the microwave if necessary.

AUTHENTIC NAANS
MAKES ENOUGH TO SERVE 8–10

You don't need a tandoor oven to make great-tasting, fluffy naans. Sure, it's nice to use a tandoor, and I often do, but this pan method is much easier and worth a try. I guarantee you that the naans you make at home on your hob will be just as good as most takeaways, if not better.

PREP TIME: 15 MINS, PLUS
    RISING TIME
COOKING TIME: 20 MINS

900g (2lb) plain (all-purpose) flour, plus extra for dusting
Scant 1 tbsp salt
2 tbsp baking powder
300ml (1¼ cups) full-fat (whole) milk
7g sachet (2½ tsp) dried yeast
2 tbsp sugar
3 eggs
270g (generous 1 cup) Greek yoghurt
Oil, for greasing
3 tbsp melted ghee
Nigella seeds (black onion seeds), to sprinkle

Sift the flour, salt and baking powder into a large bowl. Heat the milk in the microwave or on the hob until hand-hot. Pour into a jug (if heated on the hob), add the yeast and sugar, and whisk it all together. Cover with a cloth and leave in a warm place for about 20 minutes. It should foam right up. If it doesn't, don't worry, your naans will still rise.

Lightly beat the eggs and yoghurt together. Pour the yeasty milk mixture into the flour, along with the whisked eggs and yoghurt, and mix everything to combine.

Tip the dough out onto a work surface and knead for about 10 minutes until you have a soft, slightly sticky dough ball. Brush the insides of the bowl with a little oil and place the dough back in the bowl. Cover and allow to rise for 1–24 hours – longer rising times achieve a tasty sourdough.

Pull a chunk of dough, about the size of a tennis ball, from the risen dough. Using your hands or a rolling pin, roll the ball out on a lightly floured work surface into a flat, circular disc or teardrop shape, about 5mm (¼ in) thick. Slap the disc between your hands to get all the excess flour off.

Heat a dry frying pan over a high heat and, when very hot, place the naan in it. It will begin to cook on the underside then bubble on the top. Check the bottom regularly to ensure it doesn't burn. If it begins to get too dark, turn the naan over to get a bit of colour on the other side. Each naan should take no more than 3–5 minutes to cook.

Remove the cooked naan to a plate, brush with a little ghee and sprinkle with nigella seeds. Keep warm while you cook the remaining dough in the same way.

OPTIONAL EXTRA

This recipe is for fluffy, lightly browned naans. If you prefer a more charred appearance, place the finished naans under a hot grill (broiler) for about 1 minute, or to your liking.

CURRY-HOUSE NAANS

MAKES 6 NAANS, SERVES 4–6

This is how naans are made at most curry houses. The idea is to use bakers' measures so that when getting started the amount of dry ingredients is equal to the amount of wet ingredients. Following this rule, it is easy to scale the recipe up or down. As self-raising flour is used, a large or small batch can be whipped up whenever necessary. So to double this recipe you would use 1kg (2lb 3oz) of flour, 500ml (2 cups) of milk and about 400ml (scant 1¾ cups) of water and an additional egg, for example. Then just scale up the sugar, salt and nigella seeds too. You really can wing it. When you make the first batch, you might think it has gone wrong – it hasn't! Be sure to read the recipe to the end. I have a video on my YouTube channel that demonstrates this recipe cooked in a tandoor oven, but you can get outstanding results in a pan.

PREP TIME: 20 MINS, PLUS
OPTIONAL SITTING TIME
COOKING TIME: 20 MINS

250ml (1 cup) warm full-fat (whole) milk
2 eggs, lightly beaten
1 tsp salt
3 heaped tbsp caster (superfine) sugar
1 tbsp nigella seeds (black onion seeds)
500g (4 cups) self-raising (self-rising) flour, plus extra as needed
70ml (¼ cup) rapeseed (canola) oil
Ghee or butter, for brushing

Pour the milk and 150ml (generous ½ cup) warm water into a large mixing bowl. Add the eggs, salt, sugar and nigella seeds and whisk well. Start adding in the flour, whisking as you do. Once you've added all the flour, the mixture will still look very soupy and far too wet to work into dough balls. I recommend covering the dough at this time with a wet cloth and letting it sit for at least 3 hours or overnight for best results. That said, you could just jump right into finishing the recipe at this stage.

When ready to cook the naans, slowly start adding more flour. The idea here is to add just enough flour so that the dough is workable. It should be very soft and slightly sticky, but not so sticky that it sticks to your hands. If it does, dust with a little bit more flour until you can easily divide and form the dough into six spongy dough balls.

Once the dough balls are formed, you either could let them sit, covered, for about 30 minutes or you could push forward and make the naans immediately. As the dough is so soft, you shouldn't need a rolling pin. Dip your fingers in the oil and start patting the first dough ball to flatten it. Continue slapping it until it is flat. Repeat with the remaining dough balls.

Heat a dry frying pan over a medium–high heat and slap the first naan into it, oiled side up. As it cooks, bubbles will form on the surface and it will begin to look like a real naan! If you have a blow torch, use it to brown and blacken the bubbles; otherwise, just flip the naan over. This will pop a lot of the bubbles, but the naan will still be delicious. Brush with a little melted ghee or butter, keep warm and repeat with the remaining naans.

PESHAWARI NAANS

MAKES ENOUGH TO SERVE 8–10

Peshawari naans take some experimentation to get right. I don't really have a sweet tooth, so if they're too sweet, I just don't like them. That is of course not the case with many people, who love them very sweet. Therefore, please use this recipe as a guide. Feel free to adjust it to your own tastes when making the paste. With a bit of practice, you will find a recipe that is exactly as you want your Peshawari naans to be.

If you have any leftover dough, it can be kept in the fridge for up to 3 days, or frozen. If you're planning a curry evening with friends, why not make a selection of naans? Place a plate each of plain, keema and Peshawari naans on the table and you'll be everyone's best friend.

PREP TIME: 2 MINS, PLUS
   THE TIME TO PREPARE
   THE DOUGH
COOKING TIME: 10 MINS

1 quantity naan dough (see page 306*), ready to shape
Flour, for dusting
3 tbsp melted ghee
Sesame seeds, to sprinkle

FOR THE PESHAWARI PASTE
200g (2½ cups) almond flakes
2 tbsp desiccated coconut
3 tbsp single (light) cream
1 tbsp sugar, or to taste
20 sultanas (golden raisins)

*If you prefer, you could use the naan dough from the curry-house naans recipe, opposite, but you will need to double the quantities of the dough ingredients.

First make the paste. In a food processor, blend the almond flakes, coconut, cream, sugar and sultanas (golden raisins) until they form a thick paste. You may need to add more cream if it is too crumbly, or more almond flakes if too wet. Remove from the processor and knead into a pliable dough-like paste.

Pull off a ball of naan dough the size of a tennis ball, flatten slightly and place a piece of Peshawari paste slightly larger than a golf ball in the middle of the dough.

Fold the naan dough around the paste and roll out following the method on page 306 for plain naan. Cook in a hot, dry frying pan in the same way, then brush with ghee and sprinkle with sesame seeds to finish.

Keep warm while you cook the rest of the naans.

KEEMA NAANS

MAKES ENOUGH TO SERVE 8–10

I've found that keema naans are best cooked in a tandoor or very hot oven on a pizza stone. They are difficult to get right in a frying pan because of the meat inside. The trick is to roll them out while keeping the meat inside. With a little practice, you'll roll out your naans and the minced meat inside will be thin and flavourful, just like at the best restaurants.

I often substitute homemade tandoori masala for the mixed powder in the minced lamb. I like both versions, so you might like to give both a try.

PREP TIME: 25 MINS, PLUS
   THE TIME TO PREPARE
   THE DOUGH
COOKING TIME: 10 MINS

1 quantity naan dough (see page 306*), ready to shape
Flour, for dusting
Melted ghee, for brushing
Coriander (cilantro), to garnish

FOR THE KEEMA
400g (14oz) minced (ground) lamb
½ onion, finely chopped
2 green chillies, finely chopped or mashed into a paste
2 tbsp mixed powder (see page 169)
1 tsp garlic and ginger paste (see page 172)
Pinch each of salt and freshly ground black pepper

*If you prefer, you could use the naan dough from the curry-house naans recipe on page 308, but you will need to double the quantities of the dough ingredients.

Preheat the oven to its highest setting and place a pizza stone on a rack to heat for about 1 hour.

Meanwhile, combine all the keema ingredients in a large mixing bowl. Knead the meat for about 5 minutes, scraping the meat against the bottom of the bowl as you do so. You want to see streaks of minced meat clinging to the surface.

Pull off a piece of naan dough the size of a tennis ball and roll out on a floured surface to about 3mm thick. Place a ball of minced meat, slightly larger than a golf ball, in the middle of the disc and wrap the dough around it.

Lightly roll out the filled disc following the method on page 306, flipping it over a couple of times as you do. Be careful not to press too hard while rolling, or the meat will become exposed. If this happens, patch the area with a small piece of dough.

Brush the shaped naan with just a little melted ghee and place on the heated pizza stone in the oven. Bake for about 3 minutes, then flip it over and cook for another 3 minutes. Check the dough and filling are done, and cook for longer if needed.

To serve, sprinkle with coriander (cilantro) and perhaps a little more melted ghee. Keep warm while you roll and bake the remaining naans.

TIP
If you don't have a pizza stone, you can use a baking tray, although it will not get as hot.

PURIS

MAKES 6

I am hooked on puris! Especially served for breakfast with the potato curry on page 154. You will see my finished puris on that page too. There is really so much you can do with puris. Dip them into curries and dhals, or they are delicious served with pickles, like the spicy mixed vegetable pickle on page 329. At the end of the day, these are fried bread so I'm sure you'll find a use for them.

PREP TIME: 20 MINS, PLUS RESTING TIME
COOKING TIME: 10 MINS

450g (3¼ cups) chapatti flour, plus extra for dusting
Pinch of salt
Rapeseed (canola) oil, for deep-frying

Sift the chapatti flour into a large bowl with the salt. Slowly add about 250ml (1 cup) of warm water until you have a soft, pliable dough. Knead the dough for about 10 minutes, then set aside, covered with a tea (dish) towel, for about 30 minutes.

Divide the dough into six equal-size balls. Using a rolling pin, roll out the small dough balls on a floured surface until round and quite flat. Try to keep them as perfectly round as possible for best results.

Heat about 10cm (4in) of the oil in a large wok. When a piece of rolled-out puri sizzles instantly when hitting the oil, you're ready to fry. If you have an oil thermometer, you're aiming for 190°C (375°F). Don't overcrowd your pan – cook one puri at a time if necessary. Slowly lower the flat puris into the oil and deep-fry for 30 seconds, until the puris puff up and turn light brown. Tapping them lightly with the back of your spatula will help them balloon up. They are ready when lightly browned. If they are not cooked enough, they will deflate when you take them out of the oil. I usually turn my puris in the oil at least once to cook both sides evenly.

Carefully remove them with a slotted spoon or spider strainer when ready and transfer to paper towel to absorb any excess oil.

You can serve puris on their own, as you would naans, or filled with the filling of your choice. Serve immediately.

IDLIS

SERVES 6 OR MORE AS PART OF A
MULTI-COURSE MEAL

Fluffy steamed idlis taste great. They are delicious dipped into your favourite chutneys and sambar. This recipe uses a quick 'cheat's method' batter, which is a lot less work than more authentic versions that use a fermented batter. For the best results, you will need idli moulds – available online and at Asian markets. Before I invested in an idli mould set, I used a Yorkshire pudding tray placed on a brick in a large lidded pot of boiling water to steam. It worked well, so do what you have to try these. You'll be glad you did!

PREP TIME: 10 MINS
COOKING TIME: 20 MINS

Vegetable or rapeseed (canola) oil, for greasing
Chutneys or sambar, to serve (optional)

FOR THE BATTER
200g (1¼ cup) rice flour
70g (½ cup) urad dhal flour
⅛ tsp ground fenugreek
1 tsp salt
½ tsp baking powder
Juice of 1 lemon

Pour all of the batter ingredients into a bowl. Slowly pour in 410ml (1¾ cups) water, mixing until you have a thick and smooth batter. It should be thick enough to coat the back of a spoon.

When ready to cook, pour about 7.5cm (3in) depth of water into the bottom of your idli pan and bring to the boil. You want the water level to be just below the idli trays, so you might need to adjust the amount of water depending on your pan. Oil your idli trays lightly with oil, then pour the batter into the moulds.

Carefully lower the trays into the idli pan, cover and steam for 15 minutes. After 15 minutes, you should have delicious, fluffy idlis. To check for doneness, stick a toothpick or fork into the centre of one or two. If it comes out clean, your idlis are ready. If it comes out with a little batter stuck to it, continue steaming for a couple more minutes. Remove the trays from the steamer and let the steamed idlis sit, undisturbed, for about 2 minutes before removing them from the moulds. A small knife or spoon will help you lift the cooked idlis neatly out of the moulds.

Serve with chutneys and/or sambar if you like.

KERALAN PARATHAS
MAKES 6

Keralan parathas take some practice to get right, but even if yours don't look great at first, they will still taste delicious! It took me some time until I was completely happy with mine and I've enjoyed eating and serving my failed attempts. Just go for it and have fun. The preparation time is quite long, but you will get much faster if you make these often. If you would like to watch me make them, I've made a video on my YouTube channel, Dan Toombs. These parathas are good on their own or dipped into a curry.

PREP TIME: 1 HOUR, PLUS
RESTING TIME
COOKING TIME: 20 MINS

450g (3 cups) plain (all-purpose) flour
80g (½ cup) semolina flour
1 tsp salt
3 tbsp sugar
About 50g (3½ tbsp) melted warm ghee, vegetable ghee or rapeseed (canola) oil
Oil, for greasing

Pour the flours, salt and sugar into a large mixing bowl. Slowly drizzle in 300ml (1¼ cups) of warm water while working the dough with your hands into a soft but firm, easy-to-handle dough. Knead for 5 minutes, then cover and allow to rest for 20 minutes, or even overnight.

Dip your fingers in the ghee or oil and work the dough into 6 equal-size balls. The ghee or oil makes working with the dough easier, plus adds flavour. Let the dough balls rest, covered, for another 5 minutes.

Lightly oil your work surface and place one of the dough balls on top. Flatten it with your hands, then roll out into a large rectangular shape. The dough needs to be really thin so that your parathas are nice and flaky. You should be able to see the surface through it.

With the longest sides at the top and bottom, use a sharp knife to cut slits across the width of the dough at about 5mm (¼ in) intervals but leaving the edges intact, so that the dough is still joined at the sides. Lightly brush all over the surface with a little ghee or oil.

Now carefully begin to roll the dough up from the bottom into a long sausage. This will be difficult because of the slits; I find that using a sharp knife to help lift the dough from the surface helps. Once you have a long dough rope, curl that up into a spiral, so it looks like a Chelsea bun or cinnamon roll. The idea here is to get as many layers in your paratha as possible. Repeat to roll up all the dough pieces in the same way. Let each ball sit for at least 5 minutes, covered.

Flatten one of the parathas with your hands, until it is about 18cm (7in) in diameter. Be careful not to press down too hard or you will lose some of those layers. The swirls should be visible at the top.

Melt a little ghee or oil in a non-stick pan over a medium heat. Place your paratha in the pan, cook for about 30 seconds, then flip it over. You can start flattening your next paratha while this one is cooking. Continue cooking the first paratha, flipping regularly so it doesn't burn, until it is cooked through and browned on both sides – about 3–5 minutes should do. Flatten and cook the rest of the parathas, stacking the cooked ones as you make them and keeping them warm under a cloth.

Once they are all cooked, bash the stack of parathas lightly with your hands on the sides so the layers become more visible, then serve.

BHATURA
MAKES 8

These puffy breads are traditionally served with Punjabi chole (see page 57). They are similar to puris, but puris are unleavened, whereas bhatura are leavened. There is also a slight difference in texture between the two, so I hope you try both to decide which you prefer. You could use bhatura instead of puris for dishes like prawn puris.

PREP TIME: 15 MINS, PLUS SITTING TIME
COOKING TIME: ABOUT 2 MINS PER BHATURA

250g (2 cups) plain (all-purpose) flour
50g (¼ cup) fine semolina
¼ tsp baking powder
½ tsp bicarbonate of soda (baking soda)
¾ tsp salt
4 tbsp rapeseed (canola) oil, plus extra for deep-frying
2½ generous tbsp Greek yoghurt

Tip the flour and semolina into a large mixing bowl and add the baking powder, bicarbonate of soda (baking soda) and salt. Mix well with your hands, then add 2 tablespoons of rapeseed (canola) oil and mix it into the flour. Add the yoghurt and slowly pour in about 125ml (½ cup) of water while mixing with your hand. You may not need all the water, so add it slowly until you have a very soft dough that is slightly sticky to the touch but workable. Form this into a dough ball and cover. Place in a warm place to rise for about 2 hours. Don't worry if it doesn't rise much; the dough will still work.

Divide the dough into eight equal-size balls. Take a dough ball and coat it lightly with oil, then roll it out into a round tortilla/chapatti shape that is about the same thickness as a tortilla. Repeat with the remaining balls. Heat about 10cm (4in) of oil in a large saucepan or wok over a medium–high heat. The oil is hot enough when a small piece of dough sizzles and rises immediately to the top when tossed in.

Slowly lower the first bhatura into the hot oil and tap it with the back of a spoon or better, a large slotted spoon. As you do this, the bhatura will begin ballooning. Drizzle hot oil over any parts that aren't puffing up to help it inflate. Turn it over and continue tapping it with the back of the spoon until it is fully inflated. Turn it over a few more times until it is light brown – this helps the bhatura stay inflated. Transfer to a warm plate and cook the rest. Bhatura are best served immediately.

STEAMED WHITE RICE
SERVES 4

Never fill your pan more than one-third full or the rice will not cook correctly. If making a larger batch, remember the uncooked rice-to-water volume (not weight) ratio is always 1 measure of rice to 1½ measures of water.

PREP TIME: 2 MINS, PLUS SOAKING TIME
COOKING TIME: 40 MINS

370g (2 cups) basmati rice
Pinch of salt
1 tbsp ghee or butter

Put the uncooked rice in a large bowl and cover with cold water. Swirl the water around with your hands; it will become milky from the rice starch. Pour the water out and add fresh water and repeat until the water is almost clear. About five times should do the job. Leave the rice to soak in the last batch of fresh water for about 30 minutes, then drain.

Place the rice in a saucepan along with 750ml (3¼ cups) of cold water, the salt and ghee or butter in a saucepan. Cover with a tight-fitting lid and bring to a boil over a high heat. As soon as the water boils, remove from the heat and let it sit, lid on, for 40 minutes. Don't remove the lid. After 40 minutes, your rice will be perfectly done. Using a fork or chopstick, separate the rice grains, stirring very slowly. Basmati rice has a tendency to turn to mush if stirred too vigorously.

BOILED WHITE RICE
SERVES 4

You can cook a lot more rice using this method, and the water-to-rice ratio isn't as important. You need to cook with enough water so that the grains of rice can float around freely as it simmers. This is my preferred method when I am preparing rice for a fried rice recipe.

PREP TIME: 2 MINS, PLUS SOAKING TIME
COOKING TIME: 10 MINS

370g (2 cups) basmati rice
Pinch of salt
A little butter

Put the uncooked rice in a large bowl and cover with cold water. Swirl the water around with your hands; it will become milky from the rice starch. Pour the water out and add fresh water and repeat until the water is almost clear. About five times should do the job. Leave the rice to soak in the last batch of fresh water for about 30 minutes, then drain.

Bring a large saucepan of water to a boil, then add the rice. Stir in the salt and butter, reduce the heat and simmer for 7–9 minutes. To check for doneness, take out a couple of grains and press them with your fingers. They should be soft but still have a bit of resistance to them.

Carefully pour the rice into a colander. If serving immediately, transfer to a serving dish and your job is done. If storing for later, rinse with cold water, carefully stir through and place in an air-tight container in the fridge for up to 4 days.

COLOURED RICE
SERVES 4

A cookbook of curry-house recipes wouldn't be complete if I didn't explain how to make coloured rice. You probably already know it's done with food colouring, but if you don't, it is. Powdered food colouring is normally used when the rice is still moist from cooking. You can use the colours of your choice. Here is one option.

PREP TIME: 5 MINS, PLUS THE TIME TO PREPARE THE RICE

500g basmati rice, cooked
1 tsp red food colouring powder
1 tsp green food colouring powder

Place your cooked rice on a large plate and mentally divide it into quarters. Stir red food colouring powder into one quarter, green into another, and leave the rest white. Let it stand for a few minutes, then mix it all up again.

NOTE

It is important to cool leftover rice quickly (within an hour) after cooking. When reheating, take care to fully heat it all the way through before using.

PILAU RICE
SERVES 4; MAKES 370G (2 CUPS)

Pilau rice is one of those dishes I insist on cooking with ghee. I also prefer to steam it, as the flavour of the spices infuses better with the rice. If cooking for a large group, you might be better off frying cold cooked basmati rice, as in the next recipe.

PREP TIME: 10 MINS, PLUS SOAKING TIME
COOKING TIME: 50 MINS

370g (2 cups) basmati rice
3 tbsp milk
Pinch of saffron threads
3 tbsp ghee
6 green cardamom pods, lightly bruised
5cm (2in) piece of cinnamon stick or cassia bark
1 tsp cumin seeds
1 onion, finely chopped
1 garlic clove, smashed
750ml (3¼ cups) cold water or unsalted chicken stock
2 Indian bay leaves (cassia leaves)
Salt, to taste

Put the uncooked rice in a large bowl and cover with cold water. Swirl the water with your hands; it will become milky from the rice starch. Pour the water out and add fresh water and repeat until the water is almost clear – five times should do the job. Leave to soak in the final batch of water for about 30 minutes, then drain.

While the rice is soaking, heat the milk in a small pan until it begins to simmer. Take off the heat and stir in the saffron. Leave to infuse for about 15 minutes.

Melt the ghee over a medium–high heat in a saucepan with a tight-fitting lid. When starting to give off a nutty aroma, toss in the whole spices and cook for about 30 seconds until fragrant. Add the onion and sizzle for about 5 minutes until translucent and soft.

Add the garlic to the pan, followed by the drained rice. Stir this all up so that the rice is evenly coated in the ghee. Pour in the water or stock, add the bay leaves, then cover the pan. When the rice begins to boil and the water foams, remove from the heat and let it sit, covered and undisturbed, for 40 minutes.

After 40 minutes, lift the lid and pour the saffron milk mixture on top. Carefully stir through the rice using a fork or chopstick until nice and fluffy. Don't stir too vigorously as the basmati rice may split. Season with salt and transfer to a warm bowl to serve.

Clockwise from top left: boiled white rice (page 315); fried rice (above); and pilau rice (above, left)

FRIED RICE
SERVES 2 OR MORE AS PART OF A
MULTI-COURSE MEAL

You can get really creative with fried rice. For onion fried rice, simply fry some onion in the oil and then stir in your cold, cooked rice. You could also make a fried rice version of the pilau rice above using this method. The following lemon rice recipe is the perfect accompaniment for fish curries.

PREP TIME: 5 MINS
COOKING TIME: 5 MINS

3 tbsp rapeseed (canola) oil or ghee
1 tsp garlic and ginger paste (see page 172)
Finely grated zest of 2 lemons
500ml (2 cups) cold cooked basmati rice*
Juice of 1–2 lemons
Salt, to taste
3 chives, finely chopped

Heat the oil or ghee in a large frying pan over a medium–high heat until bubbling hot. Add the garlic and ginger paste and lemon zest, and fry for about 30 seconds. Add the cold rice and stir gently for about 2 minutes until all the rice grains are nicely coated with the oil. When the rice is really hot, squeeze in the lemon juice. Season with salt and top with the chopped chives to serve.

NOTE
*It is important to cool leftover rice quickly (within an hour) after cooking. When reheating, take care to fully heat it all the way through before using.

MASALA CHIPS

SERVES 4 OR MORE AS PART OF A MULTI-COURSE MEAL

I love masala chips. Whether I'm serving them as a main dish or doing what I normally do, serving them as a side, they are always a big hit. This is especially so since I started using this recipe that was shown to me by my friend Alfarid 'Billy' Juma. The recipe couldn't be easier, but you've got to follow the instructions carefully – there is a reason Billy's masala chips are so good. This is true comfort food and I promise you that if you have one chip in his special masala sauce, you'll find it difficult to stop. For ease, I use shop-bought frozen chips. I prefer this recipe with deep-fried chips but you could also use oven-baked chips.

PREP TIME: 10 MINS
COOKING TIME: 20 MINS

900g (2lb) frozen chips (preferably the kind you deep-fry, but oven-bake will do)
Rapeseed (canola) oil, for deep-frying
1 tsp red chilli powder
½ tsp ground cumin
1 tsp ground coriander
Salt, to taste

FOR THE MASALA SAUCE
2 tbsp rapeseed (canola) oil
1 tbsp cumin seeds
5 tbsp tomato hamburger relish
5 tbsp tomato ketchup
1 tbsp sugar
½ onion, finely chopped
1 tbsp garlic and ginger paste (see page 172)

First make the sauce. Heat the oil in a saucepan over a medium–high heat. When visibly hot, stir in the cumin seeds and sauté in the oil for about 30 seconds until fragrant. Add the hamburger relish followed by the ketchup and bring to a simmer. Stir in the sugar and continue to cook for about 1 minute, then add the chopped onion and garlic and ginger paste and stir it all up to combine. Season with a little salt and take off the heat while your prepare your chips.

Cook your chips as per the instructions on the packet. Most takeaways use frozen chips that they deep-fry. I highly recommend doing the same, but if you're looking for a lighter or less messy option, oven chips will do. When your chips are ready, season them directly with the chilli powder, cumin, coriander and a little bit of salt. Remember there is already some salt in the masala sauce, so go easy.

While the chips are still hot, begin adding them to the pan with the sauce, stirring so that every chip is evenly covered in the sauce. Ideally, the process of coating the chips in the sauce and serving should be done in about 2 minutes. If you let them sit too long, the chips will get soggy rather than the crispy sauce-coated chips they are meant to be.

SEMOLINA FRIED POTATOES
SERVE 4–6 AS A SIDE DISH

Goan semolina fried potatoes are traditionally served with xacuti curries (see page 75), but I can assure you that they make a great side dish or snack anytime.

PREP TIME: 10 MINS, PLUS
  SOAKING TIME
COOKING TIME: 10 MINS

3 medium potatoes, washed and
  peeled
½ tsp Kashmiri chilli powder
½ tsp ground turmeric
½ tsp fine salt
Rapeseed (canola) oil, for shallow-
  frying
Flaky sea salt, to taste

FOR THE COATING
1 tsp chilli powder
½ tsp ground turmeric
½ tsp ground cumin
8 tbsp fine semolina

Slice the potatoes into 3mm (⅛in) coins. Place the slices in a bowl of cold water and move them around with your hand, then drain. Add fresh water and leave to soak for about 25 minutes. Move the slices around again with your hand and drain – this washes away the starch. Dry the inside of the bowl and put the potato slices back in and sprinkle with the chilli powder, turmeric and salt. Be sure to coat the slices evenly, then set aside for 10 minutes while you make the coating.

Mix the coating ingredients together, then coat the potato slices with this mixture. Pour about 1.5cm (½ in) of oil to completely cover the base of a large frying pan. Heat over a medium–high heat. When visibly hot, add the potato slices. Shallow-fry for about 10 minutes per side until the potato is cooked soft and the exterior is crispy. Season with flaky salt.

TARKA DHAL

SERVES 4 OR MORE AS PART OF A MULTI-COURSE MEAL

This has to be one of the most-ordered side dishes at Indian restaurants. Personally, I feel the meal just isn't complete without a good tarka dhal. A 'tarka' is a mixture of spices and/or aromatics that are tempered in oil or ghee. This mixture is then poured over the cooked dhal just before serving. So the chana dhal (see page 323) is actually a tarka dhal too.

For this quick and easy version, I use masoor dhal (split small red lentils), which, unlike other lentils, need only to be washed and rinsed under cold water before cooking. You can also use the finished tarka dhal in my chicken dhansak recipe (see page 205) instead of plain dhal.

PREP TIME: 10 MINS
COOKING TIME: 25 MINS

250g (1½ cups) masoor dhal (red lentils), rinsed
3 tbsp ghee
10 fresh or frozen curry leaves
1 tsp cumin seeds
5cm (2in) piece of cinnamon stick
1 onion, finely sliced
4 garlic cloves, finely chopped
2 tbsp garam masala (see page 167)
½ tsp ground turmeric
Salt and freshly ground black pepper, to taste

Put the dhal into a pan and pour over about 400ml (scant 1¾ cups) of water. Simmer over a medium–high heat for about 25 minutes until tender, removing any foam that forms on the top.

Meanwhile, melt the ghee in a frying pan and add the curry leaves, cumin seeds and cinnamon stick. Stir this all up so that the ghee soaks up the flavour of the spices. Add the onion and fry for about 5 minutes until light brown. Add the garlic, garam masala and turmeric, and sizzle until the garlic is soft.

Season the cooked dhal with salt and pepper, then pour the ghee mixture (the tarka) over the lentils to serve.

CHANA DHAL
SERVES 4 OR MORE AS PART OF A MULTI-COURSE MEAL

This recipe was inspired by a visit to Prashad in Bradford. The head chef Minal Patel showed me her recipe for chana dhal and it was amazing. She used four different types of lentils, cooked separately then blended together with all the other ingredients. Usually, the chana dhal you get at a curry house is made simply from chana lentils, so I've simplified Minal's recipe a little for you here. If you like chana dhal, you're going to love this one.

PREP TIME: 10 MINS, PLUS
    SOAKING THE CHANA DHAL
COOKING TIME: 1 HOUR

300g (10½ oz) chana dhal, soaked in
    water for 30 minutes
About 1 tbsp rapeseed (canola) oil or
    seasoned oil (see page 8)
3 tbsp ghee
½ tsp brown mustard seeds
1 tsp cumin seeds
Pinch of asafoetida*
1 tsp ground turmeric
½ onion, finely chopped
5 garlic cloves, cut into slivers
1 tbsp garlic and ginger paste (see
    page 172)
1–5 fresh green bullet chillies, to
    taste, finely chopped
3 tomatoes, roughly chopped
1 tbsp ground coriander
½ tsp ground cumin
½ tsp garam masala (see page 167)
Salt, to taste
Chopped coriander (cilantro), to serve

Drain the lentils and rinse in several changes of water, then place in a saucepan with 700ml (3 cups) of fresh water. Bring to a boil and drizzle the oil on top to stop the water from foaming over the top.

Reduce the heat and simmer until the lentils are soft but with just a little bite to them, 45 minutes–1 hour, skimming off any foam that does form. Do not strain; allow the water to reduce down.

Meanwhile, in a separate pan, melt the ghee over a high heat. When it is visibly very hot, toss in the mustard seeds. They will begin to pop after about 30 seconds. Reduce the heat to medium–high and add the cumin seeds and asafoetida. Temper in the oil for about 30 seconds and then add the turmeric and onion and fry until soft and translucent – 3–5 minutes should do the job. Stir in the slivered garlic, garlic and ginger paste and chillies, and cook, stirring continuously, for another 30 seconds.

Returning to the dhal, reduce the heat to medium and stir in the chopped tomatoes, coriander and cumin, and bring to a happy simmer. Keep warm.

You can leave the dhal as it is once cooked, or whisk or blend until creamy. Stir the onion and ghee mixture into the lentils and sprinkle with garam masala. To serve, season with salt and top with a little coriander (cilantro).

NOTE
*If you are gluten-free, please check the asafoetida packaging as some brands contain wheat flour.

DHAL MAKHANI
SERVES 4 OR MORE AS PART OF A MULTI-COURSE MEAL

Dhal makhani, when cooked correctly, is delicious. I've tried some amazing versions and also a few that just weren't quite there yet. If you like a good dhal makhani, I think this recipe will get you the flavour and texture you're looking for. Be warned, however, this isn't one you can just whip up on a whim. The lentils need to soak in water for at least 12 hours, then be slowly cooked until fall-apart tender. This is where many chefs go wrong. They rush the cooking process and the dhal has just a bit too much bite to it. If time permits, I recommend cooking this for 4 hours, adding water when required.

PREP TIME: 10 MINS, PLUS
    SOAKING
COOKING TIME: 3¼–4¼ HOURS

200g (7oz) black urad dhal, soaked
    overnight in cold water
5 tbsp rapeseed (canola) oil
2 onions, finely chopped
2 tbsp garlic and ginger paste (see
    page 172)
2 tomatoes, chopped
2 tsp chilli powder
1 tsp ground turmeric
1 tbsp garam masala (see page 167)
1 tsp paprika
2 tsp salt, or to taste
3 tbsp butter, or to taste
250ml (1 cup) single (light) cream
Chopped coriander (cilantro) leaves,
    to serve

In a large saucepan over a low–medium heat, simmer the urad dhal in water until fall-apart soft. You might need to top up the water from time to time while the lentils cook. After about 3–4 hours of simmering, the lentils will be perfectly soft. Strain the lentils, reserving the cooking water, and set it all aside.

To save time, the following steps can be done while your lentils are simmering. Heat the oil in a large frying pan over a medium–high heat. When visibly hot, stir in the chopped onions and fry for about 10 minutes until soft and lightly browned. Stir in the garlic and ginger paste and fry for about 30 seconds before adding the chopped tomatoes and the spices. Cook for another minute, then add about 125ml (½ cup) of the strained lentil water. Bring this to a simmer and add the cooked lentils. Cook over a high heat for 5 minutes, adding more strained water if needed. The dhal should be thick and soupy.

To finish, season with salt. I recommend about 2 teaspoons, which I think works really well, but as with all the recipes in this book, I feel how much salt you add is a personal thing. Add it to taste. Makhani means butter, so you can't leave that out. I recommend using about 3 tablespoons, but if you don't want to use that much, the dhal will still be delicious. Stir most of it into the dhal and then add whatever is left over to melt on top. Drizzle the cream over the top and sprinkle with the chopped coriander (cilantro) and you are ready to serve your masterpiece.

KACHUMBER SALAD

SERVES 4–6 AS A SIDE DISH

This is a popular salad in many Indian restaurants. Sometimes it's on the menu but often it's simply used to garnish dishes. It makes a nice side dish as it doesn't compete with the other dishes served. It is colourful and crisp, and helps bring a meal together. It is pictured on pages 93, 223 and 275.

PREP TIME: 15 MINS, PLUS SITTING TIME

1 red onion, very finely diced
1 cucumber, very finely diced
1–2 tomatoes, very finely diced
1 tsp olive oil or vegetable oil
Juice of 1 lemon
3 tbsp finely chopped coriander (cilantro)
½ tsp roasted cumin seeds (see page 163)
Salt and freshly ground black pepper, to taste

Mix the onion, cucumber and tomatoes together in a large bowl. Add the oil, lemon juice, coriander (cilantro) and cumin seeds and season with salt and black pepper. Place in the fridge for about 30 minutes before serving.

TOMATO, ONION AND MINT SALAD

SERVES 4 OR MORE AS A SIDE DISH

This simple salad (shown on pages 12 and 17) makes a perfect side for your summer barbecue.

PREP TIME: 10 MINS, PLUS STANDING TIME

5 tennis ball-size firm tomatoes, thinly sliced
1 onion, thinly sliced
2 green chilli peppers, finely chopped (optional)
1 tbsp mint sauce
2 tbsp finely chopped coriander (cilantro)
Juice and finely grated zest of 1 lime or lemon
Salt and freshly ground black pepper, to taste

Mix all the ingredients together in a bowl and season with salt and black pepper. Allow to sit for 15 minutes before serving.

PICKLES, CHUTNEYS AND SAUCES

I don't know about you, but for me a good selection of homemade pickles, chutneys and sauces makes a meal. So often, when you go out to a curry house these must-have accompaniments are bought in. At more exclusive Indian restaurants, they are usually homemade.

That's one of the reasons the prices on the menus at fancy Indian restaurants are much higher than at curry houses. The great news is that, although many of these recipes take some time to prepare, a lot of the time is passive.

I hope you enjoy making a few of these recipes. These are recipes that will most definitely impress your guests at your next curry feast!

LIME PICKLE
MAKES ABOUT 3 × 250ML (1 CUP) JARS

There are a lot of outstanding lime pickles that can be purchased, from both small producers and big-name brands. This is my recipe that I have developed over the past few years. I wouldn't say it is any better than many you can purchase but it is different and delicious. Sometimes different is good! You know you are at an outstanding restaurant if they place their own homemade pickles and chutneys on the table.

PREP TIME: 5 MINS, PLUS
   FERMENTING TIME
COOKING TIME: 15 MINS

1kg (2lb 3oz) limes
5 level tbsp salt
40 garlic cloves, peeled and smashed
50g ginger, peeled and very finely
   chopped
2 tbsp Kashmiri chilli powder

FOR THE TEMPERING
150ml (generous ½ cup) rapeseed
   (canola) oil
3 tbsp black mustard seeds
2 tbsp cumin seeds
½ tsp asafoetida*

Using a fork, stab about 20 holes in each lime, then cut each lime into 8 wedges. Place in a glass bowl and add the salt, garlic, ginger and chilli powder. Mix well, coating the limes and pressing down on them to release a lot of juice.

Transfer the limes to a steamer, leaving the juice in the bowl, and steam for about 15 minutes until quite soft.

Transfer the steamed limes back to the glass bowl and mix back into the juices. Cover tightly with cling film (plastic wrap) and leave for 2 days in a warm place, such as a window or in direct sun outside, mixing it every 8 hours to keep the limes coated with all the other ingredients.

After 2 days, heat the oil for the tempering in a large frying pan over a high heat. When very hot and almost smoking, add the mustard seeds. They will begin to pop after about 30 seconds. When they do, add the cumin seeds and asafoetida, and sizzle for about 10 seconds, being careful not to burn the spices.

Pour this tempered oil over the limes and mix well. Cover the bowl again with cling film and allow to sit for another 2 days in the sun, stirring every 8 hours or so.

After these last 2 days, scoop the lime pickle into a food processor and process to a chunky or smooth paste, whichever you prefer.

Spoon it into sterilized jars (see below), leaving about a 5cm (2in) space at the top. The pickle should be covered with oil, so add a little extra if needed. Place the jars in a cool, dark place for 2 weeks before using. The preserved limes should keep indefinitely but, once opened, store in the fridge and use within 2 months.

STERILIZING JARS
It is best to store your pickles in sterilized jars to keep them fresh. To sterilize jars, preheat the oven to 110°C (225°F/Gas ¼). If your jars have rubber sealing rings on the lid, remove them and boil in water for 5 minutes. Wash the jars thoroughly in hot, soapy water and rinse well, then place on a baking tray in the preheated oven for about 15 minutes until dry. Carefully remove them from the oven and fill them while still hot.

NOTE
*If you are gluten-free, please check the asafoetida packaging as some brands contain wheat flour.

SPICY MIXED VEGETABLE PICKLE
MAKES A 1-LITRE (4½ CUPS) JAR

I always have some of this mixed pickle on hand just in case I get unexpected guests. It is one of my favourites and goes well with everything from papadams to dosas. You can vary the vegetables you use depending on what sounds good and is in season. I've used marrow, radishes, turnips, broccoli and even pumpkin in the past with excellent results. I like my pickles to be quite spicy. If you don't, reduce the amount of chillies and chilli powder. You can always add more to taste later.

PREP TIME: 15 MINS, PLUS
   PICKLING TIME
COOKING TIME: 20 MINS

150g (5½ oz) cauliflower, cut into
   small florets
100g (3½ oz) aubergine (eggplant),
   diced
1 small carrot, cut into small pieces
1 red (bell) pepper, roughly chopped
3 green chillies, thinly sliced
1 mango, peeled, pitted and diced
6 garlic cloves
3 limes, thoroughly washed
1 tbsp black mustard seeds
3 tbsp chilli powder
1 tsp ground turmeric
½ tsp ground fenugreek
3 tbsp flaky sea salt

FOR THE TARKA
125ml (½ cup) rapeseed (canola) oil,
   plus extra if needed
2 tsp black mustard seeds
1 tsp cumin seeds
2 Kashmiri dried red chillies, each
   broken into 3 pieces
10 curry leaves, finely chopped

Mix all the chopped vegetables, chillies, mango and garlic in a glass or ceramic mixing bowl. Quarter the limes and squeeze as much of the juice out of them as you can over the ingredients.

Heat some water in a pan with a steamer basket and steam the squeezed lime quarters as they are for about 15 minutes to soften them. You can add the steamed lime quarters as they are to the bowl or cut them into even smaller pieces before adding.

Using a pestle and mortar, grind the 1 tablespoon of black mustard seeds to a coarse powder. Pour this powder, along with the chilli powder, turmeric, fenugreek and salt, over the vegetables and fruit in the bowl. Stir well to combine.

Now, in a small frying pan, bring about 3 tablespoons of the tarka oil to a bubble over a high heat. Add the mustard seeds. When they begin to pop (after about 30 seconds), reduce the temperature to medium–high and stir in the cumin seeds, Kashmiri chillies and curry leaves. When these become fragrant – about 30 seconds should do – pour in the remaining oil, stir well and pour it all over the chopped vegetables and fruit.

Mix really well. The vegetables and fruit should be submerged in the oil. If not, add a little more and then cover with cling film (plastic wrap).

In the summer months, you can place this outside in the sun. In colder months, place it all by a sunny window. Leave to ferment for 3 days, stirring every 8 hours or so. Then scoop it all into a sterilized jar (see note on page 328) with a tight-fitting lid. You can taste it now but wait for at least a week if you can. It gets better!

This pickle will keep in the fridge for at least three months. Make sure that the vegetables and fruit are always covered in oil to avoid it going off.

EASY MANGO PICKLE
MAKES ABOUT 3¼ LITRES (3½ US QUARTS)

A while back, I was in California visiting my parents and met their friend Sharon Iyer. Sharon is married to a man from Tamil Nadu and this is her mother-in-law's recipe. It's her husband's favourite pickle, so she made sure to learn the recipe. He likes it so much she makes huge batches of it, but it doesn't last for long. You could of course scale it down, but as it takes about 90 minutes to make, why not make this large batch as I did when she showed me the recipe. Stored correctly, it keeps forever in the fridge. The spicy pickle is so good with papadams, samosas or simply stirred into rice. It is pictured on page 12.

PREP TIME: 30 MINS
COOKING TIME: 1 HOUR

10 green mangos
5 tbsp rapeseed (canola) oil, plus extra for topping up the pickle
4 tbsp salt
1 tbsp fenugreek seeds
1 tbsp black mustard seeds
1 tsp ground turmeric
4 tbsp Kashmiri chilli powder, or to taste

Peel and pit the mangos and cut the fruit into 5cm (2in) pieces. Heat 4 tablespoons of the oil in a large saucepan over a medium heat and add the mango pieces and salt. Stir, cover the pan and simmer for about 10 minutes.

Meanwhile, pour the fenugreek seeds into a small dry frying pan and toast them over a medium heat for about 1 minute until fragrant. Be sure to move the seeds around in the pan so that they toast evenly. Allow to cool, then grind them with a spice grinder or pestle and mortar into a fine powder. Set aside.

Now heat the remaining oil over a high heat and add the mustard seeds. When the seeds begin to crackle (after about 30 seconds), stir in the turmeric. Lift the lid of the mango saucepan and pour this flavoured oil in. Stir well, then add the fenugreek powder and stir some more.

Now you're in for a waiting game. You need to simmer the mangos, covered, until they break down into a mushy consistency. This could take 30 minutes–1 hour. You should stir regularly and speed up the process by breaking the mangos up with a wooden spoon.

Once the mangos have all broken down into a mush, it's time to add the Kashmiri chilli powder. You might only want to add 1 tablespoon, but this is supposed to be a spicy pickle! Add 1 tablespoon of chilli powder, stir and repeat until you are happy with the spiciness. Me? I like it spicy, so I add 4 generous tablespoons.

Pour the finished pickle into sterilized glass jars (see note on page 328). Fill them almost to the top and be sure to press the pickle down with a spoon to get rid of any air holes. Pour a little rapeseed (canola) oil over the top and allow to cool before sealing. This delicious pickle will keep for months in the fridge.

MANGO CHUTNEY

MAKES ABOUT 1.5L (6¼ CUPS)

Mango chutney is easy to prepare. You can make it either sweet, or sweet and spicy – adding a teaspoon or so of chilli powder really gives this chutney a kick. Once you have finished cooking the chutney, you can serve it chunky or blend it until smooth. I usually make both versions from one batch. The resulting chutney is great served with papadams and kebabs. The smooth version tastes amazing stirred into madras and jalfrezi curries at the end of cooking. Don't add the chunky version to curries as the mango pieces will become hard and rubbery.

PREP TIME: 15 MINS, PLUS SITTING TIME
COOKING TIME: 1 HOUR

400g (2 cups) caster sugar
250ml (1 cup) distilled white vinegar
4–5 green mangos, peeled and cubed
1 onion, finely chopped
Large handful of raisins
5cm (2in) piece of ginger, peeled and finely chopped
3 garlic cloves, finely chopped
1 tsp black mustard seeds
1 tsp chilli powder (optional)
Salt (optional)

Put the sugar and vinegar in a large saucepan and bring to a boil, stirring continuously until the sugar dissolves. Add the remaining ingredients and simmer for about 1 hour, stirring regularly until syrupy.

When it is sticky and thick to your liking you can either leave it as it is or blend until smooth (or blend half, see introduction). Transfer to hot sterilized jars (see page 328), leaving a little space at the top.

GREEN COCONUT CHUTNEY

MAKES ABOUT 300ML (1¼ CUPS)

I can't get enough of this mildly spiced chutney, pictured on page 12.

PREP TIME: 10 MINS, PLUS SOAKING TIME IF
    USING DRIED COCONUT FLAKES
COOKING TIME: 2 MINS

4 tbsp chana dhal
100g (1 cup) grated fresh coconut, frozen shredded coconut or dried coconut flakes (if using dried, rinse and soak in 250ml/1 cup water for about 30 minutes before using)
40g (¾ cup) coriander (cilantro), chopped
2 green chillies, roughly chopped
2cm (¾ in) piece of ginger, peeled and roughly chopped
¼ tsp sugar (or to taste)
Juice of ½ lemon
Salt, to taste

FOR THE TEMPERING
1 tbsp coconut oil or rapeseed (canola) oil
½ tsp mustard seeds
½ tsp white split urad dhal
¼ tsp asafoetida*
4–5 curry leaves

Toast the chana dhal in a dry frying pan over a medium–high heat until fragrant and lightly browned, about 1½–2 minutes. Transfer to a plate to cool slightly.

Put the coconut, coriander (cilantro), green chillies, ginger and toasted chana dhal in a blender or spice grinder and blend with 125ml (½ cup) of water. This should be a runny chutney so add more water until the consistency is right. Add the sugar and lemon juice and season with salt.

Heat the oil in a small pan over a high heat. When hot, add the mustard seeds. When they begin to pop, reduce the temperature to medium–high and stir in the white urad dhal. Let the dhal toast until light brown – about 1 minute should do. Stir in the asafoetida and curry leaves and let this all sizzle in the oil for about 20 seconds. Your kitchen will smell amazing.

Pour the spiced oil over the chutney to serve.

NOTE
*If you are gluten-free, please check the asafoetida packaging as some brands contain wheat flour.

KASHMIRI RED CHILLI AND GARLIC CHUTNEY

MAKES ENOUGH FOR 4–6 AS AN ACCOMPANIMENT

This is a hot one! You only need to dab a bit on your papadam and you'll see what I mean. As you can see from the ingredients list, there isn't much to this chutney. It's all about the chilli. Give it a go if you like it hot. Don't if you don't. It is pictured opposite, on the top right.

PREP TIME: 5 MINS, PLUS SOAKING TIME
COOKING TIME: 1 MIN

20 Kashmiri dried red chillies
10 garlic cloves, peeled and smashed
½ tsp ground cumin
½ tsp salt, or to taste

Split the chillies open and remove as many seeds as you can. (There's no need to remove them all as they will sink when you soak the chillies.) Toast the chillies for about 1 minute in a dry frying pan, pressing them down so that they are equally toasted. Tip into a bowl and add hot water from the kettle to cover. Leave to soak for 30 minutes.

Strain the chillies, reserving the soaking water, and place in a spice grinder or food processor with the garlic, cumin and salt. Taste the soaking water, and unless it is really bitter, add just enough to blend the mixture to a smooth, ketchup consistency. If the soaking water tastes bitter, discard it and use fresh water instead. Check for seasoning and it's ready to serve.

RED ONION CHUTNEY

MAKES ENOUGH FOR 4–6 AS AN ACCOMPANIMENT

This onion chutney is about as easy as it gets. It's too simple for words, but then who said that delicious Indian dinners had to be complicated? Find yourself a nice, fresh red onion and it will do all the work for you. This is a very popular accompaniment, often served with papadams or piled high on kebabs and naans. It is essential to serve it very cold. It is pictured opposite on the top left.

PREP TIME: 5 MINS, PLUS SITTING TIME

1 large red onion, halved and finely sliced
Pinch of salt
Pinch of sugar (optional)
Juice of 1 lemon
1 fresh green chilli, finely chopped (optional)

Put the sliced onion in a bowl of cold water with ice cubes added, and put in the fridge for about 1 hour. Once good and cold, drain and pat the slices dry with a clean cloth.

Season with salt, and sugar (if using) and squeeze the lemon juice over the top. For a spicier chutney, mix in the finely chopped chilli. Serve very cold right from the fridge.

Clockwise from top left: red onion chutney (above); Kashmiri red chilli and garlic chutney (above); mint, coriander and mango chutney (page 335); and tamarind chutney (page 336)

COLD ONION CHUTNEY

MAKES ENOUGH FOR 4–6 AS AN ACCOMPANIMENT

You know those sliced onions that are served in a red sauce with papadams before the meal at Indian restaurants? Well, this simple chutney is a lot more popular than you might think.

This simple recipe is actually the most popular one on my blog. For me, that's still quite difficult to take in! Out of all of the recipes on my blog, this is the one people look up most. I have to say I love it too. If you're planning a curry night anytime soon, you won't want to leave this onion chutney off the menu. It's so easy to make!

PREP TIME: 5 MINS, PLUS SITTING TIME

1 large onion, finely sliced
3 tbsp tomato ketchup
1 tbsp tomato purée (see page 172)
1 tsp chilli powder, or to taste
Pinch of salt
1 tsp roasted cumin seeds (see page 163)

Put the sliced onions in a bowl of cold water with ice cubes added, and put in the fridge for about 1 hour. Once good and cold, drain and pat the slices dry with a clean cloth.

Now mix the ketchup, tomato purée, chilli powder and salt together. Stir in the sliced onions and roasted cumin seeds.

Stick in the fridge for about 45 minutes before serving, to allow the ingredients to get to know each other, and serve with papadams or whatever you fancy.

MINT CHUTNEY

MAKES ENOUGH FOR 4–6 AS AN ACCOMPANIMENT

This is probably the most popular chutney served in Indian restaurants. Some chefs add a little food colouring to make it bright green.

PREP TIME: 5 MINS

270g (generous 1 cup) plain yoghurt
1 tbsp garlic and ginger paste (see page 172)
1–3 bird's eye green chillies, to taste, very finely chopped
Juice of 1 lime
1–2 tbsp shop-bought mint sauce, to taste
Pinch of salt

Place the ingredients in a mixing bowl and whisk to combine until smooth. Cover and place in the fridge for at least 30 minutes before serving.

PODINA CORIANDER AND MINT CHUTNEY

MAKES 600ML

You really can't go wrong with a nice podina. It is delicious served really cold with hot homemade bora (see page 22). Or you can serve it with samosas, papadams, onion bhajis, on top of kebabs... anything really!

PREP TIME: 5 MINS, PLUS SITTING TIME

½ bunch of mint
½ bunch of coriander (cilantro)
10–15 fresh green chillies, to taste
420g (scant 1¾ cups) plain yoghurt
Salt, to taste

Put the mint, coriander (cilantro), green chillies and 2 tablespoons of water in a blender and blitz to a paste. Add this to the yoghurt in a bowl and mix until smooth, seasoning with salt. Refrigerate until really cold.

MINT, CORIANDER AND MANGO CHUTNEY

MAKES ENOUGH FOR 4 AS AN ACCOMPANIMENT

I love this simple chutney, pictured on page 333 on the bottom right. It's so good spooned over the lamb seekh kebabs on page 277 – you will be amazed how the flavours work together. If you're serving this to guests, they'll probably be wondering what the heck went into it, it's such an interesting flavour combo. Admittedly, the first time I tried a similar chutney, I couldn't figure it out either. I'm usually quite good at recognizing ingredients but not with this one.

PREP TIME: 5 MINS

Small bunch of coriander (cilantro), leaves only
Large bunch of mint, leaves only
200ml (generous ¾ cup) smooth mango chutney (see page 331 or shop-bought)
1–4 fresh green chillies, to taste, finely chopped
2 garlic cloves, finely chopped
Juice of 1 lime
Salt, to taste

Finely chop the coriander (cilantro) and mint leaves and place in a blender with the remaining ingredients, seasoning with salt. Blend until smooth and use within three days.

MINT AND CORIANDER SAUCE

MAKES 250ML (1 CUP)

This is a sauce I make all the time. It is available at Asian shops but nothing beats taking it all up a notch with your own homemade version. You can adjust the recipe too. Vary the coriander-to-mint ratio, add more or fewer chillies, use yoghurt or leave it out... this sauce is a good'n! I store it in a squeezy bottle for convenience, but that isn't essential. It is pictured on page 17.

PREP TIME: 5 MINS
COOKING TIME: 5 MINS

2 tsp cumin seeds
Very large bunch (about 100g/3½oz) of mint
Very large bunch (about 100g/3½oz) of coriander (cilantro)
6 green chillies (more or less to taste)
4 garlic cloves
5cm (2in) piece of ginger, peeled and roughly chopped
Juice of 2 lemons
150g (generous ½ cup) plain yoghurt (shop-bought or make your own – see below) (optional)
Salt, to taste

In a dry frying pan, roast the cumin seeds over a medium–high heat until warm to the touch and fragrant but not yet smoking.

Pour the roasted seeds into a blender or spice grinder with the mint, coriander (cilantro), green chillies, garlic, ginger, lemon juice and 2 tablespoons of the yoghurt (if using). Blend to a paste. If you are having trouble getting the ingredients to blend, add a little more lemon juice or a drop or two of water until you have a thick green paste.

You could now use the sauce to spread over sandwiches and wraps but if you are making chaats or like a smoother, thinner sauce, whisk the remaining yoghurt into the paste until very smooth. (You could even add more yoghurt if you prefer.) Season with salt.

I like to store this sauce for up to 3 days in restaurant-style squirt bottles for squeezing over lots of different dishes.

MAKE IT VEGAN
You could leave out the yoghurt for a stronger but very delicious flavour, or try a soy or coconut yoghurt.

TAMARIND CHUTNEY

MAKES 2 JARS

Tamarind chutney simply has to be on the table when my wife and I plan a curry party. It's sweet, sour, savoury and spicy, and also has a nice crunch to it. What more could you ask for in a chutney?

PREP TIME: 5 MINS, PLUS SITTING TIME

1–2 tbsp tamarind concentrate
2 tbsp water
3 tbsp sugar
4 tbsp tomato ketchup
Juice of 1 lemon
3 fresh green chillies, finely chopped
½ onion, finely chopped
3 spring onions (scallions), finely chopped
4 tbsp finely chopped coriander (cilantro)
1 large carrot, grated
1 tsp madras curry powder (see page 171)
Salt, to taste

Put all the ingredients into a small bowl and mix well. Refrigerate for at least 1 hour before serving.

TAMARIND SAUCE

MAKES ABOUT 200ML (GENEROUS ¾ CUP)

Good-quality tamarind sauce is commercially available. It is delicious squeezed over different chaats like my aloo tikki chaat on page 49. If you fancy having a go at making your own, this recipe gets great results.

PREP TIME: 5 MINS
COOKING TIME: 30 MINS

1 tbsp rapeseed (canola) oil
1 tsp cumin seeds
1 tsp cayenne pepper
1 tsp ground ginger
½ tsp asafoetida* or garlic powder
½ tsp fennel seeds
½ tsp garam masala (see page 167)
200g (1 cup) caster sugar
40g (3 tbsp) tamarind concentrate

Heat the oil in a saucepan over a medium–high heat. When visibly hot, stir in the cumin, cayenne, ginger, asafoetida or garlic powder, fennel seeds and garam masala. Stir the spices around in the oil to flavour it for about 30 seconds, then pour in the sugar and tamarind concentrate along with 450ml (scant 2 cups) of water.

Bring to a rolling simmer and let the sauce reduce until it has a chocolatey colour and is thick enough to coat the back of a spoon. This should take about 20–30 minutes. The sauce will be thin but will thicken once cooled. Store in the fridge in a squeezy bottle, if you have one, and use as required. This sauce will keep for 2 weeks.

NOTE
*If you are gluten-free, please check the asafoetida packaging as some brands contain wheat flour.

TAMARIND (BLACK) PANI

MAKES 250ML (1 CUP)

You can purchase good-quality tamarind pani (water) at Asian shops and online. It is delicious served with pani puri (see page 71). I often make my own and this is my go-to recipe. There are a lot more complicated and fussy recipes out there but the end results are about the same.

Block tamarind will achieve a superior flavour but tamarind concentrate works well too and it is a lot easier. Just stir it into 1 litre (4½ cups) of water with the other ingredients.

PREP TIME: 10 MINS, PLUS SOAKING TIME
COOKING TIME: 15 MINS

200g (7oz) block of tamarind or 80g (6 tbsp) tamarind
    concentrate
1 tbsp ground cumin
1 tbsp ground coriander
2 tsp salt (or to taste)
2 tsp chaat masala (see page 168)
2 tsp chilli powder
1 tbsp mint sauce
3 tbsp finely chopped coriander (cilantro) leaves
Sugar, to taste (optional)

Tamarind is quite fibrous and there are usually seeds in the block, so it needs to soak to break down the fibre and release the edible pulp. Break up the tamarind into a large bowl and cover with hot water – about 200ml (generous ¾ cup) should do. Let it sit for 2 hours. After this time the tamarind will be really soft.

Using your hands, squeeze the tamarind until it melts into the water and breaks away from the seeds and fibres. Pass this brown tamarind water through a fine sieve into another bowl, pressing down as you do to get all of the delicious, sweet-and-sour pulp out.

Now add 800ml (3½ cups) of fresh water to the tamarind water. Stir in the rest of the ingredients. This will keep in an air-tight container in the fridge for at least 1 week. It can also be frozen.

GREEN PANI

MAKES 700ML (3 CUPS)

Green pani (green water) is delicious poured into pani puri (see page 71). It can be made in minutes, though leaving it in the fridge for about 2 hours before serving will allow the flavours to develop. I don't strain the pani but some people do. I'll leave that up to you.

Green pani has other uses besides pani puri. Try steaming rice (see page 314) using the green pani instead of water. If you don't feel like making it, you can purchase excellent-quality green pani at Asian grocers.

PREP TIME: 10 MINS, PLUS CHILLING TIME

Large bunch of mint leaves
Large bunch of coriander (cilantro) leaves
3 green chillies (or more if you like things spicy)
1 tsp chaat masala (see page 168) (optional)
1 tbsp ground cumin
½ tsp salt
1 tsp roughly chopped ginger
1 tsp amchoor (dried mango powder)
2 tbsp sugar, or to taste
Salt, to taste
Chilli powder (optional)

Put all the ingredients up to the salt in a blender with 250ml (1 cup) of water and blend for 1 minute. If you're in a rush for the deliciousness, you could add 250ml (1 cup) more water and run it all through a sieve, check for seasoning and enjoy immediately. For best results and a stronger flavour, place the paste with the additional water in the fridge for about 1 hour. Then run it through a sieve and check for seasoning. Season with salt and perhaps a little chilli powder. If you prefer a sweeter flavour, stir in some more sugar.

Your green pani is now ready to serve. It can also be frozen for up to 3 months to use later. I always have some on hand because my pani puri parties just tend to happen late at night after a few beers with friends without any planning.

TAKEAWAY-STYLE PAKORA SAUCE
MAKES ABOUT 300ML (1¼ CUPS)

If it's Indian takeaway-style pakora sauce you like, this is a good one. Usually this sweet-and-sour sauce is red from food colouring, and does look the part when bright red. The mango chutney and ketchup are already quite sweet but you might want to add a little sugar. The sour flavours come from the lemon and mint sauce. Just try it and adjust until you are happy with the flavour.

PREP TIME: 5 MINS

1 onion, finely chopped
2 tbsp smooth mango chutney (see page 331)
3 tbsp tomato ketchup
1 tsp mint sauce
200g (¾ cup) plain yoghurt
½ tsp roasted cumin seeds (see page 163)
½ tsp chilli powder, or to taste
1 tbsp sugar
Lemon juice, to taste
Salt, to taste
½ tsp red food colouring powder (optional)
Full-fat (whole) milk (optional)

Whisk all the ingredients up to and including the lemon juice together. Once the sauce is nicely combined, season with salt, if needed. Add the food colouring (if using). If the sauce is too thick, stir in a little milk until you are happy with the consistency.

YOGHURT SAUCE
MAKES 250ML (1 CUP)

This is essentially a raita, but I call it a sauce because that's what it is referred to at many of my local kebab shops. It's that white sauce in a squeezy bottle that tastes amazing squirted all over your kebab. You must know the one? It also has soured cream in it, which I've never seen in a raita. Whatever you call it, I'm almost certain you will recognize the flavour if you frequently find yourself in the queue for a delicious kebab. Some places substitute mayonnaise for the soured cream, which you might want to try. For me though, it has to be soured cream.

PREP TIME: 5 MINS, PLUS CHILLING TIME

125g (½ cup) plain yoghurt
125ml (½ cup) soured cream
Juice of 1 lime
2 garlic cloves, crushed
1 tbsp hot sauce of your choice
¼ tsp ground cumin
1 tbsp finely chopped coriander (cilantro) leaves
Salt and freshly ground black pepper, to taste

Place all the ingredients in a large bowl and whisk until thoroughly blended into one very tasty sauce. Check for seasoning and place in the fridge for at least 30 minutes before serving.

HONEY MUSTARD RAITA

MAKES JUST OVER 250ML (1 CUP)

This is a delicious dip for papadams, kebabs, samosas and chicken pakoras. I love to serve it with my tandoori-style king prawns (see page 291).

PREP TIME: 5 MINS
COOKING TIME: 5 MINS

200g (¾ cup) plain yoghurt
3 tbsp finely chopped coriander (cilantro)
1 tbsp honey
Juice of 1 lime
2 tbsp rapeseed (canola) oil
1 tbsp mustard seeds
10 fresh curry leaves (optional, but don't use dried)
½ tsp ground turmeric
1 tbsp garlic and ginger paste (see page 172)
Salt, to taste

Put the yoghurt, coriander (cilantro), honey and lime juice in a bowl and whisk until smooth and creamy. Set aside.

Heat the oil in a small frying pan over a high heat and add the mustard seeds. When they begin to pop (after about 30 seconds), reduce the heat and add the curry leaves, turmeric and garlic and ginger paste. Stir for about 30 seconds.

Pour the hot oil over the yoghurt mixture and whisk briskly again to prevent the yoghurt from curdling. Season with salt, if needed. Place in the fridge for about 1 hour before serving.

CUCUMBER RAITA

MAKES 550ML (GENEROUS 2¼ CUPS)

This is delicious spooned over biryanis and kebabs. If you want to make it even more exciting, try adding a few small chunks of cooked potato and/or finely chopped green chilli.

PREP TIME: 5 MINS

420g (scant 1¾ cups) Greek yoghurt
3 garlic cloves, finely chopped
½ English cucumber, grated
Juice of 1–2 limes
Pinch each of salt and freshly ground black pepper

Put all the ingredients into a bowl and whisk them together with a fork. Place in the fridge for about 1 hour before serving.

CORIANDER, GARLIC AND CHILLI RAITA

MAKES 500–550ML (2 CUPS)

My favourite raita. Nothing more to be said.

PREP TIME: 5 MINS

Bunch of fresh coriander (cilantro), leaves only
1–2 garlic cloves, to taste
2 tbsp lime juice
2 fresh green chillies, or to taste, roughly chopped
375g (1¾ cups) plain yoghurt
Salt, to taste

In a spice grinder or small food processor, blend the coriander (cilantro) leaves, garlic, lime juice and chillies to a paste. You can also use a pestle and mortar to do this, which is a little more work.

Whisk the yoghurt with a fork until creamy smooth, then stir in the coriander paste. Season with salt to taste and chill in the fridge for about 30 minutes before serving.

LIST OF INGREDIENTS

AJWAIN (CAROM) SEEDS
Ajwain 'seeds' are actually small fruit. They smell like thyme but their flavour is more of a cross between fennel seeds and oregano, but much stronger. They have a pungent, bitter flavour, so should be used sparingly.

AMCHOOR (DRIED MANGO POWDER)
Amchoor powder, made from dried and ground mango, has a strong citric flavour and is really good added to tandoori masalas or any curry that benefits from a citric kick.

ASAFOETIDA
In its raw powder form, asafoetida smells terrible. Once fried, its aroma and flavour are more pleasing, like fried onions. This spice is quite strong, so should be used sparingly. It is often tempered in oil with other ingredients to make a tarka for dishes such as tarka dhal. Please note that some brands contain wheat flour, so please check the packaging if you are gluten-free.

BASMATI RICE
The rice you serve with these recipes has got to be basmati. It has a nutty flavour all its own. Basmati benefits from aging, so look for the longest-grain, aged basmati rice you can find. It's a little more expensive but worth every penny. Both Tilda and East End Foods supply top-quality basmati rice.

BASSAR CURRY MASALA
This is a spicy blend often substituted for chilli powder in Punjabi and Pakistani cooking. As it contains mustard oil, it shouldn't be eaten raw. I have suggested it in a few recipes but feel free to experiment, adding it with or instead of chilli powder. It is available from most Asian grocers.

BAY LEAVES (ASIAN, WESTERN)
Indian bay leaves come from the cassia tree and taste like cassia and cinnamon. They are available from Asian grocers and some larger supermarkets. Western bay leaves are what you probably already use in your spaghetti Bolognese and meat stews. I don't think any more explanation is necessary.

BLACK SALT
This fine salt has the disadvantage of smelling like eggs gone off, due to its high sulphur content. Don't be put off by the smell, though. It is a key ingredient for homemade chaat masala and also tastes fantastic sprinkled sparingly over a host of other dishes. There is no substitute, so if a recipe calls for it, do your best to source it. It's available from Asian grocers and online.

CARDAMOM (BLACK AND GREEN)
By weight, cardamom is the third most expensive spice in the world, beaten only by vanilla and saffron. Green cardamom is most often used in BIR cooking, added to garam masalas and tempered whole in oil. The seeds are what impart the flavour, so the pods are often lightly crushed before adding to get that flavour into the dish. Black cardamom is bigger and has a stronger, smoky flavour. If you need to substitute one type for the other, use half as many black as green.

CASSIA BARK
See cinnamon.

CHILLIES (FRESH)
Fresh chillies range in heat from quite mild to numbingly spicy. I usually use green bird's eye and bullet chillies for the recipes in this book. That said, I do like to experiment with other chillies as they all have their own unique flavour in addition to their heat level. Fresh chillies can be used simply split down the middle, finely or roughly chopped, or blended into a chilli paste.

CHILLI POWDER
The preferred chilli powder at most curry houses is Kashmiri chilli powder. It is quite spicy and has a nice flavour too. Kashmiri chilli powder is available at Asian grocers and also some supermarkets. How spicy your curries are is really a personal thing. I use Kashmiri chilli powder in my cooking but you might like to experiment with milder or hotter chilli powders.

CINNAMON
Almost all of the cinnamon powder sold around the world is actually made from cassia bark. More often than not, the labelling is not deceptive, with cassia often labelled 'cinnamon cassia'. Powdered cassia can be used in both savoury and

sweet recipes for a nice, warming kick, and it tastes almost identical to real cinnamon powder. Although cassia tastes great, there is new medical evidence that consuming it in regular doses can cause liver damage. I don't feel there is much to worry about if you only cook with it ocasionally, but I'm not a medical expert. If you use cinnamon regularly, use Ceylon or 'true cinnamon'. It costs a little more and it's what I use.

If you are looking for 'true cinnamon', it will usually be stated on the label. If in doubt, 'true cinnamon' is only grown in Sri Lanka, the Seychelles and Madagascar. Cassia bark comes from China and Indonesia.

CLOVES

These offer a sweet, recognizable flavour that is excellent in spice masalas and for tempering in oil. Cloves have a low smoking point, so they can burn faster than most spices and need to be watched if roasting.

COCONUT MILK, FLOUR AND BLOCK

Coconut flour and block coconut are most often used in BIR curries, whereas coconut milk is more popular in authentic Indian curries. You can substitute one for the other, but when using coconut milk, you might need to reduce the sauce down more.

CUMIN

White cumin seeds have a strong flavour and aroma that are hugely popular in Indian and other cooking. Cumin is in fact the second most popular spice in the world, second only to black pepper. The seeds can be tempered whole and are also nice added in ground form to many dishes.

Black cumin seeds (royal cumin) are darker and thinner than the white seeds. They are sweeter and nuttier than white and also stronger in flavour, so are used sparingly. They add a nice touch to special dishes.

CURRY LEAVES

My favourite ingredient, these small leaves smell amazing when tempered in a little oil. They are used more in southern Indian cooking, but many British curry-house chefs have started adding them to their northern Indian, Pakistani and Bangladeshi dishes too. Use fresh or frozen leaves, as the dried leaves have a weaker flavour.

FENNEL SEEDS

Fennel seeds have a nice flavour, similar to black liquorice and star anise. Star anise is slightly stronger but I do use the two spices together and also substitute the whole spices for each other if I've run out of one. Fennel seeds can be tempered whole in oil and also added later to a sauce as a ground spice.

FENUGREEK (METHI)

You can purchase fenugreek as a powder, whole seeds or as dried leaves. The dried leaves are used most in British Indian cookery.

GHEE

This is clarified butter but it doesn't taste like homemade clarified butter. They must feed the cows something different over there in India. It is available from Asian grocers, and many supermarkets now stock it. Ghee doesn't need to be refrigerated and should last, covered, for months. There was a time when curry-house curries were sodden in the stuff. Nowadays, healthier alternatives are being used, like rapeseed (canola) oil, but ghee is still hugely popular and a great way of getting a nice buttery flavour into your dishes.

KOKUM

In all my years of cooking Indian food, there are a handful of ingredients that just blow me away because of their amazing and unique flavours. Kokum is one of them. Used mainly in south-Indian cooking, kokum is the dried rind of the kokum berry. The rinds are dried and used as a souring agent in sauces, just like tamarind is used in so many Indian dishes. I love it for its slightly smoky and sour flavour. The kokum rinds are not supposed to be eaten because they are so sour, though before I knew that I ate a few and actually quite liked them! Kokum can be hard to come by outside India, but it is available online, so please take the time to order and try it in the recipes that call for it. As I mention in the recipes, you can substitute other souring agents like tamarind or lemon/lime juice, but in those recipes calling for kokum, there is a delicious and even eye-opening reason for it.

MACE

See nutmeg.

MUSTARD OIL

There's no substitute for mustard oil and I love the stuff. It has a pungent and strong flavour and has been used for centuries in northern Indian and Bangladeshi cooking. It is available here in the UK but has not been approved for human consumption. If you decide to go for it and break the rules, be sure to heat it up until it smokes and then let it cool before heating up again to use in your cooking.

MUSTARD SEEDS (BLACK)

Mustard seeds are available as black or yellow, but I use the black variety in the recipes in this book, which need to be tempered in very hot oil. Once they start popping, the heat can be reduced and their pungent flavour will be released into the oil. Mustard seeds require this high heat but most whole spices don't. Once the mustard seeds have begun popping in the oil (this takes about 30 seconds), other whole spices with lower smoking points can be added.

NIGELLA SEEDS (BLACK ONION SEEDS)

Although nigella seeds are often called black onion seeds, they aren't actually from the onion family. Whatever you call them, they are excellent sprinkled over homemade naans.

NUTMEG AND MACE

Like most spices, nutmeg is best purchased whole and then ground as, once ground, it loses its flavour quickly. The small, hard, round nutmeg is the seed of the nutmeg tree and is harvested from the inside of the nutmeg fruit. Crack one of the fruits open and you'll find a red, lacy covering around the seed. This is mace. Mace and nutmeg are similar in flavour but nutmeg is a lot stronger than the more delicate mace, and should be added to curries only in small doses. Dried mace is nice tempered in oil and is often used ground with cardamom seeds to make cardamom and mace powder.

PANEER

Indian paneer is the most simple of cheeses and is now widely available in Asian shops and in supermarkets.

For the recipes in this book, shop-bought paneer will do fine, but if you want to try making your own there are instructions on page 180.

RICE FLOUR

Rice flour is gluten-free and helps make fried food extra crispy. You can substitute cornflour (cornstarch) if you have trouble finding it. Likewise, it works really well as a gluten-free substitute for cornflour. It is available at Asian grocers, online and in many larger supermarkets.

ROSE WATER

Rose water is made by steeping rose petals in water, and is cheap, so there's no need to go out picking rose petals. This fragrant water is added to rice, biryanis, kormas and other dishes to make them taste and smell even better.

SAFFRON

By weight, saffron is the most expensive spice on the planet, worth more than gold. Luckily, you don't need a lot, as a little goes a long way. Saffron consists of the stigma of the crocus flower. Only three stigma grow on each flower, which have to be picked by hand. That's why it's so expensive. Many restaurants use turmeric instead of saffron to give their food colour. I use saffron threads in my recipes, which add a much better flavour than powdered.

STAR ANISE

See fennel seeds.

TAMARIND

Tamarind is available both in block form and as a concentrated paste. Tamarind concentrate will work fine in my recipes and it's a lot less work. It has a strong acidic flavour like a strong vinegar.

TURMERIC

Turmeric is one of the spices that make Indian food what it is. Its deep yellow colour gives food an appetizing appearance. It is often used as a substitute for saffron, for its colour, though it tastes nothing like it. It has a distinctive woody, bitter flavour that is popular in curries and rice. As it is quite bitter, it is used sparingly.

YOGHURT (GREEK AND NATURAL)

Full-fat Greek yoghurt is perfect for marinating meat, poultry, seafood, paneer and vegetables. I also prepare thick raitas with it. For thinner raitas and for use in sauces, use plain yoghurt, which doesn't curdle as easily.

SUPPLIERS AND CLASSES

INGREDIENTS

SPICE KITCHEN ONLINE LTD

Spice Kitchen supplies excellent-quality spices that can be purchased online. Not only that, it has begun producing the spice blends from my books, such as mixed powder, curry powder, garam masala, tandoori masala and chaat masala. It is also supplies kokum, which is called for in many of my recipes. You can also order spice tins/masala dabbas filled with whole spices or their own spice blends from around the world, which are all blended in-house.
www.spicekitchenuk.com; 07729 116102
soldwithlove@spicekitchenuk.com

EAST END FOODS

East End Foods has been a much-valued sponsor of my blog for many years. I have visited its production facilities and can trust it to deliver excellent-quality spices, pulses, flours and rice. Their whole and ground spices are available at supermarkets, Asian grocers and from online retailers all over the UK.
https://eastendfoods.co.uk

SPICES OF INDIA

You will love shopping on this site. In addition to all the groceries and spices they supply, you will also find a fantastic range of Indian kitchen and tableware.
www.spicesofindia.co.uk

PLANTS4PRESENTS

This company supplies plants, such as curry leaf plants and different chilli plants, which you can have delivered to your home.
https://plants4presents.co.uk

BALTI BOWLS

THE BIRMINGHAM BALTI BOWL COMPANY

Birmingham steel-pressed balti bowls come stylishly presented in a gift box. Once again, you can purchase authentic balti bowls that are manufactured in Birmingham.
www.thebirminghambaltibowlco.com

BARBECUE AND GRILLING

THÜROS BARBECUES

If you love kebabs, you've got to check out Thüros Kebab Grills. I love mine.
www.thueros.com

TRAEGER BARBECUES

The easy way to get delicious smoky flavour into your barbecued foods. Traeger barbecues use wood pellets to cook the food. You can set the preferred temperature and let the Traeger do all the work. This is the perfect barbecue for easy indirect cooking.
www.thealfrescochef.co.uk/find-a-dealer

KAMADO JOE BARBECUES

I have only recently started cooking on the Kamado Joe Classic barbecue and love it. In fact, the new barbecue recipes in this cookbook were all cooked on the Kamado Joe. You can find more information here:
https://kamadojoe.co.uk/

MY UK CURRY CLASSES

I teach cooking classes around the UK. For more information, please visit my website:
www.greatcurryrecipes.net

US SOURCES

PENZEYS

Large range of spices that can be purchased online.
www.penzeys.com

SAVORY SPICE

Large range of spices.
www.savoryspiceshop.com

ISHOPINDIAN.COM

Groceries and Indian cooking utensils.
www.ishopindian.com

ANCIENT COOKWARE

A large range of cookware from India and around the world.
www.ancientcookware.com

INDEX

ACKNOWLEDGEMENTS

It was a pleasure to work with everyone at Quadrille again to produce this cookbook. I would like to thank Sarah Lavelle for commissioning the project, copy-editor Corinne Masciocchi and my editor, Louise Francis, for all of her help with my words and bringing the book together.

Thanks to Kris Kirkham, who photographed each of my cookbooks. I love your work, Kris! I would also like to thank food stylists Rosie Reynolds, Amber De Florio and Tamara Vos for making my recipes look so good on the page.

Many of my recipes were either taught to me or influenced by the outstanding chefs I've met. Unfortunately, I can't mention them all by name in this small space but thank you! Some chefs and foodie friends deserve a special mention as they have been so influential in how my recipes developed, often sharing their own recipes. Thank you very much Eshan 'Mo' Miah from Zaman's in Newquay, Bob Arora from Sachins in Newcastle, Syed Ahmed from Duke Bombay Café in Darlington, Milon Miah from Spice Island in Barnard Castle, Ajay Kenth from Zindiya Streatery & Bar in Birmingham, Usman Butt and Talib Hussain from Imrans in Birmingham, Zafar Hussain from Shababs in Birmingham, Jomon Kuriakose from Baluchi in London, Tariq Malik from Al-Faisal Tandoori in Manchester, Hussain Rashid from The Balti House Rishton, Minal Patel from Prashad in Bradford, Shabaz Ali from Vijaya Krishna in Tooting, Shihabudeen V. M., Vipin V. U. and Rahul Krishnan Muttumpuram.

I would also like to thank the many new friends I've met through my travels, on my Facebook, Twitter and Instagram pages, as well as in my cooking classes. I love talking food, and I've learned a lot through people testing my blog recipes and also sharing some of their own. Special thanks to Roxanne Bamboat, Vivek Kashiwale, Palash Mitra, Richard Sayce, Andy Munro, Madhup Sinha, Alfarid 'Billy' Juma, Hasan Chaudhry, Alex Wilke and Sharon Iyer.

Thank you also to my literary agent, Clare Hulton, who once again made this all happen.

Thank you to my wife, Caroline, for helping in the background and being a great sous chef!

Most of all, I would like to thank all of you curry fans out there for picking up this book. I appreciate it so much and I hope you enjoy this collection of recipes.

Publishing Director: Sarah Lavelle
Project Editor: Louise Francis
Senior Designer: Nicola Ellis
Junior Designer: Alicia House
Cover Design: Smith & Gilmour
Photographer: Kris Kirkham
Photography Assistant: Eyder Rosso Gonçalves
Food Stylist: Rosie Reynolds
Props Stylist: Faye Wears
Head of Production: Stephen Lang
Production Controller: Nikolaus Ginelli

First published in 2020 by Quadrille, an imprint of Hardie Grant Publishing

Quadrille
52–54 Southwark Street,
London SE1 1UN
www.quadrille.com

Cataloguing-in-Publication Data. A catalogue record for this book is available from the British Library.

ISBN 978-1-78713-463-8

Reprinted in 2020 (three times), 2021 (four times), 2022
12 11 10 9

Printed in China